Field Archaeology:
An Introduction

Other archaeology titles from UCL Press include:

The Origins and Spread of Agriculture and Pastoralism in Eurasia edited by David R. Harris (1996)

The Origins and Development of African Livestock edited by Roger Blench and Kevin MacDonald (1999)

A Breton Landscape: From the Romans to the Second Empire in Eastern Brittany by Grenville Astill and Wendy Davies (1997)

The Jewellery of Roman Britain: Celtic and Classical Traditions by Catherine Johns (1996)

Field Archaeology:
An Introduction

Peter L. Drewett
University College London

First published 1999 by UCL Press
11 New Fetter Lane, London EC4P 4EE

The name of University College London (UCL) is a registered trade mark used by UCL Press with the consent of the owner.

UCL Press is an imprint of the Taylor & Francis Group

Typeset by Graphicraft Limited, Hong Kong
Printed and bound in Great Britain by T.J. International Ltd, Padstow, Cornwall

British Library Cataloguing in Publication Data
A catalogue record for this book is available from the British Library

Library of Congress Cataloging in Publication Data
A catalogue record for this book has been requested

ISBNs: 1-85728-737-1 (hbk)
       1-85728-738-X (pbk)

Contents

Figures

(Source: author unless acknowledged)

Cover: Excavation of medieval great hall at Hadleigh Castle, Essex.

Acknowledgements

Having taught field archaeology for many years it is often difficult to remember the exact source of a particular idea, method or technique. Clearly much is derived from digging in my student days in the 1960s, particularly with Peter Fowler, Henry Cleere, Geoffrey Wainwright and John Lewis. Since then I have gained much from working in the field with Luiz Oosterbeek (Portugal), Siu Tsan Chiu (Hong Kong), Wu Zengde (People's Republic of China), Brian Bates (USA) and Sue Hamilton (UK), together with the hundreds of students I have worked with over the years. If any recognize their thoughts, ideas or techniques not acknowledged elsewhere, please accept this as a full acknowledgement.

Much relating to the management of archaeology, particularly SMRs, is derived from my annual visit with students to the Archaeology Section of the Essex County Council. From here the deep knowledge and experience of the Section, and particularly David Buckley and Paul Gilman, is acknowledged. Much was also gleaned over the years from colleagues from the Institute of Archaeology, University College London, visiting the undergraduate field courses I ran for twenty years. In particular I should like to thank Ken Thomas (environment), Harry Stewart (surveying) and Stuart Laidlaw (photography). The section on illustration greatly benefited from Lys Drewett's ten years' experience teaching archaeological illustration at the Institute of Archaeology and as illustrator on all my archaeological projects. Most of the illustrations derive from my field projects but, where not, these are gratefully acknowledged under the illustration. To any other archaeologists who feel I may have used their knowledge, published or not published, without full acknowledgement please accept this general thanks as full acknowledgement.

Finally I gratefully acknowledge the support and expertise of Christine Crickmore who for twenty-six years served the Institute of Archaeology as Secretary to the Department of Prehistoric Archaeology and the Sussex Archaeological Field Unit (later the Field Archaeology Unit). She even kindly typed and corrected the text of this book.

Peter Drewett
Institute of Archaeology
University College London
February 1999

Preface

Field archaeology can only be properly learnt in the field, through using techniques and looking at and thinking about archaeological remains. What, then, is the point of a textbook on field archaeology? When I came into field archaeology some thirty-five years ago, it was still possible for a raw recruit to spend afternoons with the director of an excavation sitting in front of a section as the mysteries of stratigraphy were revealed. Increasingly such luxury is unavailable to newcomers. So how do those who want to become field archaeologists learn their skills? Although there are many courses, field schools and training excavations, most still learn 'on the job'.

Obviously there are advantages in attending classes in field techniques and then attending a field school. You will be lectured at, demonstrated to, and no doubt practise a range of skills often, for financial reasons, in regrettably large groups. Generally gone is the one-to-one session with a well-established and vastly experienced field archaeologist. You will then arrive on your first real excavation as a volunteer, crew member or poorly-paid archaeological labourer. At this point often nobody really has the time to spend explaining all those strange things which go on on excavations.

This book is designed to help all those people coming into field archaeology. Hopefully it will be a useful guide to those arriving at a first class in field techniques, those arriving at a first field school in archaeology and then those working on a real excavation or field project for the first time. It may be a useful textbook for those teaching field techniques at introductory level. Those with vast experience will only find it an amusing diversion: "Does he really do *that*?!"

This brings me to the problem of what field techniques to introduce. Although British techniques of field archaeology have a good reputation in many parts of the world, approaches vary throughout the world. An American archaeologist trained at Berkeley will do things differently from one trained at the Institute of Archaeology in London, who will in turn do things differently from one trained at the Institute of Archaeology in Beijing. There is clearly bad practice, there is not recording what you see and not publishing results. However, there are many equally good practices when it comes to digging, recording and publishing. Having worked in the Americas, Europe (especially Britain), and the Far East with Chinese archaeologists, it is clear to me that many varied approaches are equally valid. This book is therefore not aimed at attempting to explain how to excavate a Roman villa or a Tang tomb. Instead I hope to provide an elementary introduction to general principles, approaches and techniques, but with sufficient detail on, for example, how to dig a posthole whether that posthole is in the Caribbean, Britain or China.

A word of warning, however. When you arrive on your first excavation you may be told, "This is how I dig", "This is the 'right' way to dig", or "This is how we are required to dig by our funding agency or by the State Archaeological Service". Clearly you must dig that way on that project, but read on in your evenings and consider other ways of doing it. Remember that the greatest field archaeologists should be flexible in approaches and techniques, lateral thinkers and not slaves to dogma. Those that are not will never rise above the level of competent field technicians and they are not truly field archaeologists, as I hope one day you will be.

CHAPTER ONE

Introduction

What is archaeology?

It is unlikely that you will ever come across two archaeologists who will agree exactly what archaeology is. Some do not even see it as a subject in its own right. Obviously the word 'archaeology' – or 'archeology' if you prefer – has a dictionary meaning, but even here agreement is not universal. The *Concise Oxford Dictionary* (7th edn, 1985), for example, states that archaeology is the "study of human antiquities, especially of the prehistoric period and usually by excavation": a good traditional view of the subject! *Webster's International Dictionary* (3rd edn, 1986), however, sees archaeology as "the scientific study of extinct peoples or of past phases of the culture of historic peoples through skeletal remains and objects of human workmanship found in the earth". To non-archaeologists, archaeology involves three crucial elements: 'the past', 'material remains' and 'excavation'. To many archaeologists, however, the meaning of the word and the discipline is more flexible and has shifting meaning. When exactly is 'the past'? It is not *now*, but it certainly was when you read the last sentence.

Most archaeologists agree that archaeology must have a material element – for example, "Archaeology: a sub-discipline of anthropology involving the study of the human past through its material remains" (Renfrew and Bahn 1991) or "Archaeology: use of human remains to solve the problems of another discipline, such as anthropology or art history" (Rouse 1992). It is the study of human material *remains* that makes archaeology different from anthropology which, among other things, can study intact human material culture, not just its *remains*. Archaeology is different from history in that it requires the *remains* to be studied, not just written descriptions of these remains. Not all *remains* have, however, been lost or buried and require excavation to reveal them. The Great Wall of China (Fig. 1.1) or the Parthenon in Athens are *remains,* but neither has ever been 'lost' or required much in the way of excavation to reveal them. Clearly, the study of material remains can be used in other disciplines: anthropology, art history or history – but archaeological methodology, theory and aims make it essentially different from these other disciplines. The fact that economists use the techniques of mathematicians in no ways makes mathematics a sub-discipline of economics. Equally, the fact that archaeology provides data for anthropology or history in no way makes it a sub-discipline of

1

Figure 1.1   The Great Wall of China: an archaeological site never 'lost'. (photo: A. Drewett)

these subjects. Archaeology is its own subject with its own theory, methodology and aims.

Archaeologists are therefore dealing with the *remains* of past peoples, societies and cultures. Remains have a tendency to be lost, buried and forgotten, so archaeology has developed a range of methods to recover partial remains. It has borrowed and adapted techniques, methods and theories from other disciplines but made them very much its own. In addition it has developed its own methods of studying palimpsests in the landscape and its own unique methods of excavation. Archaeological excavation has its own theoretical basis, often passed by word of mouth from excavator to excavator rather than formally set down in textbooks. In addition, archaeology has adopted, adapted and evolved its own theoretical basis for the interpretation of the past through the study of material remains.

If we consider archaeology to be the study of the past through the study of material remains, clearly archaeology becomes an enormous subject with time-depth back to the dawn of human existence and up to just before *now*. Geographically it covers the whole of the world's surface, the surface of the moon and all those scraps of failed hardware lost in space. Archaeology, however, is not just rubbish-collection. Not all material remains left by humans have the same value to archaeologists. To merely collect rubbish is not only a waste of the resources available to archaeologists but also gets archaeology a bad name with the wider public who generally, although they often do not know it, are footing the bill. Archaeologists who systematically record the position of a coke bottle or tin foil from a cigarette wrapper and then carefully bag and curate it as part of the archaeology of the site just make themselves (and other archaeologists) look silly. The presence of such artefacts may be significant in indicating modern disturbance, but nothing more. Note it and return it to a new archaeological context, your site backfill.

Even within the archaeological context of a period like the neolithic in Europe or the archaic in North America, not all material remains have the same value to archaeologists. A few broken shells on a coastal site may have less significance than the same shells hundreds of miles inland. On a medieval site the bulk of the material remains may be shattered roof-tiles which, although important, will not provide as much information as the much smaller assemblages of pottery or metal-work. Not all remains of human activity are of equal importance in the interpreta-tion of the past. It is the job of the archaeologist to select what he or she considers to be important and then concentrate effort on that material.

Archaeologists therefore locate rubbish in the landscape, carefully select and record that rubbish and then, through analysis of that rubbish and the application of a variety of theoretical perspectives, produce a story about the past. Archaeologists cannot 'reconstruct' the past; the past is gone for ever. What they can do is create a series of stories or interpretations about what it may have been like in the past. They do this by collecting as many 'facts' about the past as they can. A pot is a fact. We can say how it is made, what it is made of, perhaps where it was made and, from residues, what it contained. We can perhaps say what date it was made. From then on it can be woven into a story of what life was like in, say, the neolithic period.

To produce a story about what it was like in the past, archaeologists must put their material remains into the context of natural remains also surviving in the landscape. Were the people you are studying living in a forest, on grassland, by a river or by a former shoreline? This environmental context can be studied through the associated discipline of environmental archaeology. Through the study of natur-ally occurring – although perhaps humanly modified – remains like pollen, shells or soils, an environmental story can also be built up. Both the human story and the environmental story have 'facts', theories and interpretations. This book will con-centrate on the recovery of 'facts' but they have no value unless they form part of evolving theories and interpretations about the past.

What is field archaeology?

Field archaeology is, not surprisingly, what archaeologists do in the field. How-ever, it also has a considerable pre-field element and an even more considerable post-field element. Sometimes the term 'field archaeology' is used only to refer to techniques, other than excavation, used by archaeologists in the field. 'Field archae-ology' used in this way refers essentially to the battery of non-destructive field techniques used to locate areas of archaeological interest (sites). Excavation is, however, one of the techniques available to field archaeologists and so is part of field archaeology. Excavation remains, however, both the most detailed and the most destructive, and yet potentially the most informative, technique available to the field archaeologist.

Field archaeology starts with the location of archaeological sites. Immediately this runs into the problem of what is an archaeological 'site'. Most archaeologists see sites as places where there are clusters of artefacts, often – but depending on what period they are dealing with – associated with humanly made structures or features like dug pits. There may also be some human modification of the natural environment in or around the 'site'. How small, however, does a cluster of artefacts have to be to constitute a site? Is a single projectile point found in a woodland environment a site? Clearly it constitutes the material remains of a specific human activity, presumably hunting, taking place at a specific place in the landscape. It clearly is a 'site', but equally clearly it is not going to provide the archaeologists with as much information as, say, a tell site in the Near East. In many ways one could see the whole surface of the earth as an archaeological 'site' with varying concentrations of humanly produced remains. Even areas with no remains are part of the human story of the region. Why was there no human activity in a particular area? A field archaeologist therefore has to look at data of different levels in the field. An 'empty' area or a single projectile point provides some, but minimal, data. Sites with high concentrations of artefacts, features and a modified environment potentially provide masses of raw data about the past. These are the ones on which field archaeologists are likely to concentrate.

So what are the elements of field archaeology which make some archaeologists consider themselves to be field archaeologists while others are not? Clearly it is perfectly possible to be an archaeologist studying material remains from the past without ever stepping into the field. Many people are surprised that out of the 42 or so faculty members of the Institute of Archaeology at University College, London (the largest university department in Britain), only about a dozen could be safely let out to direct an excavation. This says nothing about their competence as archaeologists, just that they do not engage in field archaeology.

The first element of field archaeology is to decide 'why?' There is little point in simply going into the field to do field archaeology without having any questions to answer. At its simplest, the question may be 'is there any archaeology there?' Clearly, if an area of the earth's surface is to be removed by, say, an industrial development, such a question would be the first to be asked. If there is no archaeology there it becomes somewhat difficult to ask any further questions, except perhaps, 'why not?' This question – 'is there any archaeology there?' – forms the basis of many site or landscape evaluation projects undertaken within the area of salvage or rescue archaeology. Such a question may, however, be equally valid when considering a research project. Clearly if no archaeology is present, no further questions can be asked.

The first element of field archaeology is therefore to design the project. This involves the creation of a research design. The actual content of each research design is naturally going to be very different; there are, however, certain elements that should be common to all. A common format starts with a general introduction to the project. This will locate the project area, tying it into the national grid and preferably locating it on a map incorporated into the research design. The introduction should include information about site ownership and any legal restrictions in place on the site: in Britain it should ask, is the site protected as a Scheduled Ancient Monument under the 1979 Ancient Monuments and Archaeological Areas Act? It is usually useful to have had preliminary discussions with the landowner and statutory authorities before you prepare your research design. If you are simply not going to be allowed access to the land, then there is little point in proceeding in the preparation of a research design.

The second element of the research design should consider all previous archaeological work that has taken place in the area or on the site. Excavation, even of the highest standard, will destroy some archaeological information while recovering other. Having dug a site, the *in situ* evidence is destroyed, even if recorded on paper. Excavation is an unrepeatable experiment. Even surface archaeology like artefact collection from the plough zone diminishes the archaeological resource. Therefore if there has already been sufficient archaeology done in the area to answer all or some of your questions, then is it responsible to proceed with your destructive project? Naturally, when considering previous work in the area, its quality will have to be assessed. Was the project well executed and published? Even if an excellent project for its time, are there now techniques available which were not available at that time? Was the site dug before environmental samples were collected or before carbonized material could be radiocarbon dated? On the basis of all this previous work it may be possible for section three of the research design to outline the sequence of occupation on the site or in the region. This will form the starting point for your project.

The fourth, and perhaps most important, element of the research design should outline the aims and objectives of the project. This element will be different in every case and may involve both broad and specific questions. You will, however, be designing your project on the basis of very imperfect knowledge, and if the project involves excavation you will have only one attempt, as the process of excavation destroys the site even as it reveals it.

However careful your design, the fieldwork will inevitably throw up expected information and new questions. This is where archaeology differs from most other associated disciplines like history or anthropology. A historian, when searching for evidence of the wool trade in fifteenth-century Europe, say, can reasonably ignore a reference he or she finds to the seventeenth-century wool trade or fifteenth-century pottery trade. An archaeologist working in the field cannot do this. If the evidence is found on or in the ground, then removed, but not recorded, it is gone for ever. Historians can return to the documents later; the archaeologist cannot return to the dug site and find data *in situ* to re-read it. Aims and objectives must therefore be flexible enough to allow redesign as the project progresses. The fieldwork may throw up new questions you had not even thought to ask. Field archaeology requires flexibility. An over-rigid research design at best leads to disaster, at worst to archaeological irresponsibility. Unfortunately some funding bodies, and especially in the realm of 'contract' archaeology in Britain and the United States, often require very rigid research designs. These designs are more often related to tight financial controls than good archaeology.

Having decided what your aims and objectives are, the fifth element of a research design for a field archaeology project should cover methods. How are you going to achieve your aims and objectives? What techniques are you going to apply to the site or area? Are the techniques available and will they work in your area? The techniques available may simply not work. If techniques are not available to answer the questions you want to ask, you have three possibilities. You can either develop new techniques, ask new questions, or forget the field project.

The time spent on the field element of a field archaeology project may, of course, be only a fragment of the time spent on the whole project. The bulk of the time spent on the project will be on post-fieldwork analysis and publication. The sixth element of the research design should therefore consider the post-fieldwork or post-excavation and publication programme. Here you immediately run into a problem. As you have not yet undertaken the field survey or dug the site, you do not yet know what will be found, so what needs what analysis, or how such information should be appropriately published. With experience, however, it is usually possible to predict a surprisingly accurate picture of what may be found. On a palaeolithic site you will find lithics, but no pottery. On a dry, acid site organics will not survive unless they are carbonized. Organics will survive if the site is waterlogged or desiccated. Within certain parameters you can estimate the broad range of material and structures that could be expected. Your research design for the post-field element of the project must, however, remain flexible enough to incorporate the unexpected: the unique neolithic deposits with pottery found dug into your palaeolithic site, for example.

The publication element of the field archaeology research design is in many ways there purely to remind you of your commitment, and to remind your funding agencies of the potential cost of publication. Publication in some form, on the printed page, in electronic journals or even on CD-ROM, must be seen as the final element of any field project. The data you recover in the field cannot be regarded as yours. You briefly hold it in trust for all humanity. If you do not make it available to other archaeologists and the public at large, you have in effect destroyed that information. The only truly bad archaeologist is one who does not publish the results of his or her field investigations. All else is opinion. By publication, of course, I mean making publicly known rather than necessarily words printed on the pages of a book like this one. A properly curated archive in a public museum may constitute publication. The obsessive secrecy some archaeologists have for 'their own' data is not only unprofessional: it is also immoral.

The final element of a research design for any field archaeology project should consider requirements of staff, time and money. This is a requirement of the real world. It is not, however, straightforward. If you were building a bridge you could accurately determine exact quantities of materials and exactly how long it should take how many people to put the various elements together. In excavation you can only define broad parameters. A dry site may suddenly reveal a perched water table containing preserved organic artefacts. The cost of the excavation may then double overnight. Your staffing, budget and timetable should therefore be kept as flexible as your funding agencies will allow. Even then a contingency amount should be built in.

Who does field archaeology?

Field archaeologists can be broadly divided into three groups: those involved in 'pure' archaeological research; those undertaking field archaeology as part of cultural resource management; and those essentially doing it for fun, that is as a leisure-time pursuit or hobby. All three groups can and do make a major contribution to archaeology. Although one group often makes disparaging remarks about another, all three groups contain good, bad and indifferent field archaeologists. All three groups profess an interest in archaeological knowledge, and therefore are clearly differentiated from treasure hunters whose main interest is in the objects themselves – often, but not always, coupled with the monetary value of the objects. An essential interest in the context of an object makes the field archaeologist different. The treasure hunter may, however, be interested in the context if it enhances the value of the object. They are not usually interested in passing on the knowledge gained to the wider public.

The group of field archaeologists involved in 'pure' field archaeology is the smallest, and usually engage in their field archaeology as part of a much wider project. They may be university lecturers or professors, or sometimes museum curators. Their projects may be funded by the state, mainly through the British Academy in Britain, or the National Science Foundation in America. Funds are limited and fiercely fought for. Some universities and museums have their own limited funds available for field archaeology. This group should, in theory, have the knowledge, backup, time and resources to design and execute field projects to answer specific research questions. The reality is often very different with limited resources, insufficient time, and diminishing backup. They often, therefore, have to compromise by running field schools or operating within a threatened area in order to gain access to alternative funding sources.

Perhaps the largest group of field archaeologists comprises those that undertake field archaeology as part of cultural resource management. 'Cultural Resource Management' (CRM) is a catch-all term coined in America to cover all aspects of the management of cultural resources. These include both objects produced by human activity in the past, and sites of human activity. Humanly-modified landscapes, even those given mythological significance like a natural rock or a cave, can be considered cultural resources. The need to manage these resources comes from the realization that they are finite and diminishing. No new bronze-age sites are being created in Europe, but each year many are being lost.

Field archaeology is an essential element of cultural resource management, or as it is sometimes known in Britain, archaeological resource management. It employs more field archaeologists than any other area of archaeology. There are five basic elements to cultural resource management. Firstly the resource cannot be managed until it has been found. Field archaeologists are therefore required to locate the resource. This will involve a search of existing knowledge including the analysis of existing aerial photographs of the region being considered. New surveys may then be undertaken using all the non-destructive techniques considered in Chapter Three. Techniques must be non-destructive as the value of the resource can be reduced by intrusive techniques like excavation.

Having located the resource, Cultural Resource Managers must then record the resource in a user-friendly, but readily enhanceable, way. This will require the creation of some form of Sites and Monuments Record (SMR). Usually this will involve a map locating the site and a written description of the site. Most Sites and Monuments Records in Britain are held at county level and are computerized to enable rapid data retrieval, cross-referencing, and enhancement. Britain also has a non-intensive National Monuments Record (NMR) held by the Royal Commission on Historical Monuments for England at Swindon. It can be accessed via computer terminals in their London office.

Having located and recorded the resource (a continuous ongoing activity), cultural resource managers must then consider the use and protection of the resource, and mitigation procedures should the resource be threatened. All elements require field archaeologists. The resource needs legal and practical protection. Most countries in the world now have some form of legislation in place aimed at the protection of the cultural heritage. In Britain the cultural heritage is protected through the Ancient Monuments and Archaeological Areas Act of 1979 and the Town and Country Planning Acts, and in the United States of America by the Archaeological Resources Protection Act of 1979 and related laws and regulations. Valuable as these laws are, sites cannot be protected simply by passing laws; they also require practical management. The law may stop people doing things to a site, ploughing it or building on it, but without practical management the site could become overgrown, with roots damaging the buried archaeology, or animals burrowing through archaeological deposits.

The use of the resource also has to be managed. Archaeologists may wish to use the site for damaging research through excavation, and teachers may want more information about the site to use it for educational purposes. Tourists and visitors will want access to the site. Any use of the site may result in damage, so the cultural resource manager will have to weigh up conflicts between use and preservation.

In addition to threats to the site through use, the site may be threatened through development or natural processes. Development threats often create the greatest impact on archaeological sites and this area involves the greatest employment of field archaeologists. In countries with the principle 'the polluter should pay' (as through Planning Policy Guidance Note 16 in England), large sums are often made available to undertake field archaeology in advance of development. Often the field archaeologist is involved initially in a desk-top assessment of known information, followed by a field evaluation of the development area. This may lead to a major salvage or rescue excavation, and often an enormous post-excavation project leading to publication.

The third group of people who do field archaeology are those doing it as a hobby. These are the traditional 'amateurs' of British archaeology. They form the backbone of British archaeology based on the county archaeological societies – some, like the Sussex Archaeological Society, with over 2,000 members. Some work in the field with professional archaeologists and others work on their own field projects. Their contribution in Britain is enormous as they are largely unfettered by the constraints of time, money and policy inflicted on many professionals. Unfortunately, many countries have no such tradition of amateur field archaeology.

Theoretical basis of field archaeology

Much has been written in recent years about the apparent split between archaeological theory and practice, as if the practice of field archaeology has no theoretical basis. Even the newest crew member on an excavation, digging her trowel into the ground for the first time, is working within a theoretical framework. If not, she would be simply a treasure hunter. This is not the place to review in detail the major theoretical movements in recent archaeology, although many of these, particularly the culture-historical, processual and post-processual schools have, or are in the process of, impacting on field archaeology. Alternative texts are available to make these theoretical positions accessible to the field archaeologist (for example, Trigger 1994).

Field archaeologists deal first and foremost with data: fragments of fired clay; pieces of chipped stone; round, linear and oval holes in the ground; small piles of stones sometimes held together with mortar. At the moment the excavator starts revealing them in the ground, he or she begins the process of interpretation. The fired clay fragments become sherds from pots; the chipped stones become hand axes or bifaces; the round, linear and oval holes become 'postholes', 'ditches' and 'storage pits'. The piles of stones become 'walls'. Theories are being applied to the data.

Theoretical archaeology starts at the most abstract, but ends up by impacting on everything a field archaeologist does. A consideration of the limits and validity of the methods and grounds of knowledge (epistemology) is fundamental to how field archaeologists work. Essentially, can the field archaeologist prove or disprove what he or she is claiming? Archaeologists working in what became known as 'New Archaeology' in the 1960s, particularly in the United States, believed that hypotheses could be proved or disproved, essentially like a chemical experiment. These archaeologists, sometimes referred to as positivists, asserted that it was possible to test an archaeological theory and so 'prove' it to be either true or false (Binford and Binford 1968).

Some archaeologists maintain that, as the past is gone, we can never really prove that our ideas about it are true, or even that the certain function of a small round hole packed with stones (a posthole?) can be proved or disproved. Some maintain that it is possible to prove that an idea about the past is untrue, but that one can never really prove that it is true. The more times we find small round holes packed with stones (postholes?) and arranged in round, square or rectangular patterns, the more likely we judge ourselves to be dealing with timber buildings. It would be difficult, however, actually to prove that what we had found were not simply round, square or rectangular patterns of small round holes packed with stones.

The culture-historical approach to archaeology began as an attempt by the early archaeologists to use the approaches used by traditional historians. Archaeology was seen as a way of simply projecting history back into periods when there was no writing. The culture-historical approach attempts to 'reconstruct' the history of peoples. As much of the world consists of nation-states and much archaeology is, and has been for some time, state-funded, the 'culture-historical' approach remains important in much of the world. The 'culture-historical' approach is dominated by the description and 'testing' of theories by applying them to data. Essential for this approach is the gathering of detailed cultural data: pots, metalwork, house plans and the like, and their classification. From this database 'archaeological cultures' were defined. These were then seen by many as representing different peoples.

The 'culture-historical' approach requires field archaeologists to provide detailed local sequences of artefacts and information about their geographic distribution. Led by nineteenth-century pioneers like General Pitt-Rivers, archaeological features such as ditches were sectioned at right angles to create a vertical section through the site. Artefacts were then carefully plotted against the observed stratigraphy to give a sequence. The 'culture-historical' approach therefore required field archaeologists to do certain things in certain ways. Known, or unknown to the excavator he or she is working within a theoretical framework.

Field archaeologists working within a 'processual' theoretical framework do things rather differently to those working within a culture-historical framework, although field techniques inevitably overlap. Processual archaeology emphasizes the interaction between human culture and the environment, and sees this interaction as essential for understanding culture change. As you will immediately see if working within this theoretical framework, every seed, shell and bone becomes essential data in the way that it was perhaps not so significant to traditional culture-historical archaeologists. Processual archaeologists are positivists, believing that hypotheses about the past can be tested. Initially processual archaeologists largely ignored the ideological and symbolic nature of some of the data they recovered, but this area has been incorporated by some processual archaeologists into a theoretical framework sometimes referred to as 'cognitive–processual' archaeology. Processual archaeology remains the dominant theoretical framework in which most field archaeologists in Britain and America work.

For some archaeologists, processual archaeology placed too many limits on the way data could be looked at. Particularly, the attempts to derive broad 'laws' from the data were seen to exclude the importance of the individual and of individual actions in the past. A mass of detailed criticism of the processual methods was loosely brought together under the umbrella of 'post-processual' archaeology. The symbolic nature of much material culture found by archaeologists was stressed by post-processual archaeologists, and indeed, this area was adopted as important by archaeologists who retained essentially a processual framework, that is 'cognitive–processual' archaeology. Post-processual archaeology, however, goes very much further and is impacting on how field archaeology is practised in the field.

At the simplest level, field archaeologists working within a post-processual framework will, for example, record not only the plan of a stone circle or stone row, but also how it is placed in the landscape in relation to natural stones, prominent peaks, short and long views. The context in the widest sense of the term is brought into play in the interpretation. Equally, when digging a site a processual archaeologist will be happy to recover every bone, small and large, from a defined deposit. A post-processual archaeologist will see intention in how certain bones or bone groups are deposited in the ground, both in relation to each other and other elements of the site. The processual archaeologist is interested in big processes, the post-processual archaeologist is also interested in an individual's action: the careful placing of a bone or axe. As you can see, what a field archaeologist does in the field will be determined to some extent by the theoretical framework in which she or he is working.

In addition to the broad theoretical frameworks in which a field archaeologist works, there is also, within the process of excavation itself, a considerable body of theory. A crew member or volunteer picking up potsherds in a ploughed field, or carefully cleaning a layer of soil off a wall foundation may not always be thinking of the theoretical basis of what is being done, but nevertheless the theory is present in the practice. One area of theory is of such central relevance to the field archae-ologist that the whole of Chapter Two is devoted to it. This relates to how an archaeological site is formed and then transformed into what may be located in the landscape or dug up today.

Stratigraphy is a core concept within field archaeology and has a strong theoret-ical basis going back into the eighteenth century. J. Hutton's *Theory of the earth with proofs and illustrations*, published in Edinburgh in 1795, is in many ways a starting point in the evolution of stratigraphic theory. Surprisingly, however, many archaeologists failed to see the theoretical importance of the notions of stratigraphy being developed in geology. Indeed the real importance of stratigraphy was not widely accepted until the work of the American Alfred Kidder and the British archaeologists Mortimer Wheeler and Kathleen Kenyon this century. Even today some archaeologists dig in arbitrary horizontal spits (levels of identical thickness), regardless of the natural contours of the site's stratification.

The basic theory behind archaeological stratification is that, as originally depos-ited, the layer at the bottom of a sequence is the earliest and each layer above it is progressively younger. The layer at the top of the sequence is the youngest. A layer has to be deposited on something and that something has to be there first. Archae-ological stratification, however, includes more than layers of soil or whatever. It also includes cultural interfaces like walls, ditches and pits, all of which are part of the stratigraphy. We shall return to this in Chapter Six.

On excavations, therefore, virtually all aspects of what field archaeologists do are theory-laden. This includes both broad theoretical approaches like 'processualism' but also specific theoretical concepts like stratigraphy. Non-excavation fieldwork is also theory-laden. Much of this is tied up with the interpretation of field data, but unless the theoretical framework is evident in the field practice, then often the data will not be collected in a way which will enable it to be interpreted in a particular theoretical framework.

Polished stone axes, for example, are found by field archaeologists working in many parts of the world, from the Caribbean, through Europe, to the Far East. They are found widely scattered throughout the landscape. Culture-historical archae-ologists would see their value for dating, perhaps through classification. Processual archaeologists may see them as tools for cutting down trees to clear forests for agriculture. Post-processual archaeologists, while accepting their value for dating or chopping down trees, would also recognize that as they are often found unused, they are not all casual losses. Some at least may have had a symbolic or ritual role. If this is the case, where they are deposited and even the orientation of the blade may be significant.

When working on a field survey around the neolithic–bronze age settlement at Man Kok, Lantau Island, with a group of Chinese archaeologists, we found two polished stone axes on the hill above the settlement. Working within a processual framework, the group carefully recorded the position of the axes in the landscape. Their interpretation was self-evident. They were axes. Axes are used to cut down trees. They were, therefore, lost in an area being cleared for agriculture. The fact that both blades were clearly facing away from the settlement was not formally recorded. Indeed, the orientation of stone axes is rarely recorded in field surveys. Are unused stone axes regularly found with blades facing away from settlement areas? Were they placed there to symbolize the limit of clearance or human control of the landscape? Do they mark the junction of tame and wild? The way one records field data may expand or limit how one can interpret it.

The same will apply to the recording of archaeological features in the landscape. How they are recorded will limit or expand the range of possible interpretations. Take an enclosure on the top of a hill: a British iron-age hillfort, for example. Mount Caburn, in Sussex, England, is a good example. Here a small 'hillfort' has been studied by archaeologists since General Pitt-Rivers first dug here in September 1877. This prominent hill has a bank and ditch dug around the top and has a single entrance (Fig. 1.2). Clearly it is a defended enclosure: a 'fort'. But is it? Two elements have been taken: hilltop and bank-with-ditch. Little else was considered in the field survey and publications, which show these two elements only. What was not recorded was the shape of the hill, which in fact makes the site largely indefensible. Within the enclosure is the top of a dome-shaped hill, whose convex slopes make it virtually impossible to see anything other than a very small area within the enclosure or very short lengths of its ramparts at any one time. Unless defended by hundreds of people, it could quite easily be attacked unknown to the defenders. Given the general absence of contemporary material within the enclosure and apparently low local population (based on site densities), what was being defended anyway?

If one is working within a theoretical framework which sees bank-and-ditch as indicating defence, then they will be recorded in such a way that it will be difficult to see them as anything other than for defence. However, if you are working within a theoretical framework which recognizes the potential for symbolism in both constructions and artefacts, you may see the bank or ditch simply as a boundary, a dividing line, between different spaces in the landscape. How these spaces relate to the natural landscape may be of crucial importance in their understanding.

Superficially similar enclosures may have very different functions, depending on where they are in the landscape. Take British neolithic causewayed enclosures, for example. When first studied in the 1920s and 1930s they were carefully surveyed,

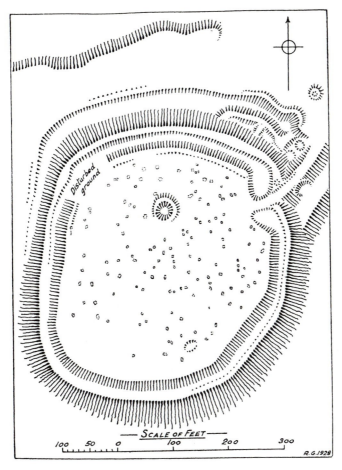

Figure 1.2 An early plan of Mount Caburn, Sussex, an iron-age hill 'fort'. (Sussex Archaeological Society)

and all their plans looked remarkably similar: one to four circles of interrupted ditches. When groups of such enclosures are examined locally in their landscape context, it becomes clear that some were false-crested (apparently on a crest but actually below it) overlooking dense clay forest, while others were on hilltops overlooking thin chalk soils suitable for neolithic agriculture. Visibility both from and to the enclosures is significant in their interpretation. Depending on the theoretical perspective of the field archaeologist, such data may or may not be recorded.

Some field archaeologists may claim that one must simply be 'objective' and record 'everything'. Clearly such an approach is unrealistic in terms of time and money, but also what does 'everything' mean? In the 1920s everything thought to be archaeologically relevant about causewayed enclosures was recorded. Now we realize that much more is potentially relevant than just the archaeology as such ('the archaeology' is the remains that are the subject of 'archaeology'). Location and orientation of sites and artefacts may be as significant as their sequence of occupation and date. The field archaeologists' theoretical perspective will, up to a point, always determine where and how he or she practises field archaeology.

Project management

It may seem odd to find a section on 'management' in an introductory textbook on field archaeology. Indeed, if one looks back at the classic textbooks on field archaeology, 'managment' appears nowhere. Anyone running a field project, or even a section of a field project like a trench supervisor, is, however, a manager. 'Management' – like 'archaeology' – means different things to different practitioners but essentially it is the process of planning, organizing, directing, co-ordinating, controlling and supervising any activity with responsibility for results. It is usually seen in terms of business, making and selling ice-creams or constructing a housing estate. Its concepts are, however, equally significant for archaeological field projects. Each project has to be planned, undertaken and productive of results.

Project management was developed by industrialists like Frederick Taylor in America early this century (Taylor 1911). The aim was to design specific work processes and sequences of work to get a job done in the most efficient manner. This generally involved specialist workers doing specific jobs in a predefined order. This, of course, was exactly what the great British field archaeologists like General Pitt-Rivers and Sir Mortimer Wheeler, with their military training, had been doing or were about to do. A gunner would shoot, a quartermaster would supply, a sapper would sap (dig trenches). So on their excavations, labourers would dig, photographers would photograph and surveyors would survey.

Classic project management, often known as scientific management, blended well with the objective nature of 'processual' archaeology. Each element in the field could be dealt with by a specialist in their own area or field. Essentially, everything could be done in the field by highly-trained technicians. The results could then be interpreted and re-interpreted after the field project, as 'all' the field data had been objectively recorded. Field archaeology, however, is not like making ice-creams or building housing estates, so the mindless adoption of 'scientific management' in some areas of archaeology, especially in British and American public archaeology, resulted in much dull, repetitive archaeology and a bored work-force. Archaeologists were often adopting 'scientific managment' at times when industry was moving on into newer concepts like matrix management. Archaeology has always been good at adopting and adapting from other disciplines. Its success in this process rests largely on its ability to adapt, modify and use only those elements that are really applicable and not blindly to accept theories and practices from other disciplines.

There are two main elements to the management of field projects. One relates to the process: what order will what be done in, with what techniques and equipment? The second is: who will do it with whom? People cannot simply be slotted in like a piece of equipment, such as a back hoe. The back hoe is hired, the hole is dug, the back hoe is laid off. People can be treated in a similar way, but rarely will a project benefit from this approach to people. People need to feel involved and be responsible for their actions within the project.

Managing the process of a field project is relatively straightforward; it just needs forethought and organizational ability. Certain things clearly have to be done before others. In 1991 English Heritage produced its model of scientific management as applied to archaeological projects (Andrews 1991). *MAP2*, as it has become known, following an earlier version known simply as *MAP*, argued that archaeological projects should be organized in clearly defined phases. Each phase should have clearly defined objectives and have adequate staff, equipment, time and costs allocated to them. Five phases were proposed (Andrews 1991):

Phase 1: Project planning
Phase 2: Fieldwork
Phase 3: Assessment of potential for analysis
Phase 4: Analysis and report preparation
Phase 5: Dissemination

The importance of reviewing results of the developing project is particularly stressed, with each phase being carefully documented. Particularly important is the need to update the project design as information becomes available from the field or preliminary analysis, that is, be flexible. The desirability of external monitoring of the project and some form of quality control is stressed.

One of the most important aspects of archaeological project management is the ability to control time and money. A timescale for the project and individual elements of it must be defined, together with the order in which tasks should be performed. This information must be clearly and simply available to all those involved in the project. The best way to do this is visually. Such charts have been used in industry for almost a hundred years, but rarely appeared in the management of archaeological projects until the 1980s. One of the most widely used was designed by the American engineer Henry Gantt (1861–1919) and is named after him – the Gantt chart. A Gantt chart deals essentially with scheduling as relating to time (Coventry and Barker 1981). The Gantt chart is a bar chart with individual activities identified and arranged along the y-axis while time is arranged along the x-axis. For example, within a whole project, say 30 days would be allocated to excavation. This would be represented as a 30-day bar. This could be broken down into smaller time allocations, say three days for machine-stripping overburden on the site, 20 days hand-digging, five days final planning and photography, and two days machine-backfilling. People, or groups of people, can be allocated to the specific tasks.

An alternative to the Gantt chart would be to use a Critical Path Analysis (CPA) chart. This, rather than using bar charts, uses an arrow diagram which is sometimes also known as 'network analysis'. This involves producing a diagramatic model of the real process of doing the project from start to finish. The idea is to produce a 'critical path' through the maze of individual activities required in any project (Coventry and Barker 1981). For example a site may need to be cleared and fenced before the site accommodation and facilities for the labour force are put in place. This may take two or three days with perhaps only three or four people, so all of this appears on your chart before the arrival of the back hoe to dig off the overburden. Only at this stage should the larger digging crew arrive. The critical path analysis chart, therefore, provides a graphic model of the most efficient way of getting the job done.

For archaeology, with all its unforeseen elements like suddenly discovering a waterlogged element to the site, a third management technique may be most appropriate; this is the Programme Evaluation and Review Technique, or PERT. Like critical path analysis, PERT involves a model or network linked by arrows to represent all activities in a logical order. CPA provides one time estimate for each activity, while PERT is more flexible and therefore perhaps more appropriate to archaeology. PERT defines not one but three time-estimates for all tasks. It provides the most likely time, but also indicates minimum and maximum possible times. Rain can seriously slow down the progress of excavation, while if a deposit turns out to be shallower than anticipated it will be dug very much more quickly.

A sound field project, therefore, requires a clear aim and a clear management plan to achieve that aim.

CHAPTER TWO

What is an archaeological site? How is it formed and transformed?

Archaeological sites consist essentially of activity areas and rubbish. That is where people have done things in the past and left some residue of having done something. This may have been a great 'something' like constructing Machu Picchu or Stonehenge, or a very minor 'something' like flaking a flint axe or eating a shellfish. Some activity areas, like a sacred rock, may involve no surviving residue other than the natural rock, so one can never be certain that it was an activity area. Unless there is clear oral tradition or documentary evidence that it was a sacred rock, then it cannot be considered an archaeological site, simply a site that could have been used. What we now see as archaeological sites are of course not intact activity areas. They have been changed through time. They are being changed during the life of the activity area, changed at the point of discard or abandonment and changed after discard. Archaeological sites are therefore transformed or changed activity areas and rubbish. The American scholar Michael Schiffer, among others, has been very influential in the consideration of the processes of transformation, and what follows is loosely based on much of his work (for example, Schiffer 1976 and Schiffer 1987) but consideration of transformation processes goes right back to Charles Darwin and his study of earthworm activity (Darwin 1881).

Primary and secondary uses

It is important to remember that few artefacts or features have a single use throughout their life. Objects and structures can change in both their use and their meaning over both short and long periods of time. The first range of transformation processes takes place in the living context of the community making and using the artefacts and structures. Take a pot, for example. It could start its life as a container to eat from. It might then become cracked and considered no longer suitable for use as tableware. If in a very rich household, it might be discarded at this stage. Alternatively it could be relegated to the kitchen, perhaps to hold wooden spoons. In due course it might be replaced by a chipped but less damaged pot. The first pot could then be relegated to an outbuilding, perhaps to hold chicken-feed. Finally it is broken and can no longer be used as a container. The sherds could be discarded at this stage, or could be broken up to make hard core for the farmyard, or perhaps

Figure 2.1   Medieval sagging-based cooking pot buried behind the farmhouse on Bullock Down, East Sussex. Re-cycled as a chicken feeder?

pulverized to make grog and added as a filler in some new pottery being made. The pot, therefore, has a primary use and then a range of secondary uses, ending up being recycled in new pots. Often this process cannot be detected in the archaeological record. There would be no way of telling whether the grog in the new pots had been through this cycle of use or was the remains of kiln wasters that had gone straight from firing to second firing as grog. As a field archaeologist, however, one must be aware of possibilities of secondary use and the recycling of materials.

Sometimes secondary use is obvious in the archaeological context. Take, for example, the medieval sagging-based cooking pot in Fig. 2.1. When found it was rimless and carefully buried in the surface of the chalk behind a medieval house. In it were a few carbonized grains of wheat, barley, oats and vetch seeds. When removed from the ground, signs of burning on the bottom of the pot showed that it had been used for what sagging-based pots were made for in the middle ages, that is, as a cooking pot. However, the context of discovery indicates it was no longer being used as a cooking pot but had been put to a secondary use. Its context in a farmyard suggested an agricultural use. Perhaps it had been re-used as a feeding bowl for chickens? Could the carbonized seeds have been the residue of chicken feed, including some accidentally burnt during a drying process?

Building materials can often be seen put to a secondary use. Any inorganic material from a demolished building, like bricks or tiles, could be re-used as hard core for the construction of a new building. Alternatively, particular types of material can be re-used for specific purposes for which they are well suited. Fired

Figure 2.2 Medieval roof-tiles re-cycled in the sixteenth century to make a lead-melting hearth.

roof-tiles, for example, withstand heat so are excellent for flooring or backing for hearths. Figure 2.2 shows medieval roof-tiles from a hall carefully re-used in the sixteenth century to make a hearth for melting lead during the destruction phase in a medieval castle. Of course here again we have the problem that although clearly made as roof-tiles (each has two peg-holes), there is no evidence that they were actually ever used on a roof. They may have been excess tiles, coming straight from the kiln. Clearly, however, they had a primary function and – whether used in that way or not – were put to a secondary use.

Grog, the recycling of old pots as filler in new pots, is easy to identify, but recognizing the recycling of other materials is more difficult. Bronze is a good example. Tools made out of bronze have a relatively short life because bronze itself is fairly soft. A bronze axe in regular use will quickly become blunt, chipped or even broken. Although they can be re-sharpened, when the damage is too great the axe is likely to be mixed with other broken bronze tools, remelted and recast into new axes. The material itself has been recycled in such a way that there is no way of establishing its original function. Was it originally an axe, chisel, pin or mixture of many different broken tools?

Sometimes, of course, objects are not used in such a way that they get damaged. A special pot, for example, could be carefully preserved unused on a shelf or only brought out for rare special occasions. It might be passed from generation to generation, achieving added value with age. It could become a cherished heirloom. Such an object might never reach the archaeological record or might do so hundreds of years after its manufacture. Such objects can change in meaning through time, but they can also totally confuse archaeological dating as they appear in the archaeological record hundreds of years later than their date of manufacture. If this form of cultural transformation process is not recognized, then it can create severe problems when dating an archaeological deposit. The first problem to be aware of, when considering the creation of an archaeological site, is that it is the result of changing use of materials and features during the life of the site.

Rubbish and accidental loss

Secondly, archaeological sites result from how people discarded things and features during the life of the site, and how they finally abandoned the site. Rubbish, meaning anything considered of no further use in the living context, can be disposed of in a variety of ways. Essentially rubbish can be disposed of either where it is generated or somewhere else. An activity can generate rubbish and then those generating that rubbish can simply walk away from it. This could be considered rubbish in its primary position. Alternatively, the rubbish could be collected up and disposed of somewhere else, that is, in a secondary location. Rubbish in a primary location provides at least two pieces of basic information: what activity took place and where it took place. The second type of rubbish, redeposited or secondary rubbish, only indicates what activity took place, not where it took place. Clearly primary rubbish is of more value to archaeologists than secondary rubbish.

Figure 2.3 shows a good example of primary rubbish. Here a flint-knapper has prepared an axe and walked away from the rubbish, that is, flint flakes generated during the manufacturing process. If this material remains *in situ*, is rapidly buried and not subjected to natural movements and changes in its buried context, it may provide even more information than *what* happened *where*. It may also provide some '*how*' information. Was the flint-knapper crouching, sitting or standing? The pattern of the flakes may provide such information.

Rubbish can be disposed of in a secondary context more or less anywhere. In certain societies there may, of course, be rules or taboos relating to all rubbish or particular classes of rubbish. Clear differentiation in how and where different classes of rubbish are disposed of may hint at rules or taboos. Even if there are no such rules or taboos, rubbish can be disposed of in a variety of different ways, some of which may survive in the archaeological record and some of which may not, or only partially. Often rubbish is used to fill in unwanted holes. Although often referred to as 'rubbish pits' this is generally a secondary use of pits dug for storage, as cess pits, water holes or quarry pits. 'Rubbish pits' are of course of great importance archaeologically as although the actual rubbish may not be of the same date, it is generally, but not always, deposited in one act or over a short period of time, so the activity of rubbish deposition is of one date.

Rubbish can be disposed of in a variety of other ways. For example it can be 'middened', that is put in piles either close to or away from settlements. Unlike a pit, which has a finite volume, middens can be added to over very long periods of

Figure 2.3 Primary rubbish. *In situ* waste flakes from prehistoric flint tool manufacture.

time, and because they are above ground may be subjected to more changes than rubbish in a pit. Other types of rubbish disposal may leave little or no trace. Rubbish may, for example, be spread out over fields to enrich the soil. The organic element of the rubbish will break down and be incorporated into new growing plants. The inorganic material, pottery, flint flakes or metalwork, may survive spread over the fields' surfaces, be worm-sorted down to lower levels, or move down slopes under gravity. Coarser pottery will break up completely in this process. Rubbish dumped in rivers could totally vanish from the archaeological record or just leave odd hints in river alluvia, perhaps miles downstream from the area of deposition. Secondary rubbish disposal is therefore very varied and often difficult to interpret in more than a general way.

Some objects reach the archaeological record not through the deliberate disposal of rubbish, but through accidental loss. At first sight *loss*, being entirely accidental, would appear to be arbitrary without any associated patterns. This, however, is not strictly true. Loss has very strong biases in terms of size, value and where the object is lost. Clearly big things are less likely to be lost than small things. A cart is less likely to be lost than a coin. Even with big things there is a strong bias in favour of some objects not being lost and others being lost. This will create a strong bias in the archaeological record. Take transport, for example. There are many more boats surviving from British prehistory than carts. This, certainly from the later bronze age onwards, was probably not because there were more boats than carts, but just that boats lost in rivers and lakes are more difficult to recover than carts that tip off a track. There are clearly 'loss traps' that favour the loss and

Figure 2.4   Secondary rubbish in a latrine pit.

subsequent preservation of some classes of artefacts (for example, boats) and not others (for example, carts).

Size also plays a part in the loss of smaller artefacts. Large coins, for example, are easier to find than smaller ones. In the case of smaller objects, value also is particularly important. More effort will be put into finding a small lost gold coin than perhaps a larger copper-alloy one. Size and value are therefore factors which are important when considering loss. The value is, of course, the value to the person or community losing something, not the archaeologist's estimate of value. A scrap of bone from an ancestor may be of more value to the community owning it than any metal artefacts. If mislaid during a ritual, no stone may be left unturned in attempts to recover the bone scrap.

Where something is lost may also determine whether any effort is made to recover it. Take the Raeren copy of a Siegberg beaker found in a latrine pit in a medieval castle (Fig. 2.4). The beaker has lost its rim but is otherwise intact and certainly would still hold water. Clearly it is of no use as a drinking mug on the royal table, but as an exotic import it could be recovered and put to a new use in a servant's house. The reason no effort was made to recover it for secondary use was because of where it was lost, in a rich deposit of royal ordure!

Burials

The burial of the dead can be considered as a very specific type of rubbish disposal. There are many ways of disposing of the dead, some of which survive in the archaeological record while others do not. Sometimes human remains may be recycled as cult objects, like the bones of the medieval saints. More usually they are discarded through inhumation, cremation, excarnation or water burial. Clearly some forms of burial leave better archaeological traces than others. It should also be remembered that disposal of the dead, rather than being a single act like Christian burial, may be a process lasting over many years. In some areas of China, for example, traditional burial involves inhumation burial in wooden coffins for seven years. The bones are then dug up, put in special burial pots and placed on hill slopes overlooking the sea. These ancestors are then visited at least once a year, offerings are made and ceremonies held. Chinese may travel thousands of miles to be with their ancestors for the annual Ching Ming festival held on the 106th day after the winter solstice.

Disposal of human bodies may also involve the discard of artefacts with the body: 'grave goods'. These are extremely valuable to archaeologists as they usually represent a contemporary deposition, even if all the objects are not of the same date. Heirlooms could be put in a grave, or there might be a tradition to bury certain things even if they were no longer in current use. There is always the problem of how far grave goods actually represent real everyday objects and how far they are specially made for burial and therefore tell us something about burial practices but nothing about everyday life. Some objects are clearly made specifically for burial, like the jade suits of Imperial China, but other grave goods like beakers in the early British bronze age may have been either ritual, or everyday, drinking vessels put to a secondary use as grave goods. The actual vessels buried may, however, have been made specifically for burial in the style of those in everyday use.

Abandonment of a site

At some stage in the life of an activity area, a settlement, or even a city, it may be abandoned. At this stage all features, pits, buildings, roads, will be abandoned but also a range of artefacts, which although still perfectly usable, will be left behind. Some sites like Ozette in Washington State, or Port Royal, Jamaica, may be abandoned as the result of natural disaster without any time for the inhabitants to recover even the most valuable artefacts. All is abandoned under a mudslide or the sea. Usually, however, sites are abandoned more slowly and the inhabitants can decide what to take and what to abandon. Crucial decisions will have to be taken. These may depend partly on the relative value of artefacts and partly on how far the people are moving.

Unless specifically designed as mobile, structures are rarely taken to the new settlement unless it is very close. It is often easier to prepare new roof timbers than to salvage old timbers, which may already be in the process of decay. Specific ornamental elements may, however, be taken. Distance is clearly an important element in the decision-making process when movement is being planned. If the settlement is moving only a very short distance, even bricks could be salvaged for re-use. They are unlikely to be taken, however, if the group is moving either very

Figure 2.5   Re-usable materials in the process of being scavenged from a deserted building.

far or along a difficult route. The same applies to mobile artefacts. Those that are heavy and easily replaced are more likely to be abandoned than light and scarcer artefacts.

In the weaving process, for example, loom weights are heavy and easy to replace whether made of clay or stone. They are, therefore, often abandoned. On bronze age and Saxon sites in Britain, for example, lines of loom weights are often found, looking as though they have been simply cut off the vertical loom and abandoned. Finely-decorated bone weaving combs, with their greater labour input and the skill required in their manufacture, are more likely to be taken to the new settlement. Valuable objects may, however, be deliberately abandoned when a site is deserted if their abandonment has some specific cultural or religious meaning. Bronze arte-facts are sometimes found in abandoned later bronze age houses in Britain. Some may have been casual losses but others may have been votive offerings left as part of abandonment ritual.

Once a site has been abandoned other communities in the area may see it as a useful local resource of firewood or building materials. It may not have been considered sensible by the original community for all structural timber to be taken long distances simply for firewood. A local community, however, would see the wood as a valuable local resource. Buildings could be systematically scavenged for local use, resulting in partial or complete removal of wood, bricks, stone or indeed any other reusable materials (Fig. 2.5).

Finally, when the settlement has been levelled, it could be changed by further human actions. The site could be levelled further for new building, or cut away to make terraces for new houses or agriculture. The site could be ploughed, resulting in artefacts being moved around in the plough soil, but also moved down slopes. Any further human disturbance of the ground might result in elements of the site being moved around and redeposited.

Natural transformation processes

Even if a community simply walks away from its settlement or activity area, the site is unlikely to remain as left. Even in the case of natural disasters like Ozette, Port Royal or Pompeii, natural processes will be at work changing the remains. These processes are often known as natural or post-depositional transformation processes, as opposed to the human or cultural transformation processes already described.

Wind can be an agent both of destruction and preservation. Exposed elements of a site, like a masonry tower, may be either continuously or seasonally subjected to wind erosion. Fine particles can be blown off masonry, for example, and this material then acts as sand-blasting on the adjacent bit of masonry. Softer elements, like mortar between the stones, are likely to be abraded first, perhaps loosening stones which then fall off revealing a new surface to wind erosion (Fig. 2.6). All these particles must, however, end up somewhere and if they fall to the ground at another part of the site they may build up a deposit which protects that area from further wind erosion.

Figure 2.6   Mortar eroded out of medieval masonry through wind action.

Water is another natural agent of either destruction or preservation, depending on local conditions. If the site is permanently waterlogged even organics are likely to survive, but usually water acts as an agent of destruction. River or coastal erosion can remove whole sites, washing the remains downriver or even out to sea. The rolling action of artefacts in fast-moving water may simply abrade them, as in the case of lithics, or may totally destroy them as would happen to soft ceramics. Flash floods on otherwise dry land can also damage or remove sites.

Freezing water may also preserve or destroy. If the site is permanently frozen, the organics will survive as if put in a deep-freezer. Rapid or seasonal freezing and thawing is, however, extremely destructive. Water in the cells of organic material or within the voids in stone or ceramics will expand on freezing, blowing apart small parts of the object. Over time the whole object can be broken up in this way. Ceramics, particularly if low-fired and porous, can be broken down into their constituent elements of clay and filler and so effectively vanish back into the soil. These constituent elements will become impossible to trace if they are moved about in the soil.

Animals are one of the main causes of movement within the soil. These may be big burrowing animals like rabbits, small earthworms, or even microscopic soil mites. The effect of burrowing animals can be devastating on an archaeological site. Whole layers can be dug out of burrows and redeposited on the surface. If the burrows then collapse, all layers above can be broken up and drop into lower deposits. Burrowing animals often live in colonies which can result in large-scale destruction of buried archaeology. Usually this destruction is clear in the archaeological record, but if it happened centuries earlier and the site has re-consolidated, it may not be clear and so could result in misinterpretation of the data. Land crabs in loose sandy deposits create particular problems as their burrows often fill in with sand from above as soon as the burrow is dug. Artefacts can drop with the falling sand, moving them from one layer down into the next.

Earthworms, like wind and water, both preserve and destroy sites. Earthworms burrow to over 2 m down. They do this by swallowing the earth in front of them and then, in the absence of any underground cavities they can fill with this soil, will bring it to the surface where it is discarded as worm 'casts'. Charles Darwin (1881) calculated that in some areas ten tons of soil are dumped on the surface of each acre of land each year. This has the effect of moving objects down the profile. Objects abandoned on the surface will have soil cast above them and they will collapse as voids are made by the worms below. This process will aid the preservation of the object as it will be protected from wind, water and frost. The process may, however, move the object into a lower layer, thus confusing the dating of the site. In practice, however, objects tend to move down the profile in broadly the sequence in which they were laid down. The real problem comes in relatively shallow soils with a compact bedrock (Fig. 2.7). On the shallow, chalk soils of southern England, for example all artefacts can be worm-sorted down to the same layer just above the chalk. This gives the characteristic chalkland soil profile of stone- (and artefact-) free topsoil, the worm cast, and the stony layer (with artefacts) just above the bedrock. All stratigraphy can be lost with prehistoric, historic and modern artefacts all found in the same layer.

Figure 2.7 Effect of worm-sorting on shallow chalk downland soils (with possible posthole below).

Changes through chemical action are usually much slower than the natural processes described so far. Rainwater, even when not affected by industrial pollution to form 'acid rain', is slightly acid. This will affect particularly calcareous materials like lime mortar used in building. The mortar will be dissolved and wash away, perhaps finally resulting in the collapse of the structure. As the rainwater then passes into the soil it may take humic acids into solution from dead plant-tissues. This acid water will then affect buried artefacts and structures, dissolving away elements. These dissolved elements may survive in the soil and so could potentially be identified by archaeologists as chemical traces, but it is more likely that they will be washed out of the soil into rivers and finally the sea.

In addition to the chemical elements in soil moving down the profile and down slopes, soil itself is constantly on the move. As well as being cast onto the surface where worms are present, it is also constantly moving down slopes as the result of gravity, a process known as soil creep. The so-called 'sheep tracks' often visible on slopes are little natural terraces caused by the gradual movement of soil downslope under the influence of gravity. These natural terraces gradually move downhill. Where there is a good vegetation cover, the movement is slow as the vegetation holds soil particles on the slope. Once the vegetation cover is broken, however, the movement can be quite rapid and it is often accentuated by water washing down the slope. The effect of this process can be seen at the bottom of fields where the moving soil may be trapped to form a lynchet, or in the bottom of valleys where depths of colluvium build up. Artefacts can move down slopes as part of this process and be redeposited in the new soil deposits. As will be seen in Chapter Six, although a site on a hilltop or slope may vanish, its material remains may form an essential dating tool for the re-formed lynchet or valley-bottom deposits.

In addition to worms, insects and mites, most soils – except those desiccated or waterlogged – contain fungi and bacteria. Anything organic in the soil will be affected by these organisms and, unless they have an inorganic element like calcium in bone or silica in some plants (phytoliths), will vanish as the result of fungal and bacterial action.

Growth of any vegetation on an archaeological site can affect the archaeology, changing or even destroying it. Standing masonry can be broken up by roots grow-ing in cracks and forcing them apart. In the short term, roots and branches may hold masonry together, but when the plant dies and rots, then the masonry may collapse into the voids made by the rotting roots. If this happens above ground, the effect may be very visible and dramatic. Root action below ground is equally devastating, but may remain invisible until revealed by the field archaeologist excavating the site. Recent root action is usually straightforward to interpret, but ancient root action is not always so clear, particularly after worm-sorting and soil creep has affected the deposits. The broken-up wall may end up looking deliberately slighted by human action.

Natural earth movement can include both very minor shifting of surface layers or major movement as the result of earthquakes or volcanic action. Some deposits, like clay, have a tendency to slump down slopes, taking whatever is above with them down the slope. When this process detaches pieces of buildings it is often clear archaeologically. However, the slumping of deposits without features, like lithic scatters, is often more difficult to trace if the deposits have reconsolidated over time in their new location. Major earth movements like earthquakes usually create such devastation to archaeological deposits that their effect is easily trace-able. The same applies to transformation as the result of volcanic action.

Two examples of abandonment

We will now look at a couple of examples of these processes in action on buildings, one masonry and the other timber. Naturally every example will be different, but the broad processes are often very similar with only detail varying from site to site.

Masonry buildings can be constructed in a variety of ways. We will consider a small medieval farmhouse like Building 5 excavated at Kiln Combe, Bullock Down, Beachy Head, East Sussex, in England in 1976 (Drewett 1982a). This consisted of a small rectangular house 8.5 m × 5 m. It was constructed by cutting a level plat-form into the hill slope. The walls were then constructed on this platform without the use of foundation trenches. The walls were made of local flint held together with lime mortar made from the local chalk. The structure would have been roofed with timber, holding thatch. The doorway was in the southern corner and inside was a large bread oven and smaller cooking hearth. Furniture would have included

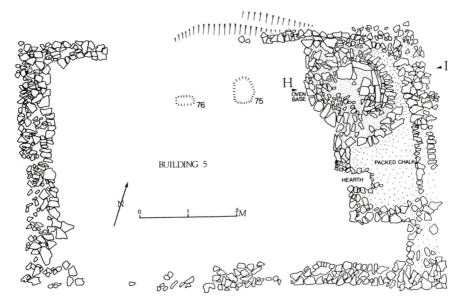

Figure 2.8   Plan of a household unit. Medieval farmhouse, Bullock Down, East Sussex.

wooden tables, benches and beds. Grain was ground between quernstones, wool spun with spindle whorls, and food cooked in large sagging-based cooking pots. A small family, perhaps a couple with several children, lived in the house (Fig. 2.8).

At some stage during the sixteenth century, probably as a result of the increasing value of sheep, the tenants of the house were evicted. One can imagine the scene of a cart being loaded up with the few portable valuables owned by the family, perhaps the table and stools, clothes, knives and cooking pots. The house was then abandoned. Some artefacts like a small chalk spindle whorl were lost in the process. The large mayen lava quernstone was abandoned as it was already beginning to shatter through age, and the evicted tenants would not expect to need it in their new urban life. Some objects were therefore lost in the process of final abandonment of the site, while others were simply left where they were.

Given the somewhat isolated location of the farmstead, human scavenging of the site is unlikely, although roof timbers may have been taken away for use as firewood. It is more likely that the site was simply left to natural processes of destruction. The untended thatch would come adrift from the roof and be blown off or collapse into the structure. The roof timbers would rot and fall in, making the mortar in the walls vulnerable to wind, water and chemical action. This would finally result in collapse of the walls, a process which would protect the lowest course or two of the wall from further erosion. As the house was constructed on a slight platform cut into the hill slope, soil creeping down the slope would be caught on the platform, thus protecting the floor and footings of the house.

While used as part of sheep runs, the remains of the house were well protected under developing downland turf. With a decline in sheep, however, scrubby bushes grew on the site with roots breaking up the buried masonry. Rabbits burrowed among these roots as earthworms cast soil onto the surface. Finally the site was ploughed up during the Second World War to provide more food in southern Britain. The preserving terrace was being slowly ploughed away when archaeologists intervened in 1975 before the site was finally obliterated. Similar sites elsewhere survive only as a spread of rubble with a few potsherds and animal bones in the modern plough soil.

Some buildings are constructed entirely of organic materials which will survive only if waterlogged or desiccated. Amerindian (native American) houses in the Caribbean were constructed entirely of organic materials. The small structure excavated at Hillcrest, Barbados, is a good example of a simple Amerindian shelter (Drewett 1991). It was constructed by setting five wooden posts, which were probably linked with some sort of ring beam, into holes dug in the ground. The structure was probably roofed with plaited leaves (Roth 1970). Most activities took place outside this small shelter, including potting, spinning cotton, cooking and making conch-shell tools. Debris from these activities was spread around the outside of the structure. Virtually everything usable was taken when the site was deserted around AD 1400. The structure itself was left to natural transformation processes. The structure may have been demolished very rapidly by hurricane action. Even if this was not the case, tropical rain and wind would soon have removed the unattended roof material. This would have exposed the posts to rapid bacterial action in the warm, humid climate. The posts would have rotted first at ground level, and then fallen onto the damp earth to rot rapidly. Deposits within and around the hut structure would have been churned about in the soil through the action of digging land-crabs and rapidly-growing tropical roots.

Every archaeological site is, therefore, the end-product of a wide range of transformation processes. These take place during the life of the site, then at the point of abandonment, and continue as ongoing processes both natural and cultural. Very rarely are archaeologists dealing with the intact remains of past activity. All remains are transformed in some way, and without recognizing these transformation processes archaeologists could totally misinterpret the nature of a deposit, or even a whole site.

CHAPTER THREE

Finding archaeological sites

Existing knowledge

Many archaeological sites have never been lost. The site may have been abandoned but it may remain clearly visible in the landscape even if, during much of its post-use life, it was not considered an archaeological site as such. Classic sites like Stonehenge, the Great Wall of China, or the Acropolis in Athens have always been known. This usually, but not always, includes the major sites in a region. In England, for example, few medieval masonry castles have been lost while most small peasant farmsteads of the same date have been lost. In general, but not always, small sites are more likely to have been 'lost' than big ones. However, big ones may also have been 'lost' to archaeologists, even if known to the local population.

Many Mayan sites 'lost' to – and then 'discovered' by – Western archaeologists were well known to local Amerindian populations. So there are sites known to everyone, those lost to archaeologists but known to local people, and then those lost to everyone until rediscovered, like the Lascaux caves. Local people remain a major source of information about sites known to them, even if this knowledge has not reached the archaeological record. A farmer, for example, will know where there are bumps (burial mounds?) in his fields or where the plough hits masonry (a Roman villa?).

Knowledge also exists in the records of any previous archaeological work undertaken in the area. This may consist of vague references by an eighteenth-century explorer, or detailed records of a recent field project. Increasingly this sort of information is brought together to form some sort of local, regional or national record prepared by archaeologists working in the area, often as part of a statutory body like a county council in England or the National Parks Service in the USA. These 'Sites and Monuments Records' provide ready access to existing knowledge.

In Britain an attempt was first made to set up a national record by establishing the Royal Commission on the Historical Monuments of England (RCHME) and its sister organizations in Wales and Scotland. These were established by royal warrants in 1908. The standard of recording was, however, so high that by 1990 only some 150,000 sites had been recorded, in contrast to the 300,000-plus sites recorded by county-based Sites and Monuments Records in the first ten years of life since they were established in the early 1970s.

The basic elements of a Sites and Monuments Record consist of a written record of each site, with an associated map locating it. With this there may, or may not, be a photographic record including ground or aerial photographs. The major fields of information required of the written record are:

1 Unique reference number
2 Administrative area
3 Address
4 Cartographic reference
5 Type of site
6 Date of site
7 Condition of site

To this basic record more and more detail can be added, depending on resources and how the record is going to be used. In Britain it should be remembered that county-based Sites and Monuments Records are essentially part of the planning process rather than a straightforward academic research tool. The quality of many SMRs, however, enables them to be used in both ways. Associated with each written record is a map locating (if possible) the exact position of each site or find recorded. Often early discoveries were, however, recorded only to a general area like a town or parish rather than in a precise location.

The first Sites and Monuments Records at a county level in Britain were estab-lished in the early 1970s, in areas like Oxfordshire and Essex. These started life as maps with associated record cards, but as computers became more readily available in the 1980s most records were computerized. Generally this involved simply putting the record card text into a computer system where the data can be accessed and maintained by a database management system.

During the 1980s, when it became possible for computers to handle all types of data in digital form, including maps and photographs, systems were developed so that all elements of SMRs could be computerized. Such data can now be incorp-orated into a Geographic Information System (GIS). At its simplest level these systems enable maps, text and photographs to be managed together. A GIS can produce layers of information. For example it could contain a base topographical map, solid geology, surface geology, soils, current land use and then archaeological sites. Data can be separated or combined in many different ways. For example all Roman settlements above 200 m on clay soils in a given region could be identified on a map on the screen. Written and photographic data about these specific sites could then be called up.

Currently few areas of the world have information about known archaeological sites readily available on a GIS, but clearly where they are available, as in parts of Ireland (Synnott 1996), this is where existing knowledge is most readily accessible. If no Sites and Monuments Record in any form is available, then existing know-ledge will have to be searched for rather in the way the data for SMRs was originally gathered. This involves firstly a literature search of books and journals. In Britain most counties have a county archaeological society, many of which have published an annual volume for a hundred years or more. The Sussex Archaeological Society, for example, published its 134th volume on the archaeology and history of Sussex in 1996. These volumes formed the basis of the Sites and Monuments Records in the counties of West and East Sussex.

Secondly, existing knowledge may survive in an unpublished form, like collections of artefacts in museums. Depending on how and when these data were collected, they may have more or less precise information about the location of the finds. Unfortunately, in the past, archaeological collections often moved well away from their place of discovery. One of the largest collections of neolithic flint axes from East Sussex, England, for example, was bought early in this century by the Royal Ontario Museum in Canada. Existing knowledge is therefore only as good as your ability to locate it.

Finally, existing knowledge is often stored in the heads of local people, and particularly local archaeologists, both professional and amateur. Farmers are often a major source of archaeological information although only if approached in the right way, as many see archaeology, and particularly archaeologists, as a potential threat to their use of their land. Often, however, archaeologists who have previously worked in the area but have failed to publish their results are more of a problem. Knowledge exists only when it is available!

Documents

Archaeologists working in historic periods will use documents as one of their main sources for the location of archaeological sites. Documents must, however, always be treated with caution. The fact that surviving fifteenth-century documents for a region made no mention of settlements in a particular area does not necessarily mean that there were none. The initial reason for the production of the document must always be considered, and whether the absence of information is simply because relevant documents have been lost.

Documentary evidence can be very detailed and specific, or very generalized, or both. Documents can also originate from within a community or be observations from an outsider looking in. The motives of the observer must always be assessed. Christopher Columbus's 'record' of prehistoric people in the Caribbean presents many of the classic problems associated with the use of documents produced by an observer looking into another community. Firstly, what is generally known as *The journal of Christopher Columbus* is an abstract made by the Dominican historian Bartolomé de las Casas, probably from a copy (now lost) made by two scribes from the original manuscript (also lost). Whether the scribes transcribed the document correctly, and what Bartolomé de las Casas edited out, will never be known. Secondly, even if we accept that the record that has come down to us was a faithful account of what Columbus actually wrote, he clearly came to the Caribbean with preconceived notions about the nature of 'primitive' peoples and the idea of the 'noble savage': "As soon as day broke, there came to the shore many of these men, all youths and all of a good height, very handsome people" (Columbus 1960).

Much of the detail recorded is perhaps more useful to archaeologists: "That day there came many boats or canoes to the ship, to barter articles of spun cotton and the nets in which they sleep, which are hammocks" (Columbus 1960). Canoes, cotton and hammocks rarely survive in the archaeological record in the warm, humid tropics.

When dealing with historic periods the documentary archive is, of course, vast but biased. A peasant farmstead in the countryside may never have been written about, while royal castles may have documents detailing the precise number of nails bought to re-roof a kitchen. In Britain the Public Record Office (PRO) and county-based Record Offices (CRO) are the main source of documentary evidence.

Property in Britain owned by the Church and State have some of the most detailed records. The problem with all this detailed data is often relating it to the actual archaeology on the ground. The royal castle constructed at Hadleigh in Essex is a good example of this problem (Drewett 1975). The castle started its life as a private castle, built by Hubert de Burgh, Earl of Kent and Justiciar of England. He was granted a licence by King Henry III in 1230 (Patent Rolls, 1225–32, in H. M. Colvin (ed.), *The history of the king's works*). We know from elsewhere, however, that these royal licences were sometimes granted to regularize a situation. Was the castle, therefore, actually built in or after 1230, or was the licence granted for a castle already in existence? Looking at the surviving remains of the castle, its earliest phase of construction – a small bailey with square angle towers – can be determined. Are these remains actually those of the 1230 castle mentioned in the document, or was that castle either elsewhere near by or destroyed to make way for the construction of what we now see as the first phase?

Records of Hadleigh castle show endless small sums of money spent on repairs and rebuilding: 25 shillings in 1240, £25 in 1270–71, construction of a new gate in the postern in 1312–13 and repairing a breach in the wall in 1320–21. None of this detail could be detected in the archaeological record (Drewett 1975). It is not until King Edward III spent £2,287 on the construction of a totally new barbican gatehouse on the northern side of the castle and two great angle towers at the eastern end of the castle that the documentary references show clearly in the archaeological record (Fig. 3.1).

The range of documents available to archaeologists in their quest for archaeological sites is enormous, and generally increases through time. Archaeologists working in medieval and post-medieval archaeology in Britain have numerous potential sources. Court rolls of manors often offer details of land use, enclosures, fields and settlements. Manorial surveys may list tenants and numbers of buildings on the manor, as well as details of stock numbers. For the late-medieval and post-medieval period, probate inventories may list details of a yeoman farmer's total property, from buildings to cooking pots. Title deeds, wills and lawsuits often provide information about site locations. For post-medieval archaeology in Britain, tithe and enclosure awards are a valuable source of information.

The main problems with using written sources to locate archaeological sites are firstly the reliability of the document itself, and secondly whether there is enough information to locate an actual site in the landscape. This is a separate problem

Figure 3.1 Documentary evidence clearly indicated that these two towers, together with a new gatehouse, were constructed at Hadleigh Castle, Essex, by Edward III at a cost of £2,287.

from that of using such documents to write history, where precise location within a parish, for example, may or may not be important.

Maps are perhaps one of the most important types of document to aid in the location of sites. The earliest surviving maps date back to about 2300 BC when the Babylonians created maps on clay tablets. Until the eighteenth century, however, maps tended to be pictorial rather than strictly accurate in detail. Earlier maps may locate countries, towns, villages and major natural features reasonably accurately, but individual structures may only be represented pictorially in their approximate position at no particular scale. Richard Ligon's 1657 map of Barbados (Ligon 1657) is a good example of this type of map. The island is very roughly the right shape, but houses are shown more or less regularly spaced around the coast, in the right order by land owner (Fig. 3.2). To locate one of these structures on the ground from this map is virtually impossible.

In Britain good maps date back to the sixteenth century, with the great cartographers like Saxton, Speed and Norden all working in the latter part of the century. For great accuracy, however, one has to wait for the publication of the first Ordnance Survey maps in 1795. These maps, of course, not only provide data about the late eighteenth century but also all notable features surviving in the landscape from earlier periods. They thus become not only a source for archaeologists trying to locate sites of historic periods, but also potentially prehistoric sites like round barrows that survived until the eighteenth century but have been destroyed since. However, it was many years before all of Britain was mapped accurately, and even then rural areas were mapped at a smaller scale than urban areas.

Figure 3.2   Extract from Richard Ligon's 1657 map of Barbados, illustrating the problem of locating buildings from historic maps.

In addition to written documents and maps, pictures may provide a good source of information about the location of sites, but only if the picture has within it something that can be clearly located in the landscape today. Thus early pictures like those that appear, for example, in the Aztecs' *Veitia Codex* provide great detail about how people did what, but not always exactly where, which is of course essential for locating sites. Again one generally has to wait until the eighteenth century, when the great illustrators like Samuel Buck produced architectural drawings with enough accurate detail to locate sites. Nineteenth-century photographs of now-demolished historic buildings, or even prehistoric sites, may also be a useful source of locational information.

Place names provide another source of information about the possible location of archaeological sites. Place-name studies are, however, not straightforward and not many interpretations of place names are totally certain. One problem is that the form of names often changes through time, so you should attempt to find as many old forms of the name as possible before attempting an explanation. In England the *Concise Oxford dictionary of English place-names* is a good starting point. Place names may refer to natural features like hills or rivers, field-names, house or village names. Sometimes a name originally applied to, say, a specific farmstead may become the name of the area or field after the farm is long gone. Saxon names may indicate a settlement, but not precisely where it was in the landscape. Often place names indicate only a general area where a settlement may have been, and then they form only the first stage in the process of finding a site by, perhaps, field walking or aerial photography.

Aerial photography

Aerial photography is the earliest, and perhaps still the most important, remote sensing tool available to archaeologists searching for new archaeological sites. Remote sensing involves any techniques which capture geographic data by sensors at some distance from the surface being recorded. The main elements of remote sensing are aerial photography, satellite images and geophysics. All data gathered through remote sensing can be separated, combined, and manipulated through the activity of image processing, which forms one of the key elements of Geographic Information Systems (GIS).

It was during the First World War that the significance of aerial photography in archaeology was first fully recognized. A key figure in this early recognition was a young observer in the Royal Flying Corps, O. G. S. Crawford. He went on, funded by the marmalade magnate, Alexander Keiller, to undertake a detailed air survey of central southern England, published in his classic *Wessex from the air* (Crawford and Keiller 1928). Crawford invented new jargon to describe what he saw, particularly the terms 'shadow sites', 'soil marks' and 'crop marks' (Fig. 3.3). Working in the period prior to the massive ploughing-up of lowland Britain in the 1950s and 1960s, shadow sites produced some of his most striking images. Today most new discoveries are of crop-mark sites.

Aerial photography is, of course, the process of recording what an observer sees. If nothing is visible from the aircraft, nothing will be visible on the photograph. To be visible as a shadow site, some of the archaeology must have variable height to cast a shadow. Any site with humps and bumps, like banks or ditches, has the potential to show as a shadow site. The conditions, however, must be right. Firstly there must be some sun, and secondly it must be low enough to cast a shadow (Fig. 3.4). This means that in the summer months photographs can generally be taken only early in the morning or late in the evening, just before sunset. For most of the day the sun will be too high and no useful shadows will be cast. In winter the sun remains lower, but in a typical British winter may not be visible for weeks on end!

It must also be remembered that shadows will only be cast more or less at right angles to the rays of the sun. A bank running parallel to the rays of the sun will be

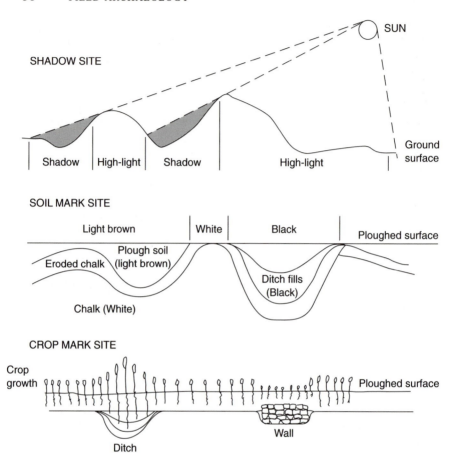

Figure 3.3 Aerial photography: shadow sites, soil marks and crop marks.

invisible at that moment. Generally, even when conditions are ideal, some bits of the site may not cast shadows, so in effect remain invisible. Several photographs taken throughout the day during a sunny winter day will produce the maximum of information. Another advantage of photographing shadow sites in the winter is that vegetation is likely to be at its thinnest during the winter months. Slight undulations covered with heather or bracken may become invisible. This will not present a problem in grazed pasture where vegetation is likely to be very thin in late summer, particularly after a dry spell.

Sites with variation in height, like standing earthworks, may also show up well after a slight dusting of snow. Snow will blow off ridges and catch in hollows, showing up banks and ditches in a very dramatic way. Conditions like this are, however, fairly rare in Britain and usually very short-lived. Torrential rain may also briefly collect in hollows, emphasising dips like pits or ditches. In this case, however, conditions may not be ideal for flying. Slight flooding in low-lying areas may persist long enough for a photographic record of water-filled hollows to be made.

Figure 3.4   Aerial photography: shadow site. Iron-age hillfort. (photo: O. Bedwin)

Soil marks may show up in any area clear of vegetation, but they are usually at their best in ploughed fields (Fig. 3.5). Each element of an archaeological site is likely to be made up of different coloured soils. Areas of burning may show up as red or black, habitation areas could be grey or black, ditches may silt in with dark, humic soil in contrast to the plough-flattened bank which will show up the colour of the parent rock, say white for chalk. Patterns of different coloured soils will reflect what is being ploughed onto the surface. These patterns may be clear, say a rectangle representing an enclosure, or very blurred as the result of long-term ploughing and mixing of the soils. Soil marks will only show up when the area is clear of crop growth, so usually the winter months are the best time to see them.

Crop marks often produce the most dramatic aerial photographs (Fig. 3.6). Crop marks are basically the result of the differential speed and quality of crop growth and ripening, depending on sub-surface conditions. Essentially if the soil is deeper in one spot in the field, the crop above will have access to more nutrients and moisture than crops above shallow soil. Crops above a ditch or pit, for example, will grow more rapidly and strongly, be taller, and ripen more slowly than those above a well or floor, which are likely to be weaker, shorter, and ripen more rapidly. Crops above deeper soils will produce positive crop marks, while those above shallow soils will produce negative crop marks.

These variations in crop growth and ripening show up best in cereal crops, although they will also show up in pulse crops like peas and beans, and even clover. Not all soils are conducive, however, to producing good crop marks. Soils on chalk and gravel produce excellent crop marks because these soils tend to dry

Figure 3.5   Aerial photography: soil mark site. Neolithic enclosure. (photo: O. Bedwin)

Figure 3.6   Aerial photography: crop mark site. Romano-British field system.

out fairly rapidly, so the contrast between the natural shallow soil and the deeper rich soils in buried archaeological features is often very pronounced. In contrast, clays do not always produce good crop marks.

Usually crop marks show up best in the early summer months as the crop begins to ripen. Every year is, however, different. Dry years may reveal excellent crop marks early in the season, while during a very wet summer very few crop marks may be visible in a given area. Sometimes, under very extreme conditions, the usual pattern of crop growth may even reverse itself. In the British drought of 1976, for example, virtually all moisture dried out of pits and ditches on shallow chalk soils, so parch marks appeared over ditches, while over the adjacent bedrock roots obtained a little moisture trapped in the shattered upper layers of chalk. Many new 'walls' discovered in 1976 turned out to be ditches.

Shadow marks, soil marks, and crop marks all produce patterns visible to the observer flying above. For record these are photographed. The actual photograph will record only what is visible, but careful selection of angle of photograph and type of film will make reading of the photograph easier. Photographs can be taken either obliquely or vertically. Vertical photographs give a plan view of the site. By taking overlapping pairs it is possible to produce a three-dimensional image of the site by using a stereoscope. This is particularly valuable to show how the site fits into the natural landscape of hills and valleys. Vertical photographs of level blocks of landscape can often be related directly to maps, so enabling the site's location and extent to be rapidly plotted.

Vertical photographs cannot normally be directly plotted, as variations in ground relief cause variations in scale at different levels. The top of a hill is closer to the camera in the plane, and therefore at a bigger scale, than the bottom of an adjacent valley which is further away so at a smaller scale. This problem of different scales on an aerial photograph has to be rectified by dividing the photograph into areas that lie in separate planes. This process is usually done with a specialist plotting machine like a Thompson-Watts plotter. The actual process of obtaining dimensional information from photographs and then producing scale drawings is known as photogrammetry. Photogrammetry is even more important when dealing with oblique photographs, where tilt creates considerable distortion which, in addition to variation in heights of the ground surface, also requires rectification. Although it is possible to rectify oblique aerial photographs manually (Hampton 1978), it is now more usual to do this with a suitable computer programme (for example, Palmer 1977).

The process of taking vertical and oblique aerial photographs obviously differs somewhat. Oblique photographs can be taken with a simple hand-held 35 mm camera through the window of a high-wing light aircraft. If the wing is not above the cabin it may well block a good shot just as it comes into view. Vertical photography requires some form of fixed mounting beside or under the aircraft. Although this can again be done with a 35 mm camera it is more usual to use a large-format camera, perhaps producing negatives up to 230 mm square. Most aerial photographs are taken with black-and-white panchromatic film which can be enhanced using a yellow filter. True colour may also be used as it has the advantage of

representing the image more or less as the observer sees it, which may aid interpretation. However, colour photographs are still more expensive to publish, and the
colour negative has a shorter life than black-and-white negatives. An alternative
is to use infra-red or 'false colour' film. The advantage of infra-red film is that it
cuts out blue light, which is strongly scattered by atmospheric haze, so the image
is often clearer than true colour. Also, vegetation has a wider range of reflection in
the near infra-red range than at green wavelengths, so slight changes of crop growth
may be clearer. The main problem is, however, that the observer must learn to think
in totally unreal colours, for example, brown soil images as green, and green crops
appearing red.

The production and plotting of aerial photographs can be done by field archaeologists themselves or contracted out to one of an increasing number of specialists.
It is the interpretation of patterns produced by crop, shadow or soil marks that
requires the specialist skills of the field archaeologist. Shadow and soil marks
essentially produce just patterns, but crop marks also provide information about
whether the pattern is produced by a hard structure like a wall or road surface, or
the soft fill of a ditch or pit. From then on you are again dealing only with patterns.
To interpret aerial photographic patterns you need to know as much as possible
about both natural and archaeological features likely to be in the area. A rectangular
parched pattern in a field in Europe could be a Roman villa. A similar pattern in
China is unlikely – to say the least – to be a Roman villa.

In Britain each period has its characteristic types of site, often easily recognizable as crop, soil or shadow sites. Enclosures with regular causeways are neolithic
causewayed enclosures. Round dark circles are likely to represent round barrows.
Rectangular ditched enclosures are likely to be Roman or later, with a few neolithic
exceptions. Rectangular walled structures with rooms are likely to be Roman villas,
and so on. Of course, not all patterns will be humanly made. Polygonal patterns
may represent the freezing and thawing of the subsurface under periglacial conditions, while meandering dark lines may represent old stream or river courses. Many
features visible on aerial photographs will be recent in origin, and indeed very
short-lived. Modern plough marks are a good example of this. Ploughing around
the four sides of a rectangular field briefly produces a pattern of diagonals like that
on the back of an envelope.

Much of the landscape is never amenable to aerial photography. Rarely do features
show up in woodland, and never when they have been built on. Even in ploughed
areas there may be problems. In undulating fields soil moves from ridges into
hollows and dry valleys. The depth of these new soil deposits may become so great
that roots of growing crops never reach the underlying archaeological features.

Ground survey

Archaeological sites may also be found by systematic ground survey. This can
be approached in a variety of ways, depending on the aims of the survey and the
available time and money. If you are surveying a specific block of land prior to a

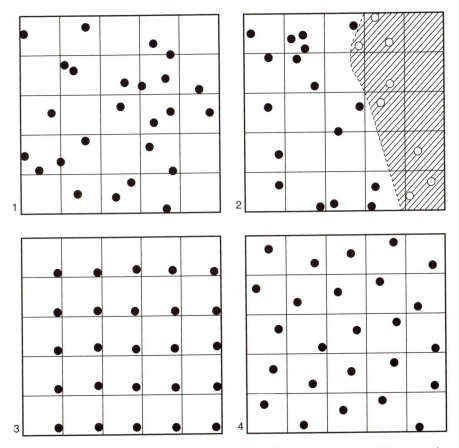

Figure 3.7 Sampling designs: (1) simple random, (2) stratified random, (3) systematic, (4) stratified systematic unaligned (after Haggett, 1965).

development like house construction, then an attempt should be made to survey the whole of the available area. If, however, you intend to survey large areas, then some type of sampling may be appropriate. Sampling a landscape to locate sites can be undertaken either by examining discrete blocks of the landscape (squares or quadrats) or by walking lines across the landscape (transects). The geographer Peter Haggett defined four basic sampling strategies in his classic *Locational analysis in human geography* (Haggett 1965).

His *simple random sample* (Fig. 3.7) involved gridding the area (on a map) and then using random number tables to select a point on the x-axis and a point on the y-axis. Where the two lines drawn out from these axis points cross is the randomly-selected spot on the landscape. How many such random spots are selected will depend on available time and resources. Also the size of the area searched at the located spot (1 m square or 100 m square for example) depends on resources. The main problem with simple random sampling to locate sites in a landscape is that as the spots may be anywhere, they could all cluster leaving great unsurveyed areas big enough to miss even the largest site. Archaeological sites are, of course, unlikely to be arbitrarily dotted over the landscape. The ranges of sites on hill tops, hill slopes, and valley bottoms, for example, are likely to be different both in type and in density. It is therefore advisable to make sure any random sample includes all geographic zones.

One way to achieve geographic coverage is to use a *stratified random sample*. To do this the area to be surveyed is broken into geographic zones, like mountains, low hills and valleys. Each zone is then sampled separately in the same way as simple random sampling. This guarantees geographic coverage. It does not, however, get around the problem of clustering.

To avoid clustering, the area could be sampled in a *systematic* way. To do this the area is gridded and a point within the first square is selected randomly. Exactly the same location is then selected in each square. An alternative to this is to select randomly a different location within each square. This design, known as *stratified systematic unaligned* has the advantage of being systematic (guaranteeing wide coverage) but with a random element.

In practice, of course, all these sampling designs present problems in the field. If you apply a sampling strategy rigidly, without looking at the landscape first, you may discover many of your points end up in factories, on motorways, or in the middle of rivers! Clearly some landscapes are more amenable to this type of sampling than others. They may work well in huge blocks of the prairies or the Australian outback, but try it around London or Birmingham and you will waste an enormous amount of time!

An alternative to examining quadrats in the landscape is to examine lines or transects across the landscape (Fig. 3.8). This could be done from randomly selected spots in the landscape, creating a random pattern of transects; but more usually it is done using a systematic pattern of transects like parallel lines across a river valley or mountain range. The actual width of the transects, and their spacing, depends on time and resources. Clearly the closer the spacing and the wider the transects, the better your coverage will be. In many areas of the world, including large areas of Britain, any attempt at sampling in a formal way will probably be a waste of time. In any given block of landscape your sample may be defined for you, as huge areas may be unavailable for survey because of towns, roads, factories, rivers, and hostile landowners refusing access. In these cases you can only survey what is available. In reality, whatever sampling strategy you select will merely be an arbitrary sample of the archaeology of the region, as many sites will have vanished or be archaeologically unlocatable under perhaps metres of alluvium or urban development. The important thing is to discover the range of sites of different levels of complexity, rather than pretending it is actually possible to discover all archaeological sites that ever existed in an area. Whether you are using random quadrats, transects or simple non-probabilistic sampling based on your experience of where sites are likely to be, the next stage is to decide what ground survey techniques to use.

If the area is ploughed, then field walking – to locate, collect and plot artefact spreads – is probably the most appropriate method. This survey should be systematic,

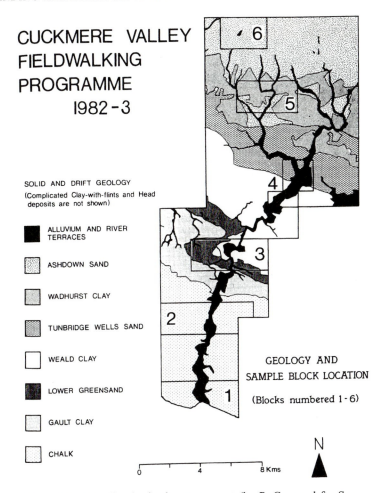

CUCKMERE VALLEY
FIELDWALKING
PROGRAMME
1982-3

SOLID AND DRIFT GEOLOGY
(Complicated Clay-with-flints and Head
deposits are not shown)

ALLUVIUM AND RIVER
TERRACES

ASHDOWN SAND

WADHURST CLAY

TUNBRIDGE WELLS SAND

WEALD CLAY

LOWER GREENSAND

GAULT CLAY

CHALK

GEOLOGY AND
SAMPLE BLOCK LOCATION

(Blocks numbered 1-6)

N

0   4   8 Kms

Figure 3.8 Sampling by landscape transect (by P. Garwood for Sussex
Archaeological Field Unit).

although at its simplest this could be a grab sample recorded by field (if they are of
relatively small size). It is more usual, however, to walk either lines or squares
(Fig. 3.9), although other shapes, like circles, have been tried.

Walking lines enables large areas to be scanned relatively rapidly. Firstly you
must select a suitable time of year and a field team. The best time for field walking
is after the ploughed area has been allowed to weather for some time. Frost will
break up the clods of clay, while rain will wash artefacts making them easier to
see. In Britain, therefore, the winter months are obviously best, but often with a
mild winter the new crop is already growing before conditions are ideal. If this
happens, the farmer, quite naturally, may refuse permission. As with aerial photography, you will need to keep almost a weekly watch on fields for conditions to be
just right.

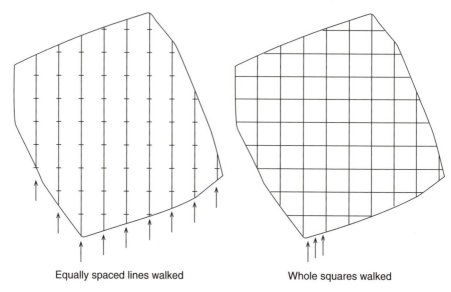

Equally spaced lines walked   Whole squares walked

Figure 3.9   Field-walking by lines and squares.

The selection and training of your field team is also of crucial importance. Clearly they must be fit enough to survive slow field-searching, often in very wet or cold conditions. More importantly, they must be able to recognize all likely artefacts that could be found in the area. They must also be trained to reduce bias as far as possible. It is always easier to see big fragments of pottery than small, and those contrasting in colour with the background soil as opposed to those of similar colour.

Walking lines enables large tracts of land to be scanned relatively quickly. Lines may be laid out either in relation to the existing field pattern, or more usually along a north–south axis. The advantage of north–south lines is that the area can be easily surveyed over a number of years and each new survey can be slotted into the existing surveys. It also looks neater on the map! In terms of results, however, there is nothing special about a north–south orientation; it could be any orientation. Lines can be easily laid out using a prismatic compass and tapes (see Chapter Four) or any of a wide range of surveying equipment. The lines are usually marked on the ground with ranging poles. How far apart you space your lines depends on the nature of your survey and available resources. Usually lines are spaced between 30 m and 100 m apart. The further apart they are, the larger the area that can be surveyed in a given time, but the greater the risk of missing small concentrations of artefacts.

Each line is broken along its length, often at the same interval as the line spacing, for recording purposes. In practice one person will walk each line, scanning about a metre each side of the line. All artefacts are collected and bagged (in a strong plastic bag as paper bags are not much use in the rain). Each bag is clearly marked with the line and segment numbers (for example, line 2, segment 4). Some surveys do not collect the artefacts but simply identify and count each type and leave them *in situ*. This may be determined by the law in a particular country or by the fact that many museums simply do not want hundreds of fragments of floor tile, for example. It is always better to discard artefacts on site rather than take them elsewhere, and then discard them to the confusion of future archaeologists.

For more intensive surveys the grid system is more appropriate. In this type of survey the area is gridded (see Chapter Four). The size of the grid square will depend on how detailed a survey you are aiming at. Usually the squares are 20 m or 30 m square, but they could be larger or smaller. The smaller the squares, however, the longer they will take to set out, more bags will be used, and analysis and plotting will take longer. Given the nature of material in ploughed fields, over-detailed recording is often a waste of time. For larger squares a team of archaeologists will line up on one side of the square and walk across the square in a line, picking up all artefacts they see. Given the way light shines on some artefacts, like flint flakes, they are often more visible from one direction than another. If time is available (which it rarely is) the squares can be walked from two directions. The number of walks across a square must, however, be the same for every square in the survey, or the quantification of the results becomes pointless.

Throughout this section on field walking the term 'artefact' has been used. This was deliberate. Artefacts can usually be at least approximately dated, so prehistoric can be separated from historic or modern. Other materials like bones and shells create more of a problem, because individually they cannot often be dated. If they are directly associated with clusters of datable artefacts one can assume an association, but one can rarely be certain. Shell may have been brought to the area by hermit crabs or bones by scavenging animals. A decision may be sensibly taken to ignore all this type of material. Bones in a ploughed field are always likely to be biased towards big bones from sheep, goats, cattle and the like, and against small fish and bird bones. Any attempt at quantification is therefore pretty meaningless. However, they may be important to indicate survival below the surface, or the position of plough-damaged human burials. All the time the field surveyor must weigh up time and cost against value of recovered information. If it is too biased, is it worth collecting?

Having recovered, recorded and identified archaeological material in ploughed fields, it should be quantified and represented in some graphic form to show variations in distribution. Either actual numbers of different classes of material can be plotted in some way, or a mean can be calculated for the whole survey area and distributions above the mean plotted.

For line surveys, densities of artefacts can be plotted by regular variation of thickness of line (Fig. 3.10). Thick lines will clearly show concentrations of artefacts while thin lines show just a thin spread. A gap in the line or a thin line would indicate either no artefacts of a particular class or none above the background mean. For gridded surveys a black circle of variable size to show quantity is often used (Fig. 3.11), but graded shading or dot-density could also be used. Contour maps of surface concentrations are an alternative way of plotting the data, but they are slightly more complex to produce, and as they involve interpolation may create somewhat spurious accuracy.

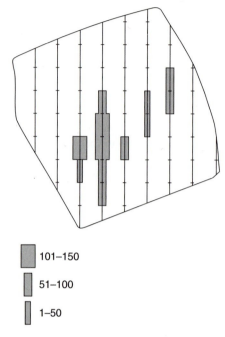

Figure 3.10   Field-walking by lines: graphic illustration of artefact densities.

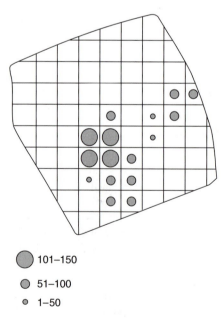

Figure 3.11   Field-walking by squares: graphic illustration of artefact densities.

The interpretation of field-walking data must always be approached with extreme caution. The absence of artefacts does not necessarily indicate the absence of sites, and the presence of artefacts at a particular spot in the landscape does not necessarily mean the presence of human activity of that date in the past at that spot. Plough soils tend to be of more or less regular depth, depending on the type of plough, soil and crop to be planted. If the archaeology is below this depth it may simply not appear in the plough soil. Also, buried archaeology is unlikely to be at a constant depth, so if it is shallower at one point on the site it may appear in the plough soil, while where it is deeper it will not. If the landscape is undulating, artefacts will tend to move down slopes and accumulate in low spots like dry valleys. Movement of objects can be partly determined by the state of the objects. The more abraded they are, the more they are likely to have been moved either downslope or round and around in the soil. Fresh, unabraded pottery is unlikely to have moved far. Artefact spreads in plough soil usually, therefore, indicate activity at that spot or further uphill. The absence of artefact spreads does not, however, necessarily mean absence of sites.

A separate problem is interpreting the nature of the artefact spread, as the term 'site' has been used to cover every type of activity area. A pottery concentration, for example, could represent a settlement site, a kiln site, a midden or rubbish dump adjacent to a settlement, or artefacts spread together with manure over fields well away from a settlement. Again the state of the artefact may help. Many small sherds mixed with other artefacts and ecofacts may represent a settlement area. If there are many misshapen sherds (wasters) in the assemblage it may represent a kiln site or waster dump. Many large, angular pot sherds with other rubbish could represent a midden, while small abraded sherds may represent manuring or simply erosion downslope from a midden. Field walking is therefore an excellent field survey method, but the interpretation of the data must always be within the local landscape context and treated with extreme caution.

Not all the landscape is, however, ploughed. Unploughed areas may contain archaeological sites surviving as earthworks or stone settings. These are more likely to show up on aerial photographs than will scatters of artefacts in ploughed fields. For a variety of reasons, however, not all earthworks or stone settings will show up on aerial photographs – or if they do, they may not be recognizable. Ground surveys may therefore be required both to locate sites and to fill in details of sites recognized on aerial photographs.

Survey of sites surviving as humps and bumps, or stone settings, requires two main elements. Firstly the site has to be located, and then recorded and intepreted. The topographical survey of these sites will be considered in Chapter Four. Location of such sites should be approached in a systematic way to ensure area coverage. If the whole area to be surveyed is unploughed, parallel transect lines could be walked across the landscape, and whenever an unnatural-looking hump or bump is seen, or stone setting located, its position would be recorded and a simple record form filled in. At the very least the record form should include a unique reference number; site name (if there is one); cartographic reference; and type, date and condition of site. Thereafter more and more detail can be recorded, depending on the nature of the survey. For example, altitude, geology, soil type, land use, aspect and orientation of site could be recorded.

Generally one is not dealing with entirely unploughed or undeveloped land-scapes, and therefore earthworks only survive in woodland, nature reserves, park-land or slopes too steep for arable. Your survey design would therefore have to be geared to the specific landscape. Walking parallel transects in woodland, for example, is often not possible and yet in areas like Britain woodland often pre-serves the best earthworks. You may have to zig-zag through woodland, recording each change in direction with a prismatic compass.

Having located an earthwork site, it can either remain as a dot on a distribution map or be subjected to an interpretative survey. This is a highly skilled process requiring an archaeological surveyor as distinct from a straight topographical sur-veyor. Earthwork surveys produced by some topographical surveyors without the required archaeological knowledge, although no doubt perfectly accurate, often look like patterns of railway embankments. The interpretative survey involves looking at relationships between humps and bumps and dips. Which bit of the pattern was there first? Which bit overlies the earlier features? How were they modified through time? As with the interpretation of aerial photographs, the surveyor is looking for identifiable patterns and relationships to build up sequences from the palimpsests left in the landscape. A skilled archaeological surveyor undertaking an interpreta-tive survey can often work out the sequence of development of a site without any damaging resort to excavation. Of course, not all archaeological features will show as humps or dips in the land surface. Even large pits and ditches could be so well filled that they simply do not show on the surface. They may also be overlain by a later bank for example. One way to 'look' into the ground without resorting to excavation is to use the wide range of geophysical techniques now available to field archaeologists.

Geophysical survey

Geophysical surveying techniques are part of the battery of remote sensing techniques which include aerial photography and satellite images. Like all remote sensing techniques, geophysical surveying is a non-destructive method of site investigation, so has obvious advantages over excavation when dealing with the finite archaeological resource.

Although General Pitt-Rivers used a primitive type of geophysics as early as 1893, the first use of instruments to record geophysical data was undertaken by Professor Richard Atkinson in 1946 at a site in Dorchester. Pitt-Rivers' technique was simply to hit the ground with the end of a pick axe and listen to variations in the returning sound. A dull thud might indicate a ditch fill, while a ringing sound might represent the underlying solid geology just below the surface. It was a rough-and-ready technique which sometimes, especially on chalk, worked well. It never, however, had the same impact as Atkinson's work on the development of non-destructive field archaeology. Atkinson's first publication of resistivity surveying in

English came in the second edition of his classic *Field archaeology* (Atkinson 1953). The remarkable advances in archaeological geophysics since 1950 are amply charted in Anthony Clark's *Seeing beneath the soil* (Clark 1990).

Resistivity surveying remains perhaps the most important technique available to archaeologists, closely followed by magnetometry. Other techniques like ground-penetrating radar, acoustic reflection and thermal sensing, for a variety of reasons remain of more restricted use. The principles behind resistivity are relatively straight-forward, although the physics and practice are more complex. Basically soils, which hold water, conduct electricity more than natural rocks like chalk, sandstone and granite. Therefore if you pass an electric current through the ground, solid materials will resist more than soil deposits. These variations in electrical resistance can be measured with a suitable meter, and patterns of variable resistance can be recorded. Solid features like walls, road surfaces and the bedrock, have a higher resistance than features filled with soil, like pits and ditches.

Although a number of instruments and probe configurations have been developed and tried since 1950, the two that have had the most success in archaeology are the Martin-Clark meter and the twin-electrode type like the Geoscan Research RM15, although the Martin-Clark meter is now rarely used.

The Martin-Clark resistivity meter is a four-terminal meter which is connected to equally-spaced steel probes pushed some six inches (15 cm) into the ground. Five probes are spaced at one-metre intervals in a straight line. Only four of the probes are active at any one time. Two of the probes pass alternating current into the ground, while the other two measure the voltage gradient created as the current passes through the ground. The advantage of having a fifth probe is that by using a turret switch on the meter, the end probe can be inactivated and leap-frogged over the other four, so only one probe has to be moved at a time rather than all four. The turret switch can be rotated one notch after each leap-frog so as to activate the moved probe and the three adjacent to it.

Two configurations of probes are generally used: the *Wenner* and the *double dipole*. In the Wenner configuration, the current is introduced into the ground through the outer two probes of the four active probes, and the resulting potential gradient is measured between the middle two. In the double-dipole configuration the current is passed through two adjacent probes and the potential gradient meas-ured between the other two adjacent probes (Fig. 3.12). The Wenner configuration was designed for geological surveying of massive structures and creates some problems with narrow archaeological features. The Wenner configuration also pro-duces double peaks over walls, making them appear much wider than they really are. The double-dipole configuration has the advantage of producing only a single peak, but has the disadvantage that penetration of the current into the soil is less than for the Wenner configuration. By using both together, the advantages of each can be gained. This is done by having a switch on the resistivity meter that can change the electrical configuration of the probes (Clark 1990).

The development of the *twin-electrode* configuration specifically for archae-ology has led to considerable time saving in the field. This configuration is a variation of Wenner in which one of the currents and one of the potential probes are

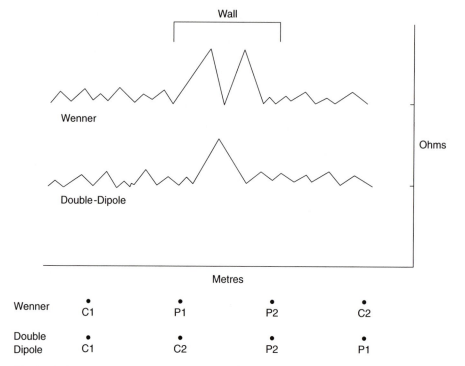

Figure 3.12   Geophysics: (1) Wenner configuration; (2) double-dipole configuration.

left fixed outside the survey area. The other two can then be attached to a simple frame and rapidly moved over the survey area (Fig. 3.13).

To undertake a resistivity survey, the area to be surveyed should be gridded (Chapter Four). For convenience 20 m- or 30 m-grid squares are usually used and laid out on a north–south alignment. If using a twin-electrode machine on a frame, then one reading is taken in each metre square with the fixed probes outside the square (Clark 1990). The reading in each square can be recorded manually or, for greater spread, using a data logger. The data can then be presented in some graphic way ready for interpretation – but we will return to this aspect of geophysics after looking at the other main methods, as finally they all produce patterns requiring similar interpretation by the field archaeologist.

The second major geophysical technique used by field archaeologists is magnetometry. This technique records minor variations in the earth's magnetic field. Many types of human activity will cause such variations in what will finally become archaeological features. Burning, where it affects clay, is particularly significant. On firing, clay becomes magnetic and retains the direction of a magnetic field of the earth at the time of firing. Also topsoil contains more magnetic oxides than subsoil, so soil silting into a ditch will locally affect the earth's magnetic field. Concentrations of iron oxides can be increased through general occupation activities resulting from burning and organic decomposition. Much of this affected

Figure 3.13   Resistivity meter.

material will accumulate in pits and other features, and so be detectable with a magnetometer. Obviously anything magnetic like iron fences, overhead cables, igneous geology, or even magnetic bits of the operator's clothing like metal zips, will create problems.

Proton magnetometry is based on the frequency with which hydrogen protons spin, which is affected by magnetic fields. Firstly, hydrogen protons in a liquid (water or alcohol) are aligned with the axis of a magnetic coil wound around the liquid's container. They are then allowed to re-align themselves to the earth's magnetic field. The protons spin during this process and the frequency at which they do this is proportional to the earth's magnetic field. The spinning protons generate a voltage in the coil which varies with the local magnetic field, and so if readings are taken at regular intervals over the site, a magnetic plan of the site can be built up which will represent the buried features.

The proton magnetometer, however, measures the absolute value of the strength of the earth's magnetic field, so the results have to be filtered for the effects of geological background, the rising and setting of the sun, and more local problems like iron fences. The development of the gradiometer partly overcomes these problems by having two bottles, both of which record the 'big' magnetic fields but only the lower one records the shallower features strongly. The electronics in the gradiometer subtract one bottle reading from the other, to produce surface readings.

Proton magnetometers and gradiometers both have the problem of discrete readings with no information recorded between reading spots. To rectify this problem the fluxgate gradiometer was developed which allows continuous output, making it

Figure 3.14   Grey-scale geophysical plot-out. (David Combes)

ideal for rapidly scanning large areas of ground. The fluxgate gradiometer is now the most frequently used type of magnetometer as its cycle of operation takes only one-thousandth of a second compared with five seconds required by a proton magnetometer (Clark 1990). The fluxgate gradiometer is a compact, lightweight instrument which measures magnetic intensity on a meter. It does this by having alloy strips which are driven in and out of magnetic saturation. As they come out of saturation, external magnetic fields can enter giving electric pulses proportional to the strength of the magnetic field. It is these variations in strength of magnetic field that are measured on a meter and can be recorded on a data logger.

The digital data recorded by both resistivity meters and fluxgate gradiometers can be transferred into graphics, showing patterns of subsurface features. This process is usually done by computer. From the 1960s until relatively recently, dot density has been the most commonly used way of showing patterns graphically. Variations in resistivity or magnetic field are represented by denser or less dense concentrations of dots, producing a 'plan' rather like a soil-mark aerial photograph. Computers can filter the dots to enhance features.

With the development of laser printers, a new graphic technique became possible. Instead of concentrations of dots of the same size, grey-scale plots can print dots of variable size on a fine regular grid (Fig. 3.14). This produces an image rather like a black-and-white photograph printed in a book. Even more startling are three-dimensional-looking images produced by draping geophysical surveys over 3-D topographic models of the same area (Synnott 1996).

Whatever plotting system is used, the final result is a pattern of shapes on a computer monitor or printed page. Geophysical surveys do not tell field archaeologists exactly what is at a particular spot in the landscape. Like aerial photographs, the patterns need interpretation. As with crop marks, it is generally possible to determine whether the buried features are walls or ditches, pits or column bases, but only by knowing the range of likely sites in an area can the field archaeologist interpret the pattern as a Roman villa or a sunken house-pit of the Hudnut phase in the western USA.

A technique related to the use of magnetometers in the field is the technique of magnetic susceptibility. Magnetometers are essentially used to locate buried features and burnt areas, whereas magnetic susceptibility locates occupation areas because of the enhancement of susceptibility by the use of an area by humans. This technique is particularly important where occupation evidence survives only in topsoil, either *in situ* or having eroded down slopes (Clark 1990).

To undertake a magnetic susceptibility survey, the area of the survey is gridded and soil samples taken on a regular grid. These are dried and sieved to remove the coarse components like stones. The magnetic susceptibility is then measured using a sensor like the Bartington MS2B (Clark 1990). Areas of high susceptibility are likely to represent areas of human interference of the soil by enhancement through the introduction of organic rubbish or flecks of burnt material. This technique is particularly important in locating activity areas and the full extent of sites where rubbish, such as pottery, has been collected up and middened at the edge of sites, or even taken away and spread over fields with manure. Simple field walking would only find the artefact spreads which might, or might not, be close to the activity areas where this rubbish was actually generated.

The least-used of the major geophysical techniques is ground-penetrating radar. Although successfully used by the Division of Remote Sensing of the US National Parks Service since the 1970s, and on well-drained pumice-derived soils in Japan (Conyers and Goodman 1997) the equipment remains expensive, the technique is not good in wet soils, and the results are often difficult to interpret. It does, however, have some value in Britain during evaluation exercises in urban contexts as it can provide images 6–8 metres deep, in the way neither resistivity or magnetometry can (Stove and Addyman 1989).

Chemical survey

An entirely different way of locating human activity in the landscape is by locating changes in soil chemistry resulting from human occupation. It has been calculated that 100 people, carrying out a range of domestic and farming activities, deposit about 124 kg of phosphorus into the landscape annually (Proudfoot 1976). All living things absorb phosphorus and then discard it as organic waste. As most waste is likely to be disposed of at or near centres of activity, by tracing

Figure 3.15   Auger survey collecting samples for phosphate analysis.

concentrations of phosphorus (unless naturally occurring) in theory one can trace human activity areas. Generally this would be done where there is some other hint at human activity like aerial photographic evidence or a pottery scatter. The area to be surveyed is gridded. If the archaeology has been clearly brought up to the surface, by ploughing for example, then a soil sample is collected in each grid square. An alternative is to use an auger to take a deeper soil sample (Fig. 3.15).

Phosphorus which entered the soil with organic waste, having been released from the waste, becomes fixed in the soil. Fortunately for survey purposes, most modern phosphates used in agriculture do not fix in this way, so are lost out of the soil (to pollute streams and rivers). The organically-derived phosphates do not leach out of the soil and remain more or less where originally deposited. Each sample of about 300 g is carefully bagged and labelled. Back at the survey base or laboratory, 50 mg of soil is placed on filter paper and a couple of drops of ammonium molybdenate in hydrochloric acid are added. A dilute solution of ascorbic acid is made by adding 0.5 g to 100 ml of distilled water, from which two drops are added to the sample after thirty seconds. A blue ring then develops on the filter paper, which is directly proportional to the amount of phosphorus in the soil. The reaction is stopped after two minutes by placing the filter paper in a 50 per cent solution of sodium citrate in water (Eidt 1977). Essentially, the deeper the blue, the more phosphorus there is present in the soil. This can be assessed very approximately by eye, or more accurately by using a colorimeter.

Although phosphorus is perhaps one of the clearest and easiest chemical residues to locate in the soil, other chemicals like copper and lead may be associated with specific types of human activity, and degraded lime mortar may be traced by higher concentrations of calcium locally in the soil (Clark 1990).

Accidental discovery

Although archaeologists have a battery of survey, remote sensing and chemical techniques available to locate archaeological sites, it remains true that many, if not most, new archaeological sites are found by accident. Classic accidental discoveries like the Lascaux painted caves or the Xian terracotta army are well known, but in virtually every disturbance of the earth's surface some archaeology is located. Some of this archaeology may be so recent, like flower-pot sherds or drain pipes, as to be of little interest to archaeologists, but much more is missed by having no trained observer to locate and record the information.

Many archaeological discoveries are made by building workers, farmers, quarry workers and just casual passers-by. A tiny fraction of these discoveries comes to the attention of archaeologists. Usually casual finds are reported to local museums. It is essential that the archaeologists in the museum or elsewhere show enthusiasm for these discoveries, even if they are not of major importance. One bad experience by a member of the public and they will never bother to bring their discoveries in again, and next time it may be a terracotta army!

There are also accidental or partly-accidental discoveries made by archaeologists. Whenever surveying an area using any techniques, field archaeologists should take the opportunity to look into any available 'keyholes' to see what lies buried. These keyholes are often very short-lived and the opportunity may not arise again.

Keyholes can be broadly divided into natural and humanly-produced. Natural keyholes include burrow upcast, thrown up by burrowing animals, the root bases of uprooted trees, and natural erosion by rivers and the sea. River banks and low cliff lines can provide a ready-made cross-section through the landscape. Human keyholes are usually even shorter-lived. These include pipe trenches, foundation trenches of new buildings, holes dug for fence posts, or even holes dug for graves.

Having located an archaeological site it is the responsibility of the archaeologist either to record it, or at least inform relevant authorities who can record it.

CHAPTER FOUR

Recording archaeological sites

The recording of archaeological sites discovered in the field essentially has three elements: a written description of the site, a survey including plans and elevations, and a photographic record. Many of these techniques are of course the same, or similar to, those that we will meet again in Chapter Seven when recording excavated features. The record described in this chapter may be as far as the field archaeologist goes, or it may be a stage before excavation. It must *not* be presumed, however, that excavation is, or should be, the final element of any fieldwork. In fact the presumption should be that excavation is only a last resort if all non-destructive techniques of investigation fail to answer the questions posed. Excavation, being totally destructive, allows questions to be asked only once. If excavation recording is very precise, as it should be, then some questions can be asked of the record, but never again of the whole site.

Written description

The written description of a site in the field should be properly integrated with survey and photographic data. Even with the finest prose, a written description inevitably can mean slightly different things to different readers, particularly if translated into other languages. As long as conventions are adhered to, surveys and photographs usually do not present this problem.

How the description of a site is written will depend very much on how the record is to be used. If you are recording the site simply to record its existence on, for example, a Sites and Monuments Record, then the use of a pre-printed record form in the format of the Sites and Monuments Record is advisable. The basic fields of record have already been described in Chapter Three and consist of a unique reference number, administrative area, address, cartographic reference, type of site, date and condition of site. This should be sufficient for future workers to locate the site again. If, however, you are attempting to interpret the site and pass your interpretation on to others, then a more detailed written description of the site will be required. Such descriptions are usually tied into a topographical survey.

Interpretative surveys and their written description go right back to the beginnings of field archaeology. As early as the seventeenth century, field archaeologists like William Stukeley (1687–1765) accurately described field monuments. At the beginning of the nineteenth century, field archaeologists such as William Cunnington were not only describing monuments, but also the sequences represented by them: "A few feet further to the west from the large tumulus are two more barrows over which the great inner *vallum* [of Battlesbury Camp] passes" (Cunnington 1975). This clearly describes a sequence of the earthworks.

The finest current descriptions of surface archaeology in Britain are those produced by the Royal Commission on Historical Monuments surveyors. Tight interpretative descriptions support fine surveys. Modern descriptions are usually more precise than those of earlier antiquaries and include measurements: "A double-lynchetted track (d), up to 9 m in width, originates from beneath the east terminal of the southern entrance and runs intermittently in a north-east to south-west direction for some 250 m before being truncated by circular hollows" (Donachie and Field 1994). However clear a description may be, it will only really make sense if accompanied by a field survey and photographs.

Archaeological surveying

Archaeological surveying uses all the techniques of land surveyors, but requires an archaeological input to interpret what is present and worth recording. Essentially, decisions have to be made throughout the survey as to what is natural as opposed to humanly-created, where the top and bottom of a bank is, whether this bit of earth-work overlaps, or is overlapped by, another earthwork.

Over the last decade or so, land surveying has been revolutionized by the introduction of Electronic Distance Measurement (EDM) equipment and the total station, together with the satellite-based Global Positioning System (GPS). However, many field archaeologists, for a variety of reasons, still have or wish to use less sophisticated and cheaper survey techniques. All survey data has the potential for inclusion in Geographic Information Systems (GIS), but naturally that collected in digital form requires less manipulation than traditional survey methods.

When selecting a traditional survey technique, the first thing to consider is precision – or how inaccurate can you be. This requires thinking about the end-product. Most surveys are presented in a reduced form. These may be drawn at a scale of 1:20 for good detail, but then reduced even further for publication. The thickness of a pencil line represents about 1 cm on the ground at a scale of 1:20, so is there any point in taking measurements less than 1 cm, particularly if surveying earthworks? More usually surveys will be undertaken at even smaller scales like 1:100, 1:500, or even 1:1 000. The significance of precision becomes even less important as the scale becomes smaller.

The simplest form of surveying is a paced or sketch survey. This can be done either with very basic equipment like tapes, ranging poles and prismatic compass, or with no equipment at all. Such surveys are really suitable only for small, simple sites where great accuracy is not too important. If you do not have access to more advanced surveying equipment, however, sufficiently accurate plans can be produced.

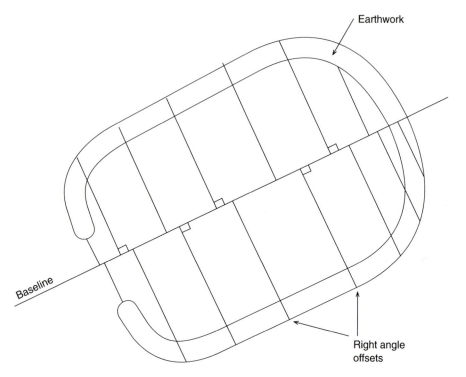

Figure 4.1 Simple surveying by offsets.

Firstly, lay out a baseline. If the site is fairly small and you have two fixed points like a tree and a corner of a building, the shortest distance between these two points gives you a straight baseline. If you have no measuring equipment, you can pace along the baseline and then pace an estimated perpendicular to the point you want to locate (Fig. 4.1). This can then be done to locate any points within reasonable distance of the baseline. You can build in more accuracy by measuring your lines with tapes rather than paces, and using tapes, optical square or crosshead to construct the perpendicular. The best tapes to use are fibreglass or similar, 20 m or 30 m long. Longer tapes, which can go up to 200 m, create problems in rough country and wind.

The crosshead consists simply of a metal cylinder with right-angle slots. You view one way along the baseline and then, viewing through the slots at right angles, lay out a perpendicular. The optical square is similar, but using prisms you can view along the baseline and at right angles at the same time. Ranging poles, red and white poles 2 m long made of wood or metal, are used as sighting markers. Using just tapes, a perpendicular can be made either by constructing a 3–4–5 triangle (as Pythagoras; see Fig. 4.2) or by putting the end of the tape on the point you want to locate and swinging the tape over the baseline. The shortest distance on the baseline as the tape is swung along it has to be a right angle (Fig. 4.3). This simple technique of surveying is reasonably accurate on level sites, but if there is any slope

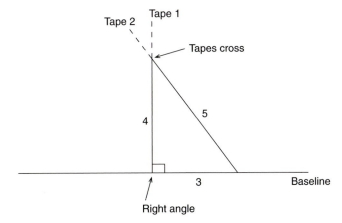

Figure 4.2   Constructing a 3-4-5 triangle.

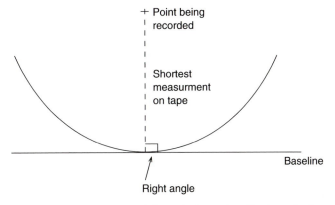

Figure 4.3   Establishing a right angle from a baseline by swinging a tape.

care must be taken to keep tapes level, and a plumb-bob should be used to locate positions on the ground below the level tape.

An alternative to offset surveying, using perpendiculars from a baseline, is triangulation. This, as the name suggests, involves constructing triangles. It can also be carried out from a baseline and is best done with two tapes. Two points are selected on the baseline and one end of each tape is pegged, at the points selected. This can be done with surveyor's arrows which are metal skewers, brightly coloured or with a flag attached to make them clearly visible. The other ends of the tapes are then crossed over the point you want to locate. By doing this you have constructed a triangle with three known sides, so you have fixed the point of the apex (Fig. 4.4).

For larger sites it is advisable to use a survey framework rather than a single baseline. In effect this consists of four baselines (the sides of the framework) with the shape of the framework fixed by measuring diagonals. Either offsets or triangles can then be laid off from the framework (Fig. 4.5).

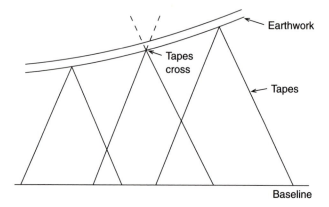

Figure 4.4   Surveying by triangulation.

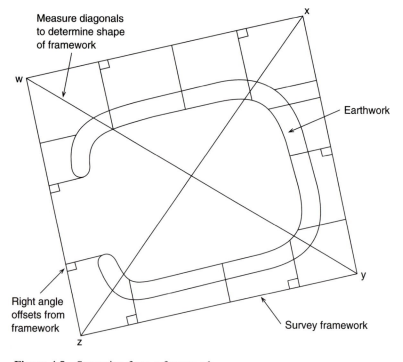

Figure 4.5   Surveying from a framework.

One of the oldest types of surveying equipment, still in use in some parts of the world and largely unchanged since its appearance in about AD 1600, is the plane table. Although rarely used where electronic surveying equipment is available, it is worth mention, partly because of its successful use over some 400 years, and partly because in many parts of the world it may be one of the most readily available pieces of survey equipment.

Figure 4.6   Plane table surveying.

The plane table consists of a drawing board (the plane table) mounted on a tripod. On this rests the alidade which is a straight edge with sights at each end. Most commonly, the plane table is used to produce plans of small earthwork sites by the radiation method. The plane table is placed level on its tripod in the middle of the earthwork. The point to be located is then sighted through the alidade and the sight line recorded by drawing a line along the edge of the alidade directly onto plastic tracing film mounted on the plane table. A tape is then used to measure from the plane table to the point being located. The distance is scaled down (say to 1:500) and measured along the sight line drawn on the plane table. The position of the first point has then been located. Each point to be measured can be located in the same way. The points are then joined up to produce the shape of the earthwork (Fig. 4.6).

An alternative way to produce a simple ground survey is to grid the site. This process can also be used to produce a field-walking grid or a grid laid out in advance of excavation. A site grid, as the name implies, involves the construction of a regular pattern of squares over the area of interest. Actual squares are, of course, never laid out; just all or some of the corners of squares are marked in some way. For a short-lived grid, as used in field walking, this can be done with ranging poles. If the grid is to survive one or more excavation seasons, then steel pegs, perhaps even set in concrete, may be required – but this will be further discussed in Chapter Seven. Having set up a survey grid, details of the site can be plotted by taking offset measurements from the grid lines, or triangulation from the lines or corner points.

To lay out a grid, a point of origin must be selected. This will be a fixed point outside the area to be surveyed. If the grid is to be used over several years for surveying, field walking and then perhaps excavation, it must be a permanent fixed spot which will not be disturbed by any future work. It is often convenient, particularly for reference and locating the grid on existing maps, for the grid to be orientated north–south. Archaeologically, however, there is nothing significant in north–south orientated grids. It is often done just for neatness.

It is possible to lay out an accurate grid using two people, half a dozen ranging poles, two tapes and, if on a sloping site, a plumb bob. For greater accuracy, particularly on sloping sites, it can be done with a theodolite or transit. Firstly lay out as long a line as you can from the point of origin along one side of the proposed grid. This can be done by sighting a line using ranging poles. A ranging pole is put in the point of origin and one surveyor stays with it. The other surveyor takes the other poles along the line to be set out. A second pole is then put in some 100 m or so along the line. If the grid is to be orientated north–south, the second pole is set out using a prismatic compass. Both in the field and in writing up data, it should made clear that magnetic (not geographical) north is being used. A prismatic compass is a simple hand-held compass with a prism, enabling you to read the compass bearing while looking between two sighting marks on the compass. These sighting marks are lined up with magnetic north and then the second ranging pole is moved into line with the sight marks. Intermediate poles can then be sighted in by eye.

The first surveyor at the point of origin will sight along the line. The second surveyor moves a pole slowly across the approximate area of the grid line. As it vanishes behind the first pole and hides the third pole, then all three poles must be in line. The line can then be projected on across the landscape by repeating the process down the line. If a 30 m grid is being laid out, then a tape is stretched from the origin along the line for 30 m and a peg put in the ground. This process is repeated along the full length of the line. It is important to tape horizontally along each 30 m length; if the ground slopes, raise the edge of the tape at the lower end until it is horizontal and then use a plumb bob to position the peg at ground level.

From this baseline, right angles are then laid out at the corner of each grid square, that is, every 30 m in the example we are considering. This can be done using two tapes and simple geometry. Either an equilateral triangle or a right-angled triangle is constructed. To construct an equilateral triangle over a 30 m point on the baseline, measure an equal distance (say 3 m) either side of the baseline peg, and fix the end of a tape at each point. Then unwind the tapes to 6 m each, and where they cross they will form an equilateral triangle with three sides of 6 m each. A line from the original peg through the apex of the triangle will therefore be at right angles to the baseline.

Alternatively a 3-4-5 triangle could be constructed from the peg on the baseline (Fig. 4.2). This is done by measuring 3 m to one side of the baseline peg along the baseline. A tape 5 m long is held with 0 m on this point. A second tape is held with its 0 m on the baseline peg and opened to 4 m. The 4 m and 5 m tapes are then crossed, and where they cross will give a right angle from the baseline peg. Right

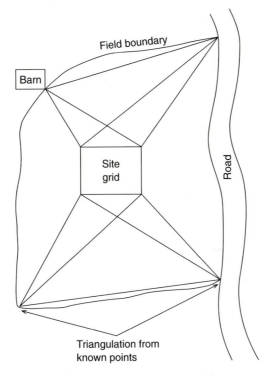

Figure 4.7   Fixing the position of a grid.

angles can, of course, also be laid out using a variety of surveying equipment, from crossheads and optical squares to transits and theodolites.

Having constructed a right angle, then a line at right angles to the baseline can be sighted out using ranging poles. This process can be repeated at every 30 m interval along the baseline until a grid of squares has been constructed. Laying out a grid using just tapes and ranging poles can be perfectly accurate, but inaccuracies can always creep in due to slope, tapes being moved by the wind, or surveyor problems (for example, misreading a tape or bad eyesight ranging out a line). To remove these problems always check the diagonals of squares created. If the length of the two diagonals are the same then it is a square. If one is significantly more than the other, recheck your layout. You must, however, consider whether a few centimetres matter. They do not matter in a field-walking grid or if surveying eroded earthworks.

A grid is only of any use, however, if you know where it is. To record this you need to fix the location of the point of origin of the grid. If you have clear, permanent fixed structures like buildings, then simply measure to a minimum of three fixed points. These points are likely to be on existing maps, so they can be located and your grid positioned in relation to them. If there are no close fixed points, then prismatic-compass bearings can be taken to fixed points further afield but clearly visible. Again a minimum of three points must be plotted (Fig. 4.7). This process can also be carried out with a transit, theodolite or total station. If

Figure 4.8 Surveyor's level.

working in an area where there are no good maps or fixed points in the landscape, then you may have to use a satellite Global Positioning System (GPS). These can be used to fix the position of any spot on the earth's surface in relation to orbiting satellites. Very cheap hand-held machines are available, particularly designed for sailors of small boats, but are accurate only to 15 m or so. More expensive systems, like the Leica System 200, however, can fix positions to an accuracy of about 1 cm.

The techniques described so far will enable you to produce a cheap, reasonably accurate plan of any simple site. They do not, however, provide any information about how the land rises and falls, how high your earthworks are, or whether the site is level or undulating. To gather this information you need to be able to record the height of different elements of the site. This is the process of levelling which, not surprisingly, can be carried out with an instrument called a level (Fig. 4.8), although it can also be done with other optical or electronic equipment to which we will return later. Although one often hears all levels on archaeological sites referred to as 'dumpy' levels, in fact there are three types which vary mainly in the way in which they are set up. These are the dumpy, quick-set and automatic levels. All three have to be set level on a solid tripod. This is done by levelling one or more spirit levels built into the machine. In the dumpy this is done by raising and lowering three screws; the quick-set uses a ball and socket, while the automatic level simply involves one small central bubble which, when centrally located in a marked ring, results in an internal mechanism levelling the sight lines.

The level itself includes a telescope. When you look through the telescope you will see a vertical line and a horizontal level line. There are also two short stadia

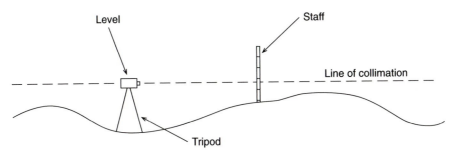

Figure 4.9 Surveying with a level: the line of collimation.

lines, but these are not used for levelling: they are used for calculating distance. When you view the landscape through the telescope, the horizontal cross-hair in effect projects an imaginary horizontal line across that landscape. In some levels this image is inverted. As the level can be rotated through 360° on the tripod, this level line can be sighted around the visible landscape. This imaginary line is really an arbitrary level plane being superimposed over the landscape, and is known as a line or plane of collimation. Both the transit and theodolite can be used in the same way as a level to throw out a plane of collimation. Their advantage over a level, however, is that they can be tilted to take readings up or down slopes while the level must remain rigidly level. From a field archaeologist's point of view, however, the level is very strong and less prone to damage than more sensitive equipment.

The second piece of equipment required for levelling is the surveyor's staff, in effect a giant ruler usually 4 m or 12 ft long, which either folds or is telescopic. The staff is marked in alternating red and black segments, divided into metres and centimetres, or feet and inches. As the staff is moved around the site, the readings taken by sighting the cross-hair in the level against the staff will be seen to vary. Lower readings indicate that the land is rising in relation to the plane of collimation, while higher readings show that the land is falling. To make sense of these rises and falls, the survey must be undertaken systematically and tied to a benchmark or, if none is available, you can create your own temporary benchmark.

The benchmark is the starting point of your levelling survey. In Britain the Ordnance Survey have cut permanent benchmarks on structures like churches and public buildings. These are an inverted 'V' with a line on top. The actual benchmark level is the horizontal line. If no benchmarks are available you can create your own temporary benchmark and give it an arbitrary value, say 50 m. This will enable you to produce a site survey with contours, but not to relate it to other sites or the wider landscape.

The level is set up as close to the site of the survey as possible, but so that the benchmark can be seen. The staff is then held on the benchmark, not on the ground below, and a reading taken. This is known as a backsight. The value of the line of collimation is then calculated by adding the reading on the staff to the value of the benchmark. If the benchmark had a value of 50 m and the staff reading is 1.4 m, then the line of collimation has a value of 51.4 m (Fig. 4.9). To establish the relative height of spots on the ground the staff is placed on these spots, readings taken on

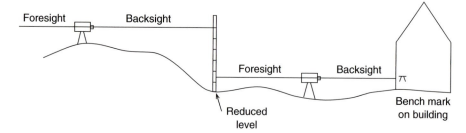

Figure 4.10   Surveying with a level: moving stations, foresight and backsight.

the staff, and then these readings are subtracted from the value of the line of collimation. So if the line of collimation has a value of 51.4 m and the staff reading is 3.2 m, then the actual height of that spot is 48.2 m. This is known as a reduced level.

If your benchmark is close to your survey site, then you may be able to turn the level from its backsight (onto the benchmark) directly into the survey area. These forward sights are then known as foresights. However, if you cannot do this, perhaps because the land rises and falls too much or there are trees in the way, you may need to move the level or 'change station'. This is done by taking a foresight to the surveyor's staff and then, with an assistant holding the staff still in the same spot, moving the level to the other side of the staff and having a reading taken back to it (a backsight). The difference between the foresight and the backsight indicates how much the new line of collimation is above or below the previous line (Fig. 4.10). This process can be repeated until the site is reached and the level of the final line of collimation calculated.

To produce a contour survey of the site you can either 'chase' a contour or interpolate contours from a grid of spot heights. To chase contours, the person holding the staff moves it along a roughly estimated contour line, moving it up and down slope until identical readings are found, say 45 m. The spot is then marked with a peg or surveyor's arrow and located using any of the techniques mentioned earlier in this chapter. This technique produces very accurate contours (although between spot heights the contours remain estimates) but can be time-consuming, particularly if the person holding the staff is not very experienced. More usually a contour survey is produced by gridding the site and taking spot heights on the corners of each grid square. The smaller the grid squares are, the more spot heights will be recorded and the more accurate the contour survey will be. The more accurate the survey is, the longer it will take to produce. To produce a contour plan the grid is drawn at a reduced scale on a plan and the reduced spot heights marked on each grid corner. Actual contours are then interpolated from these spots. This is done first by estimating their position in relation to the fixed points on the grid lines. The points on the lines with similar value, say 45 m, 45.5 m, 50 m and so on, are then joined by curved lines to produce contours.

Levels can also be used for measuring distances by using the stadia lines already mentioned. These are the short cross-hairs visible through the telescope lens (Fig. 4.11). By sighting on a staff, two readings can be taken, one with the

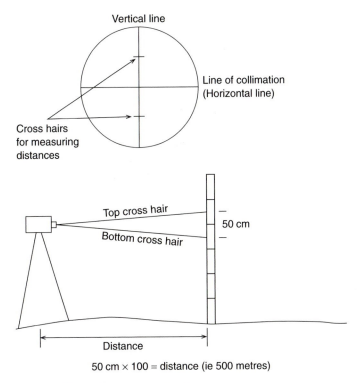

Figure 4.11   Stadia hairs in a level.

upper cross-hair and the other with the lower cross-hair. The stadia lines have been calibrated so that by subtracting the lowest staff reading from the highest and multiplying by 100, the distance from the level to the staff is calculated.

The advantage of both the transit and the theodolite over the level is that they can be tilted and so take readings above and below the line of collimation. This has obvious advantages if the site is undulating or has any steep slopes. The engineer's transit is widely used in the USA but is virtually unknown in Britain, while the theodolite is commonly used in Britain but is less common on American archae-ological surveys. They function in a very similar way. Both have three elements: the transit or theodolite, a heavy-duty tripod, and a staff. The staff is the same type as was used with a level. Both instruments are set up on their tripod and levelled using built-in spirit levels.

Reading a transit or theodolite is similar to reading a level. The centre hairline in the lens is used for taking levels, while the stadia lines are used for distance. Horizontal bearings are taken using a 360° horizontal circle. This can be used to take very precise angles. In Britain the 360° circle is divided in degrees, each degree is subdivided into 60 minutes, and each minute into 60 seconds. Angles are then quoted as 242°14′32″ which, as you can see, gives a very precise hori-zontal angle which can be used in both surface surveys and for precise excavation recording.

The additional reading that theodolites and transits can give, which levels cannot, is the vertical angle. The use of this angle introduces a need for basic trigonometry. The calculations required can be performed using formulae, but more usually tacheometric tables are used. These can be found in many surveying manuals, and appear as Appendix 3 in Martha Joukowsky's *A complete manual of field archaeology* (Joukowsky 1980).

As with most levels, the multiplication factor for distance readings for stadia is 100 in modern instruments. This factor is known as 'K'. To calculate distance, the stadia readings (that is, the top and bottom short lines in the viewfinder) are read off from the staff. The difference between these two readings is called 's'. The third reading taken is the angle the theodolite or transit has been tilted from the horizontal. This angle is known as 'V'. Distance is then calculated with the formula

Distance $= Ks \, (\cos^2)V$

Height can also be calculated using the formula:

Height $= Ks \, (\cos V) \sin V$

The importance of the transit and theodolite is that they enable you to survey more accurately where the ground surface is not level than would be possible using the previously mentioned techniques.

Much of the surveying equipment described so far is becoming redundant as electronic surveying equipment becomes more readily available, cheaper and easier to use. There will, however, always be occasions or parts of the world where simple, cheap surveying techniques will be used. A good surveyor should be able to switch methods and equipment as the need arises. If your total station dies, high in the Andes on the last day of a survey, a couple of tapes could save a very expensive revisit to the site.

Electronic Distance Measurement (EDM) equipment was first developed to be attached to theodolites but now the EDM and theodolite are built into a single housing and this is then known as a total station (Fig. 4.12). As all data can be recorded digitally, computers may be used throughout the survey to record data in the field and to draw up the final plan. The EDM or total station is set up on a solid tripod and, when switched on, a built-in transmitter throws out a beam (for example of infra-red) which is returned from a reflector held at the position you want to locate. The electronics within the machine calculate distance from the length of time the beam takes to reach the reflector and return. This time will be affected by height above sea level (or pressure) and temperature. These data will have to be entered into the EDM or total station to enable a correction to be made.

The form and key pad of EDM and total stations vary, but essentially distances, angles and heights can be recorded. Generally this is now done by automatic recording which eliminates all need for writing in the field. The EDM and total station can be used for setting out survey frameworks or grids, but area surveys are approached somewhat differently. With pre-electronic surveying, measurements were generally taken in relation to lines, baselines, triangles and survey frameworks. With electronic surveying these are not required, and the survey takes place in the area

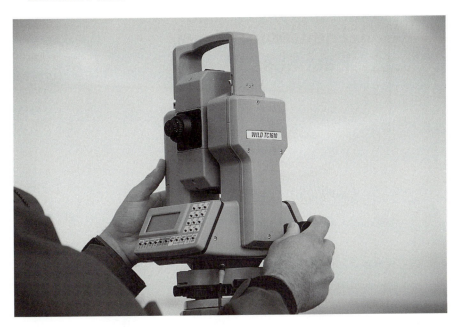

Figure 4.12   Total station.

around the equipment so there is a change from linear recording to area recording. Spots are recorded in direct relationship to the position of the surveying equipment. These areas can be very large, so the surveyor at the total station may need to communicate with the person moving the prism who could be one as much as a kilometre or so away. The only effective way to do this is to use a walkie-talkie radio.

To undertake a survey, the total station or EDM is set up at a suitable position within the survey area, preferably where all – or as much as possible – of the site can be seen. Points to be recorded on the ground are located, including buildings and field banks, together with the archaeological features. These spots are either numbered consecutively or, if the plan is to be computer-drawn, by using the codes required by the package, which will also have to inform the computer what type of feature to draw. Do the points recorded represent an earthwork to be drawn with hachures, or is it a masonry building? Many computer drafting packages can also draw contours. This generally requires level values to be recorded on a regular grid, although some can produce contours from random levels. If using random levels they must be well spread over the site, or the contours will look somewhat unconvincing. Contours are essentially lines but spot-height data can also be used to record surfaces which can produce images close to true surface representation. These are digital elevation models (DEM) sometimes known as digital terrain models (DTM). The DEM has become an important element in the construction of Geographic Information Systems (GIS).

Whatever surveying techniques are used, they will end up with an image of the site. Traditionally, and still generally for publication, conventions are used to present

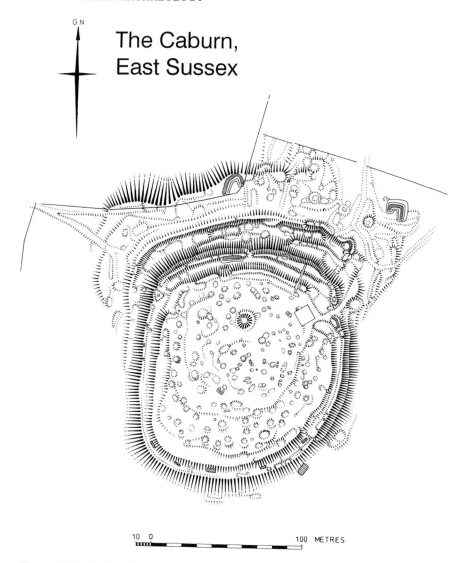

GN

The Caburn,
East Sussex

10 0   100 METRES

Figure 4.13 Hachured survey of Mount Caburn, Sussex (survey by A. Oswald and D. McOrmish. Crown copyright: RCHME).

a picture of the surface undulations of a site. Banks, ditches, pits and hollows are represented by hachures (Fig. 4.13). These enable banks and ditches, for example, to be clearly shown whereas if they were indicated by contours they might be lost in steeper natural slopes of the hillside. Used skilfully, either by a draftsperson or a computer, they can be used to show very slight variations in slope. However, computer-generated three-dimensional terrain-modelling and hill shading can generate images which no longer require conventional cartographic conventions. With vertical exaggeration even the slightest landscape features can be clearly imaged.

Photography

The third element of recording archaeological sites in the field is photography. One element of this is aerial photography, already considered in Chapter Three. The other element is producing a ground photographic record of landscapes, archaeological features and keyholes cut into the landscape, like natural river-bank sections which may show archaeological layers. Field survey, as opposed to excavation, often requires movement of equipment great distances and often by foot. A compact photographic kit is advisable for this type of work. The equipment required should be able to be packed into a standard photographic shoulder bag. A typical kit would include two 35 mm camera bodies, with either zoom lenses or 28, 50 and 200 mm lenses. Useful filters include UV (ultra-violet), polarizing, and yellow, red and green. A tripod may be taken but is often not needed in open country. Other accessories include a cable release, compass, scales and of course film (Dorrell 1989).

Films should include both black-and-white and colour. Black-and-white remains the basic film for archaeological record. The life of colour film is uncertain, and fading will occur unless storage is very carefully monitored in the long term. Panchromatic medium-speed film of 100–125 ISO is suitable for most field situations. Colour transparency or positive film is used for lecture slides and, more rarely, for publication. When it comes to colour-slide film, many photographers have their own personal preference, but in Britain Kodachrome film is widely favoured, with film speeds of 25, 64 or up to 200 ISO depending on conditions. Colour negative film is rarely used for primary field recording, although it may be used for temporary site exhibitions.

This is not the place to expand in detail on photographic principles (see, for example, Langford 1986) but certain elements should be remembered when taking photographs. Firstly a photograph does not give an exact scale image of what is in the field. Whatever is close will appear at a larger scale than what is at a distance, and if the image is all on the same plane, then the scale in the centre of the photograph will be smaller than at its edges. To produce an image more or less as the human eye sees it, a 'standard lens' should be used. This gives an angle of view of about 45°, similar to a human eye. A wide range of other lenses can be fitted to 35 mm cameras, giving very wide angles (over 180°) and very narrow angles of down to 2°. Neither of these extremes is particularly useful in archaeology, especially very wide-angle lenses which create a very distorted image. An image like a building or a river-bank section will appear very distorted if photographed very close. Distortion can be reduced by photographing from further away and then, if using negative film, printing only the part of the image required.

Photographing close images may also create problems of focus. There is only a limited distance in front and behind the spot being photographed that is in focus, that is the 'depth of field'. This may not create a problem in survey photography, but can create real problems when photographing excavations and objects (see Chapters Seven and Ten). In field survey photography, light is usually no great problem, and so by decreasing the aperture of the camera lens the depth of field is increased.

Figure 4.14   Landscape photographed in evening sun to cast shadows.

Photographing landscapes in which archaeological sites occur is relatively straight-forward, but careful selection of viewing point, time of day, weather and light conditions can greatly enhance the image, as can the use of filters. An undulating landscape will look flat if photographed with high midday sun or without any sun. Early morning or late evening sun will cast shadows, giving the landscape a three-dimensional image (Fig. 4.14). This will also apply to photographing earthworks, which may effectively vanish without any shadow. There will be spots in the landscape which give the best overviews. Usually, but not always, these are higher points. With black-and-white film, red or yellow filters can be used to reduce distant haze, as can ultra-violet filters. In colour photography of landscapes, polarizing filters will enhance the contrast between blue sky and clouds, and sharpen the distant image. Although in general all archaeological photographs should contain a clear scale, landscapes usually contain some indication of scale in the form of buildings or trees. To add an artificial scale introduces spurious accuracy as the scale in the foreground is different from that in the distance. A human figure or two may, however, enhance the composition of the photograph and give a general indication of scale. If photographing earthworks, the figures could hold ranging poles.

Photographing buildings or natural sections like cliffs creates more of a problem than general landscape photography. If photographed at ground level, the scale of the building or cliff face gets smaller higher up the face. This gives the effect of the face leaning. This effect can be reduced by taking the photograph from further away. This is, however, not always possible, in which case either a large-format camera with movements, or smaller format cameras with a shift lens will be needed to rectify the photograph (Dallas 1980). Reasonably accurate elevation drawings can be traced from these photographs.

When taking archaeological photographs, proper record-keeping is an essential part of the process. Often one landscape or cliff section looks surprisingly like another. This becomes even more important in excavation photography where hundreds of photographs of similar features may be taken (Chapter Seven). In field survey it is best to make the photographic record in a note book rather than on the sort of pre-printed loose-leaf record form often used on excavation. The record should include:

1 Film number
2 Serial number of negative
3 Full details of subject
4 Direction from which photograph was taken (compass bearing)
5 Date and time of day

In addition it may be worth recording photographic information to trace equipment problems or errors in the photographer's judgement.

6 Equipment used
7 Type of film
8 Lens
9 Stop and exposure

As with much in field archaeology, a little extra time and care spent in the field can save an enormous amount of time when attempting to sort out records for archive or publication after the field season.

CHAPTER FIVE

Planning the excavation

It must never be assumed that excavation is an essential part of any archaeological fieldwork. Indeed, if the questions under investigation can be answered using the battery of non-destructive techniques now available to archaeologists (Chapter Three), then excavation should not be considered. The archaeological resource in the field is finite and diminishing. Each excavation reduces this resource. The excavation of sites about to be destroyed for non-archaeological reasons, like building development, can usually be justified on archaeological grounds if all attempts at preservation have failed. If, however, the site is not under threat, the value of excavation in increasing knowledge must be carefully considered.

This is, however, in no way suggesting that research excavations should not be undertaken. Without proper, well-planned research excavations, archaeology as a discipline could become as fossilized as many of the sites it studies. No excavation should, however, be undertaken lightly. They are expensive, time-consuming, and often very stressful. Many of the problems encountered on excavations can be reduced by proper pre-planning and careful use of human and financial resources. Above all a flexible approach can save time, money and stress. Remember there is no right way to excavate. There is a range of possible approaches.

Permission, funding and the law

The first stage in planning an excavation is to establish whether you can actually get permission to dig the holes you want to dig, that you can afford to dig the holes, and that legally you can dig the holes and do it safely. No field archaeologist should ever dig holes without proper permission. Firstly, establish whether the site has legal protection. In some countries named archaeological sites are protected while in others all archaeological sites are protected.

Practically every country in the world has some legal control on what can and cannot be done to archaeological sites. In some countries the laws with terms like 'Ancient Monuments' or 'Archaeology' may not be either the most important or effective Acts. In Britain, for example, probably more sites are protected on a day-to-day basis under the Town and Country Planning Acts than under the Ancient Monuments and Archaeological Areas Act, 1979. This is because the Ancient

Monuments and Archaeological Areas Act requires each site to be named and defined on a schedule or list, while under the Town and Country Planning Acts the impact of the archaeology (known or yet undiscovered) of *any* piece of land considered for development can be considered during a planning application.

The top tier of archaeological sites in the world are given a measure of protection under the UNESCO Convention concerning the Protection of the World Cultural and Natural Heritage. This Convention was adopted by UNESCO on 23 November 1972, and has since been ratified by over 120 countries. Some, like the USA, were quick to ratify (7 December 1973) while some, like Britain, were more sluggish (29 May 1984). Each state party to this convention undertakes not to deliberately damage, either directly or indirectly, any sites put on the World Heritage list. This clearly should include some control on what archaeological damage (that is, excavation) is allowed by field archaeologists. In fact, however, this is usually controlled by national laws.

The World Heritage Convention established a World Heritage Committee whose role is to produce a World Heritage List, consisting of cultural and natural sites of outstanding universal value. In selecting sites, the committee must consider whether the site is unique, extremely rare or of great antiquity, or is the most characteristic example of a type of structure. In every case the state of preservation of the property is considered and authenticity proved. The Convention requires member-states to pledge to protect World Heritage Sites and to operate a World Heritage Fund to give practical support to conservation projects. World Heritage Sites are really the world's major sites like Machu Picchu in Peru, the Great Wall of China, Stonehenge in Britain and the Caholia Mounds in Illinois, USA. The list currently has just over 350 sites on it (Swadling 1992).

As a field archaeologist planning a field project, however, it is the national laws that will be most important for the success or otherwise of your project. Prosecution is likely to follow from failure to obtain the right legal permissions. It is generally best to approach professional archaeologists working in the areas of interest before approaching those actually administering the law, because how the law is interpreted locally is often as important as the law itself. Follow this with informal discussions with those administering the law and you can often save time required getting permissions.

In Britain the position is relatively simple. A small percentage of archaeological sites is scheduled (that is, listed) under the Ancient Monuments and Archaeological Areas Act 1979. These require specific permission for excavation from the Secretary of State for Culture, Media and Sport (CMS). Few of these sites are, however, owned by the State, so in addition to Scheduled Monument Consent (that is, permission from CMS, the government department responsible), you also require the permission of the land owner. In terms of archaeological law in Britain you require the land owner's permission whether or not the site is scheduled. There may, however, be other restrictions of a non-archaeological nature. For example, the area may be a Site of Special Scientific Interest (SSSI) in which case permission from the responsible body, English Nature, will be required. Also the site, although owned by one person, may be tenanted by another whose permission would also be required.

The Ancient Monuments and Archaeological Areas Act 1979, brought together some 100 years of Ancient Monuments laws in Britain. It has three parts and is basically designed to preserve sites from unwarranted destruction through, say, development, but also to control archaeological excavation. Part 1 requires the Secretary of State (of the Department of the Environment in 1979 but now the Department of Culture, Media and Sport) to compile and maintain a 'schedule' of ancient monuments. This schedule or list has been compiled in a somewhat haphazard way over the last century. When English Heritage was established in 1984 they realized that the schedule was not particularly representative of the archaeological resource as a whole. Some types of sites were grossly over-represented while others were virtually unrepresented on the list. This led to the establishment of a Scheduling Enhancement Programme which later became the Monuments Protection Programme (MPP) – the aim of which is to produce a schedule which is an academically viable sample of the whole archaeological resource in Britain (Startin 1993).

Once a site is on the schedule, it is an offence to damage it in any way unless the Secretary of State has granted written consent. Failure to obtain consent carries a fine on summary conviction. In addition to 'scheduling' an ancient monument the Secretary of State may accept it into guardianship or compulsorily acquire any ancient monument for the purpose of preserving it. In fact only about 400 sites are in guardianship and they tend to be major, visible sites like Stonehenge and many castles and abbeys.

Part 2 of the Act was designed to gain access to threatened sites for archaeological excavation rather than, as with scheduling, for permanent preservation. Any area can be designated an 'area of archaeological importance' by the Secretary of State. It is an offence to disturb the ground, flood or tip upon any area of archaeological importance without consent. To gain consent a developer must give six weeks' notice of his intention. During this period the investigating authority, appointed by the Secretary of State, has the right to inspect the site. From the end of the six-week period an operations notice can be served on the developer giving the excavating authority a maximum of four months and two weeks to excavate. Thus the whole period of statutory access to archaeologists is six months. In practice, however, direct negotiation with a developer is often more satisfactory than attempting to use Part 2 of the Act. Part 3 of the Act includes minor clauses such as that prohibiting the unauthorized use of metal detectors on any scheduled areas or on areas of archaeological importance.

In Britain the protection of most archaeological sites, given how few are scheduled, rests with the Town and Country Planning Act 1990. This Act now gives archaeologists access to threatened archaeological sites as, since the publication of Planning and Policy Guidance Note 16 (PPG 16), archaeology is deemed to be material to planning considerations. PPG 16 highlights the need for preservation of important remains *in situ*. Paragraph 25 of PPG 16, a magnificent piece of legal drafting, states what should happen if a site cannot be protected *in situ*: "Where planning authorities decide that the physical preservation *in situ* of archaeological remains is not justified in the circumstances of the case and that the development resulting in the destruction of the archaeological remains should proceed . . . it would be entirely reasonable for the planning authority to satisfy itself before granting planning permission that the developer has made appropriate and satisfactory provision for the excavation and recording the remains." Effectively the developer must pay for the destruction of any archaeology resulting from the development.

In the USA there are two key Acts to be considered when proposing an archaeological project, but advice on the specific legal position in any state should be obtained from the State Historic Preservation Officer under the National Historic Preservation Act Amendments of 1980. This amends the 1966 National Historic Preservation Act. The aim of the Archaeological Resources Protection Act is to protect archaeological resources on public lands and 'Indian' (the word used in USA law to mean native American) lands. Under this Act anyone wishing to excavate or remove an archaeological resource requires a permit. Permits will be granted only to qualified people for the "purpose of furthering archaeological knowledge in the public interest". In the case of permits to excavate on Amerindian lands they will be granted only *after* consent has been obtained from the Amerindian individual or tribe owning or having jurisdiction over such land (Hutt, Jones, McAllister 1992).

From a field archaeologist's point of view the most important aspect of the National Historic Preservation Act of 1966 and its 1980 Amended Act was the establishment of a national register of Sites of Regional, State and Local Importance. The 1980 Act requires that any State hoping to receive federal funding must designate a State Historic Preservation Officer with a staff including qualified architects, historians and archaeologists. The State Historic Preservation Officer has, of course, become the cornerstone of archaeological management in the States, rather like the County Archaeological Officer in Britain. Archaeologists working in the USA have also to consider the legal rights of the indigenous population, the Native Americans. The Native American Graves Protection and Repatriation Act 1990 requires human skeletal material as well as sacred items and objects of cultural patrimony to be returned to tribal descendants for re-interment.

If you intend to excavate a scheduled site in Britain, then Scheduled Monument Consent is required. This has to be obtained from the Secretary of State in the Department of Culture, Media and Sport. The Secretary of State is advised by English Heritage. It is therefore always advisable to discuss your project with the English Heritage Area Inspector before formally applying for consent. This will enable you to match your application to current policy within English Heritage.

The form that field archaeologists are asked to fill in when applying for Scheduled Monument Consent is the same one a developer would have to fill in, and it asks for very little archaeological information. As an archaeologist, however, you are unlikely to get Scheduled Monument Consent unless the application form is accompanied by a research design (as described in Chapter One). This is the equivalent to the development proposal put in by a developer. The current application form has only six sections, together with certificates relating to ownership. These request information about the name and address of the applicant and of the owner of site, details about the site itself, a description of the work proposed, a list of accompanying plans, and a section on any other information. Discussions on whether to allow an excavation are based very much on the research design.

If consent is granted, the permission will include both general and specific conditions. These will include details of to whom the permission is granted and for how long (usually one year), exactly what should happen to the site after excavation (usually backfilling, or consolidation if masonry found is to be displayed) and how and when the excavation should be published.

In the USA a similar procedure is required under the Archaeological Resources Protection Act of 1979 (Hutt, Jones, McAllister 1992). Application for permission to excavate on public or Amerindian lands requires a permit from the Federal Land Manager. To apply for a permit specific information has to be provided, including when the excavation will take place, the scope of the work together with precise location of the site, and specific reasons for the excavation. Most of this detail would be provided in the research design. Before issuing a permit, the Federal Land Manager would notify the relevant tribe in order to establish whether the site had religious or cultural significance to them.

Generally, in addition to legal permission under any laws designed to protect archaeological sites, you will also require permission from land owners, tenants, and anyone who may have other rights over the land. These could include individual or group grazing rights, or organizations managing aspects of the land like 'nature reserves'. The key permission is clearly that of the land owner, without which you will be unable to excavate in Britain or the USA. In some countries the law covering archaeological sites may overrule personal property rights. In Britain the land owner is the legal owner of virtually everything found on the land. In the USA, Amerindian tribes have additional rights to their objects. It is therefore advisable to consider the final deposition of artefacts when obtaining the land owner's permission to excavate. Ideally, a written agreement should be entered into, getting the land owner's permission for all archaeological objects to be given permanently to a public museum. Somewhat surprisingly, many land owners agree to this when the reasons are clearly explained by the archaeologist. If, however, the land owner insists on keeping all artefacts, then serious consideration should be given to whether to proceed with the excavation. Where reburial is an issue, however, the important element of any agreement should be the length of time the objects are to be available for study by the archaeologist.

Permission may also be required from other individuals or groups with rights to the land. In parts of Britain, particularly on open land, groups or individuals may have grazing rights over the land. These rights often go back to the middle ages and may or may not present a problem: for example, a large excavation would reduce available grazing and so compensation, or more likely a reinstatement agreement, might be required. If the area is a Site of Special Scientific Interest (SSSI) in England, then permission will be required from English Nature. Naturally any excavation which may disturb an important natural habitat could present difficulties.

In Britain two classes of archaeological material create specific problems: these are human remains and objects which come under the 1996 Treasure Act. The

Common Law position in Britain is that there is no property in human remains. This means they cannot be owned by anyone, or bought or sold: they do not, therefore, belong to the land owner of the site where they are found. They do not in fact belong to anyone. Control of what happens to human remains in England is covered by the 1857 Burial Act. (Other parts of the United Kingdom are covered by different legislation.) If, as an archaeologist, you know or suspect that you will find, and wish to remove human remains, then you are required to obtain a Licence for the Removal of Human Remains from one of Her Majesty's Principal Secretaries of State. This is currently the Secretary of State in the Home Office. The licence will include conditions relating to how the remains should be removed, how and where they may be studied, and where they should finally be deposited. This usually involves proper storage in a museum, reburial or cremation. If you find human remains during an excavation and you do not hold a licence, then you should immediately inform a coroner as required under the 1926 Coroners' Amendment Act.

The Treasure Act was given the royal assent in July 1996 and was an attempt to improve on treasure trove Common Law which had its origins in the reign of King John. This Act does not require procurement of advance permission, but if certain classes of 'valuable' objects are found, such as coins over 300 years old and containing at least 10 per cent by weight of gold or silver, then the coroner must be informed.

In addition to obtaining permission, an excavation can proceed only if adequate funding is available. Funding requirements are an essential element of the research design. An ideal position would be to obtain adequate funding for the entire project, from research design to published report. Very occasionally this is possible. More often archaeologists have to work with a mosaic of funding which develops during the life of a project. Major research projects may obtain funding from the National Science Foundation in the USA or the British Academy in Britain. Both are highly competitive. In the States, grants from private foundations or State programmes are more likely sources of funding (Joukowsky 1980). In Britain English Heritage may fund excavations of threatened sites when no developer is involved, and some museums and archaeological societies have small grants available.

The major source of funding in both Britain and the USA is from developers. Since the publication of Planning Policy Guidance Note 16 (PPG 16) in Britain in 1990, developers have effectively had to pay for archaeological excavation required as a result of their developments. This source of funding, although of major importance to archaeology, has brought its own problems. Competitive bidding for funds, with the developer often picking the cheapest quote, has resulted in some undercutting which had the effect of lowering even more the very low wages some field archaeologists receive. More difficult to assess is the lowering of field standards by groups cutting corners. More disturbing, however, is the creation in Britain of what is known in the States as 'grey literature' (Fagan 1991). That means limited, often desk-top, publication of results, of limited distribution or even confidentially produced for the developer.

Site safety

Regardless of how limited funds are, one area of an excavation that must never be skimped on is site safety. The loss of a bit of archaeology is never a justification for putting site workers at risk. Archaeological sites in Britain and the States, however, have a remarkably good safety record. The endless regulations relating to safety introduced over the last twenty-five years or so are largely the result of the poor safety record of the building industry. Properly organized archaeological excavations are by their very nature basically safe. Just compare an average archaeological excavation with a typical building site and you will see where many hazards lie. Having said that, obviously any legal requirement must be adhered to, but an obsession with safety can waste much time and money. Making a site safe is often based on good organization and common sense.

Much safety law in Britain is based on the Health and Safety at Work Act, 1974. Even if working in a country without safety laws, any responsible archaeologist should work within the framework of this Act. The general principles within the Health and Safety at Work Act can be summed up as follows: firstly, an employer (the excavation director) must provide proper premises (the site) in which, and proper plant and appliances (tools) by means of which, the worker's duty can be performed; secondly, the employer must maintain the premises, plant and apparatus in a proper condition; thirdly, the employer must establish and enforce a proper system of working.

The two potentially most dangerous aspects of archaeological excavations are deep holes and machinery on site. The safety aspects of both must be taken extremely seriously. Deep holes are dangerous, and basically the deeper they are, the more dangerous they may be. Under the Health and Safety at Work Act 1974 the director of an excavation (as 'employer') should take 'reasonable care'. What is 'reasonable' is often arguable, but by using British Standards you can make a case of 'reasonable care'. British Standards cover all sorts of things from electric kettles to methods of work. BS6031: 1981 Earthworks considers the digging of holes. This states that "where the sides of excavations cannot be battered (sloped) back to a safe angle, their continued stability should not be assumed, and where the depth of the excavation is greater than 1.2 m the omission of supports to a vertical or steep face should be a matter of positive instruction rather than acceptance without instruction".

The 1.2 m is only a guide. The work situation may be dangerous at less than 1.2 m or it may be perfectly safe at 2 m. The point of BS6031 is to make people digging holes think about the stability of those holes. There are occasions when excavations shallower than 1.2 m require support. This is particularly the case when soil is non-cohesive (for example, sand or gravel) or when work is done by persons crouching, kneeling or lying in the bottom of an excavation. Decisions on when to shore should take many factors into consideration. These include the nature of the soil, moisture, time of year (likely weather conditions), type of excavation (narrow trench or area excavation), proximity of buildings, location of buried services, sources of vibration (for example, adjacent roads) and duration of the work. One of

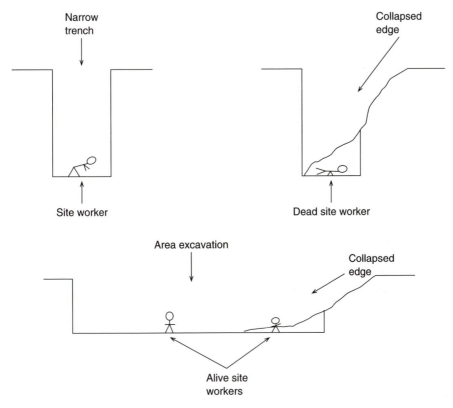

Figure 5.1   Site safety: (1) a dangerous narrow trench, (2) a safer area excavation.

the major factors in making an excavation safe is the shape of the hole dug. A long narrow trench is far more dangerous than a large, square open-area excavation. A trench edge collapsing into a narrow trench can totally bury anyone working in the bottom of the trench, whereas in a large area excavation the soil from a collapsing edge can spread much further (Fig. 5.1). If you do decide to shore your trench it is often better to employ a specialist contractor, as poor shoring may be worse than no shoring at all. Shoring is generally done with good quality planks and steel acroprops (Fig. 5.2) although it can all be done with timber.

If you do not have the resources for shoring, particularly if the trench is fairly shallow or if the soil is very loose (like sand), battering may be a sensible altern- ative. This is widely and successfully used on the loose sand sites in South China. Battering involves cutting the trench edges back to a safe angle of 45° or more. This does create some recording problems as the face is not vertical, but this can be overcome either by building up a cumulative section as the site is dug, or by recording the section with a level. If the site is buried under colluvium or other types of overburden, then the overburden could be dug with a battered trench while the actual archaeology would be within a vertical-sided trench in the bottom of the hole created (Fig. 5.3). An alternative is to dig a step trench with no vertical face

Figure 5.2   Site safety: shoring of a narrow trench.

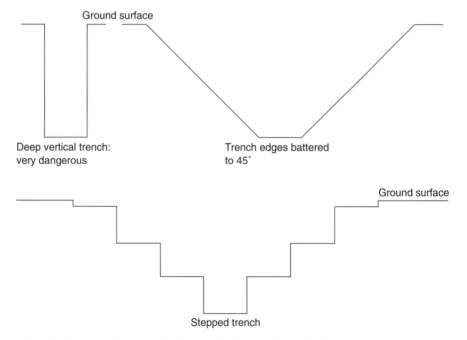

Figure 5.3   Site safety: trench edges cut back to a safe angle (battered) or stepped.

Figure 5.4 Site safety: unshored baulks can collapse and kill. (Don't worry, this is not what it appears to be and the 'body' went on to direct the Boxgrove project!)

deeper than 1.2 m. How to dig a safe hole can really only be learnt by experience, but if in doubt it is always worth consulting a civil engineer. The money involved could save lives (Fig. 5.4).

Safety helmets must be worn in all excavations greater than 1.2 m deep, or shallower if the excavator's head is lower than the top of the trench. If you are kneeling and trowelling in the bottom of a trench a metre deep, your head will be below the top of the trench and could be hit by objects knocked off the edge. This is one of several reasons why the area around the trench should be kept clear of tools, buckets, stones and the like. Helmets should comply with BS 5240: 1975 General-purpose industrial safety helmet.

Other protective clothing is required in particular circumstances, in particular if machinery is used on site. Digging equipment, like machines with back actors (rear-mounted hydraulic arms with a narrow bucket), such as the JCB 3c – or, for smaller sites, the Bobcat – can be particularly dangerous if a proper work pattern is not enforced. It is particularly important that the machine-operator should be able to see people moving about the site, but also that he or she knows that nobody will be in the area where the machine is working. To be sure you can be seen is extremely important, so a brightly-coloured (orange) overvest or other clothing should be worn. Overvests can be purchased from general building-supply merchants. Steel toe-capped boots should also be worn if working with heavy plant, in dangerous areas, or with tools like picks, mattocks or forks.

To be certain that machinery on site is safe requires the enforcement of proper working practice. This comes clearly under the Health and Safety at Work Act's requirements on the employer to establish and enforce a proper system of working. Ideally all machine operation should be undertaken before the main labour force arrives on the excavation. The fewer people on site the better, when machinery is in use. If the labour force is present, it should be deployed well away from the machine's area of work. Machines with back actors are favoured by many archaeologists (except for large-area stripping). These, when stationary and digging, have a clear zone of working which is the maximum radius of the outstretched back-actor arm. Nobody should ever be allowed to work in this zone. If the archaeologist wishes to enter this zone it should be done only after the back actor has been rested on the ground and the driver informed. Ideally the machine should be turned off. Observers, if required while the machine is working, should be stationed outside the zone of working. Machines with back actors are often used in conjunction with dumper trucks to take the soil away. These create their own hazards, both for the dumper driver and site workers. The dumper truck should always be parked for loading so that the soil can be dumped in it, but in such a position that the back actor could never hit the driver. A marked and agreed dumper run is then required to get the soil away from the site, but keeping the dumper well away from any site workers.

The Health and Safety at Work Act also considers the welfare of workers. Most archaeological excavations are in the open air, so shelter should be provided for adverse weather conditions. This may include a dry and warm shelter, or in some parts of the world shelter from the midday sun. Toilets, if not available locally, will have to be provided. Associated with these, adequate washing facilities are needed on site or near by. Small excavations, particularly urban ones, may have all these facilities available near by. Larger sites will require them to be brought onto site.

Adequate first aid is required under the Health and Safety (First Aid) Regulation of 1981. This requires employers to provide equipment and facilities adequate and appropriate for the proposed work. On excavations a first-aid box is usually adequate. In Britain statutory first-aid boxes (green with a white cross on them) can be bought, containing a basic first-aid kit. This does not contain anything which could create an allergic reaction, so has no antiseptics, creams or pills (for example, aspirin or paracetamol). It may be worth warning site workers of this in advance and advising them to bring their own tailor-made kit for personal use. The site first-aid box should be in the charge of an 'appointed person', preferably a trained first-aider.

In Britain you are required to report certain accidents which happen on sites. This is required by the RIDDOR Regulation 1985 (the Reporting of Injuries, Diseases and Dangerous Occurrences Regulation). The report has to be made to the Health and Safety Executive. Notifiable accidents include death, fractures of bones (other than hand or foot), amputation, and loss of an eye or any other injury requiring hospitalization for more than 24 hours. Dangerous occurrences requiring notification include most involving machinery, including mechanical excavators turning over. Notifiable diseases are any scheduled diseases diagnosed by a doctor, such as typhoid or hepatitis. To facilitate reporting, a responsible person is required to keep records of the accident. The record should include date and time, full name and occupation of the injured person, nature of injury or accident, place where it occurred, and a brief description of the circumstances.

As a result of joining the European Union, the British Health and Safety at Work Act has been enhanced by new regulations which came into force on 1 January 1993. These regulations implement the European Directive No. 89/391/EEC of 29 May 1990. These are long and complex but should be examined by those proposing to excavate in Europe. Important elements include a requirement that employers make a suitable and sufficient assessment of the health and safety risks of employees ('risk assessments'). Also all employees should be provided with adequate health and safety training. As part of the risk assessment, ergonomic solutions to problems like lifting and transporting loads (for example, buckets of soil) should be addressed.

Outside Europe many countries have health and safety-type laws but some do not, and others enforce them only erratically. Whatever the legal position, however, you should always aim at the highest standard of health and safety on a site. Much of it is common sense and would happen as a natural part of a well-run excavation, so obsession with health and safety should not be allowed to dominate every decision, but consideration of health and safety must be part of any decision. Remember that practically all the regulations were brought in because of poor standards in the building industry and in factories, not on archaeological excavations.

Staff, equipment and logistics

For safety reasons the minimum number of staff on site should be three, so that if one is injured, one can stay with the injured person, and one can go and get help. With a mobile phone this could be reduced to two. From that point onwards the number of staff required on an excavation depends entirely on the size of the excavation and the nature of the job to be undertaken. Generally a project will have an overall Director or Principal Investigator. This person is in charge of policy-making on all aspects of the project, academic, practical and logistical. On big sites this post may be too great for one person; if so, an assistant or deputy director may be appointed to share – or take over – certain aspects of the project.

Beneath these people there may be discrete sections or groups of people with overlapping roles. One line will involve those actually digging. These will include

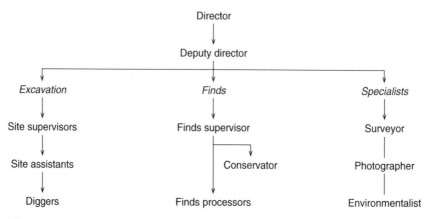

Figure 5.5   Excavation management diagram.

supervisors (assistant, site, trench, unit, and so on) and excavators (volunteers, field assistants, crew members). Another line will involve those managing the finds recovered. This group would be organized by a finds supervisor or assistant. Site conservation and photographers (if used) may be in this group, or in the third section which includes the specialists like environmental archaeologists and surveyors. The final group may be established to organize site public relations, including tours, temporary exhibitions and dealing with the media (Fig. 5.5). In practice many of these are multiple roles with a director, for example, dealing with public relations and photography.

The most important aspect of the field staff structure is to establish exact, clear, unambiguous lines of communication. Who is responsible to whom for what? Who has powers to tell whom what to do? On all field projects a light, friendly atmosphere will always result in a better-run excavation than one run on rigid hierarchical lines, with the director, for example, never speaking to crew members. It must, however, be remembered that the excavation is a serious job, even if the crew members are students on holiday. Field archaeology does attract some odd, difficult and even deranged characters so, assuming the director is not in one of these categories, he or she must expect to spend some time in dealing with personal problems. Many potential problems, like alcohol on site or over-tired crew-members arriving on site directly from a nightclub, must be dealt with swiftly on basic health and safety grounds.

In 1946 Richard Atkinson stated, "An excavator's ability can be measured by the way he chooses, uses and cares for his tools." (Atkinson 1953). Apart from the political incorrectness of ignoring his female contemporaries (like Kathleen Kenyon digging at Jericho), he made a good point. The actual selection of tools depends very much on the type of site being dug, where it is being dug, and available resources. Equipment required can generally be divided into four main groups: digging equipment, recording equipment, finds-processing equipment and general site equipment. It is a good idea to produce a checklist of equipment as there are few things more annoying than arriving on site without, for example, any string!

Figure 5.6   Small digging tools: the mason's pointing trowel and hand shovel.

For excavation, both heavy and fine digging equipment will be needed. Machinery like a JCB 3c or Bobcat is usually hired with driver. Adequate lead time is required for this as machinery is not always available at short notice. Heavy digging equipment includes spades, shovels, mattocks, pickaxes and forks. Each field archaeologist will have preferred tools, but basically spades are for cutting, shovels for shovelling, and mattocks, pickaxes and forks for breaking up the soil. Long-handled shovels are less damaging to the digger's back than the usual short-handled shovels used in Britain. To remove soil, wheelbarrows are generally used, unless the soil heap is close to the trench when it can be thrown or bucketed.

For finer digging a 3–4 inch (7–10 cm) mason's pointing trowel is the usual tool used in the USA and Britain (Fig. 5.6). The blade must be cast in one piece with the tang; rivetted or welded blades will break sooner or later. Many British archaeologists favour the WHS trowel, while in the USA the Marshalltown trowel is a favourite. The problem with using trowels as scraping tools, however, is that your knuckles are very close to the ground and can easily be cut on jagged stones. For some sites mini-hoes (Fig. 5.7) and picks may be more sensible. Soil can then be scraped or brushed onto hand shovels – or strong plastic or metal dustpans – to be emptied into buckets. If large areas are to be cleaned, yard brooms are sometimes used and soil shovelled into wheelbarrows to be run along planked walkways.

Axes and root-cutters may be required to deal with roots, while very fine excavation will require blades, dental picks and fine soft paint brushes. For finer recovery, sieves or sift screens will be required for dry sieving, while for recovering organic material a water flotation system may be required on site.

Figure 5.7   Small digging tools: mini-hoe and hand shovel.

Recording equipment includes whatever surveying equipment you have decided upon (Chapter Four). This must include at least one piece of equipment, like a level or theodolite, for recording levels on the site. Other basic recording equipment will include 30 m Fibron (or similar) tapes, 2 m steel tapes, drawing frames (1 m string grids), drawing boards, plastic drafting film and drafting tape, scale rules, rulers, pencils and erasers, string, spirit levels, plumb bobs and nails. The recording equipment should include any pre-printed record forms being used (Chapter Seven) and photographic equipment, including ranging poles for large scales and a variety of small photographic scales. Letterboards or chalk boards will be required if you want excavation data within your photographs (Chapter Seven).

Finds-processing equipment involves ziplock plastic bags (paper is unsatisfactory in damp conditions or for long-term storage), boxes, washing-up bowls and tooth brushes for cleaning objects. If you are employing an on-site conservator they are likely to provide their own equipment; if not, basic site conservation requires careful lifting and packing. Acid-free packing is needed for metals, which should be kept dry with silica gel. Tinfoil is a good inert wrapping material. Rigid plastic boxes are good for transporting fragile objects.

General site equipment includes the range of things one would expect on a well organized camp: tables, chairs, gas burners, kettles, mugs, tea, coffee, washing-up liquid, matches, water containers (if there is no on-site tap) and rubbish bags. If the site is to be fenced, then posts and fencing are required. All this equipment will be stored in the on-site accommodation. The ideal is a lockable site office, a secure storage unit and chemical toilets (Fig. 5.8). In many parts of the world this is not

Figure 5.8   Site accommodation: site office, secure unit, toilets and site vehicle.

required or not available. Sometimes just a tent or canvas shelter is adequate. Theft is often a major problem if the site is left unattended at night times or over weekends. If a secure unit is not available, tools can be chained together to increase security, but still it is advisable to take particularly valuable equipment, like surveying and photographic items, away each night.

The logistics of setting up an excavation can be quite complex, depending where in the world the project is. If you are working within easy driving distance of your home base, the logistics are obviously more straightforward than on the other side of the world. When working away from your home base, the main logistical problems relate to getting equipment and people to the site and then servicing the excavation on a day-to-day basis. Unless working in the Amazon or some such area, it is generally best to hire site accommodation and machinery. The responsibility of getting it to and away from the site then rests with the hire company who probably also insure it, although always check this.

If you come from a first-world country and are working in a second- or third-world country, there are good practical and political reasons for trying to buy as much as possible locally. This will not only reduce the amount of equipment you have to take, but also can make a real contribution to local communities. There is nothing worse than rich foreign archaeologists arriving with all their own equipment and even food. Buckets, nails, string and the like are usually available locally. Certain bits of equipment may not be available locally, so to reduce weight look for lightweight or folding versions of the equipment you usually use. The KDS Minirod, made by the Japanese Kyoto Measuring Instruments Corporation, for example, weighs ounces compared with the normal heavyweight surveyor's staff. Specialist companies (like Archmat in the States) retail 1 m folding string grids (drawing frames). Imagination and flexibility will greatly reduce the logistics of moving equipment to an excavation. If you are working locally to your base, however, there may be no problem. Simply load everything you need into a suitable vehicle and take it to the site.

Adequate transportation is of course essential. What it is depends on where you are working. If working close to your home base with good road access, most vehicles of a suitable size are usually suitable. If working further afield, and particularly in difficult terrain, then the vehicle must be selected with great care. Normally a robust four-wheel-drive vehicle of the Land-Rover, Jeep or pick-up type will be needed. If working in isolated areas, then your team should always include a mechanic with suitable tools and spare parts. Dillon (1989) lists a hundred essential tools and spare parts required for extended trips! Vehicle access is not always possible to all sites, so you may also have to consider pack animals, people, or even boats (Meighan and Dillon 1989) to get to your site. Usually all these types of transportation are best hired locally.

There may well be legal constraints concerning what you can move from one country to another. Always check these before you arrive at customs. It is illegal, for example, to bring soil into Britain although sediments can be imported, leading to potentially interesting discussions of terminology with customs officers. Many countries require a licence to import any organic materials, including prehistoric bones. Archaeologists themselves may need work permits to dig in a country of which they are not a national. Finally, the question of insurance should be considered carefully. This includes both insurance of the field team and third-party insurance in case your activities damage others, like visitors falling into trenches.

Approaches to excavation

There is no 'right' way to excavate a site. There are favoured approaches in different parts of the world. In China the 5 m square, orientated north–south, is the norm. In India the Wheeler grid system is widely used. In Holland and Britain open-area excavation dominates, while in the USA the 1 m unit is common. All approaches can produce both good and bad archaeology. Unfortunately, however, some state archaeological organizations have enshrined certain approaches in their permits and permissions. This is unfortunate as every site is different and, like being able to select the most appropriate remote-sensing techniques from a wide range, the excavator should be able to select the most appropriate excavation approach from a range. These decisions will be based both on the archaeology but also on available time and money.

It would be absurd to hand-sieve all soil from a 1 m unit on a deep urban site if only weeks were available for its total excavation. A decision may have to be made either to go for sequence (perhaps a machine-dug trench) or event (are the water-logged Saxon levels going to produce more valuable information than the eighteenth-century layers?). The decision on how to dig what shape hole depends on many factors, the first being whether your excavation is exploratory or total (if such a thing exists). It also depends on how much knowledge about the extent of the site has been gleaned from non-destructive techniques like remote sensing and field walking. Broadly the aim of exploratory excavation is to establish the horizontal spread of cultural materials and deposits and to establish the vertical sequence of cultural material. That is the sequence of the events that took place on the site.

To establish the horizontal extent of a site, a spread of samples across the area of the likely site and beyond is required. These can be laid out using the same sampling strategies outlined for ground survey in Chapter Three, namely simple random, stratified, systematic or stratified systematic unaligned. Most usually a systematic grid is used, the grid size depending on the size of the site. A broad idea of the horizontal extent of a site could be obtained by undertaking an auger survey. A core of soil is taken out of the site at every grid intersection. If possible the auger should reach bed rock before being pulled out. Artefacts, charcoal flecks, or humanly-modified soils (for example, high phosphate) can be identified and the extent of the site determined.

An alternative approach, favoured on shallow sites in the USA and elsewhere, is the shovel test survey. Again the site is gridded and at each grid intersection a square hole with sides the length of a shovel blade is dug. Ideally, these should be dug only to the surface of any *in situ* archaeology, which is then recorded and the hole backfilled. Often the hole is dug through the archaeology, which results in a site covered with small holes which could damage important relationships between as-yet unlocated features. In salvage archaeology shovel tests are usually dug very fast, with all soil being screened for artefacts. On extensive, shallower sites, if used carefully, shovel tests can give a good view of the extent of a site very cost-effectively. It is, however, of little use on sites of more than a spade's depth.

An alternative to the shovel test survey is the small square or rectangular unit, usually 1 m square or 1 × 2 m (Fig. 5.9). Again, in salvage archaeology these are often shovelled with the soil passed through screens. Given the size of test-pits, however, they really should be more carefully excavated by natural stratigraphic layers. Artefacts from each natural stratigraphic layer should be kept separate. The unit level method – where artefacts are recorded by arbitrary horizontal layers – is methodologically totally unsound, except when the soil deposits are identical through-out the profile. Test pits, sometimes known as sondages, are simply to obtain broad stratigraphic information or – if laid out in a regular grid – they will give some information about the extent of the site. Where a site has any complexity, however (and most do), they must be used with great care. Ideally they should be used only to establish the extent of the archaeology by excavating down to the surface of any *in situ* archaeology but not into it, as this may damage stratigraphic or feature relationships not apparent in small holes. If used to establish depths of deposits, they will inevitably do some damage – but as all excavation is damaging, likely gains, in relation to potential damage, have to be carefully weighed up.

Figure 5.9   Site sampling by test pit.

Test units, test pits or sondages are all various types of trench. Another, regularly used in evaluation excavations in British contract archaeology, is the long
narrow trench or transect (Fig. 5.10). Usually either regularly spaced or randomly
located, such trenches are machine-stripped to the top of any visible archaeology,
which is then evaluated without further excavation. This information is used to
negotiate further with developers for a full excavation or, if of limited value, the
site may be archaeologically abandoned. The trench can also be used to answer
specific research questions on a site.

If a site appears on an aerial photograph as a network of ditches, for example,
then trenches can be dug at right angles across the ditches to obtain details about
size, shape, infilling and recutting sequences. From this a broad date can be deduced – although see Chapter Six for problems in dating ditches. Trenches can also
be used to obtain broad sequences from linear earthworks or field banks. Digging
trenches 'blind' into archaeological sites can, however, be a very dangerous and
damaging process. They are best used only for evaluation or where you have
sufficient data, from aerial photographs or geophysical survey, to be certain that the
trench will be sensibly related to buried features.

The grid or box system of excavation was designed by Mortimer Wheeler in
an attempt to reconcile the problem of needing to excavate both horizontally to
obtain spatial information about events, and vertically to reveal a sequence of those
events. Although it has severe methodological problems, it was quite a clever idea.
The site is laid out with a grid of squares with strips of undug site between them.
As the squares are dug these become standing soil sections or baulks. The trenches

Figure 5.10   Site sampling by narrow trenches or transects.

provide information in the horizontal plane while the vertical sections provide the vertical sequence. In practice the baulks or vertical sections are nearly always in the wrong place, burying important feature relationships and postholes, without which the posthole scatters within trenches make no sense. The sections invariably cut across features and layers at obtuse angles, providing sections often impossible to interpret. The grid system was a clever idea which basically makes the understanding of even relatively simple sites almost impossible unless baulks are removed. Naturally the baulks could be carefully excavated after the grid squares are dug and the plans then completed, but often crucial relationships will have already been dug away in the squares, so if the sections are not particularly useful anyway, or provide endless repetition, why bother to make the excavation more complex than it need be?

A modified version of the grid system, the quadrant system, is however a simple, efficient way to investigate small round mounds, such as round barrows or burial

Figure 5.11   Quadrant excavation of round mounds.

mounds. The quadrant system involves cutting the mound into four segments and leaving standing baulks between them. To ensure a continuous cross-section each way, the baulks should be offset. This is done by first laying out a string cross, across the centre of the mound, and then laying out the baulks within two opposed quadrants (Fig. 5.11). The four quadrants are then excavated, the sections drawn (Chapter Seven), the baulks removed, and the whole area is planned. This method provides clear vertical information about the construction sequence of the mound, together with information in the horizontal plane concerning activity both before and during the construction of the mound.

All the approaches described so far, other than perhaps the quadrant system for excavating small round burial mounds, can be accused of being like cutting a 1 cm square out of a medieval document and trying to interpret it (Barker 1977). Of course, if the whole document is about to be burnt (the equivalent of a site being destroyed for development), a case could be made that some information is better than none. Unfortunately, however, small holes can produce very misleading information and one section across a ditch can give a totally different sequence to one only a metre away. We therefore have the problem, is misleading information really better than no information?

The dangers of digging small holes in archaeological sites have been known for decades, particularly through the work of Gerhard Bersu (Bersu 1940). Telephone-booth digging in MesoAmerica was roundly condemned by Kent Flannery in the mid-1970s (Flannery 1976) and similarly in Britain by Philip Barker (Barker 1977). Most archaeologists now agree that for settlement sites, and many other types of

Figure 5.12   Open-area excavation.

site, open-area excavation is the best approach. For some types of site, or for
preliminary evaluation, other approaches may be more appropriate but must be
used carefully, selectively, and flexibly. At the end of the day a well excavated,
well recorded, fully published 1 × 1 m unit does considerably less harm than a
huge, badly controlled, unpublished area excavation. Time, resources and ability
remain crucial elements in deciding excavation strategy.

The principle behind open-area excavation is ideally to clear the whole of a
site (Fig. 5.12) revealing, recording and removing each archaeological deposit in
broadly the reverse order of their deposition. There are either no, or only temporary,
soil sections on site. The sequence or stratigraphy of the site is carefully recorded
through continuous recording of surfaces of deposits (Chapter Seven). The size and
shape of the area excavated is in no way predetermined by the field archaeologist.
It will depend entirely on the size and shape of the site. As a public relations
exercise, however, archaeologists usually edge the area with straight, vertically cut

sides. To the wider public this will make the excavation look 'serious' and not like a building site.

Generally, because of the scale of open-area excavations, deposits above *in situ* archaeology are removed by machine. Sometimes this is a highly efficient way to start an excavation, saving huge labour costs. On shallow, arable sites there is, however, the problem that by machine-stripping all the plough soil off the site you may only be left with sub-surface features. A surprising amount of site detail can survive in plough soil and be recovered through magnetic susceptibility, phosphate analysis and careful artefact recovery. People in the past, as today, lived and under-took their daily tasks on surfaces, not down pits and postholes (Clarke 1990, 106–7). We shall return to the details of excavation in Chapter Six.

Levels of recovery

Having decided upon a broad approach to an excavation and the size and shape of holes, or the hole, to be dug, then levels of recovery should be considered. In fact this has to be considered as every single discrete archaeological entity (or context) is located whether it is plough soil, an *in situ* floor, or the contents of a pit. Even in 'total' area excavation you will be sampling only aspects of the site. You may attempt to recover all walls on a site, or all potsherds (at least those visible to the human eye) but is there any point in collecting every pollen grain, even if it were possible?

Levels of recovery range from very coarse to very fine. The coarsest form of recovery is to use heavy earth-moving machinery. This can be used to locate fea-tures like walls, but virtually the entire archaeological content of the soil machined out is lost. Picking up odd bones or potsherds from machined-out soil is almost pointless as the sample will be so biased. There will, however, always be contexts which can be safely machined off, like concrete floors in an urban context, wind-blown sand on a desert site, or perhaps plough soil moved down a slope to bury an archaeological site below. In a rescue or salvage situation it may be the only way to get enough dug in the time available to make sense of the site. For archaeological work the best types of machine, some would say the only types, are those which pull soil off the site rather than pushing it off. Machines with a back actor (a hydraulic arm with bucket) are frequently used (Fig. 5.13) but any machine with a blade that can be pulled away from the archaeology could be used. Bulldozers which push the soil forward and then drive over the cleared archaeology are not to be recommended.

The next level of recovery up from machinery comprises hand-held heavy digging tools like picks, mattocks, hoes and shovels. Used skilfully these can be considered precision tools, but generally they are used for disturbed contexts rather than, for example, *in situ* floors. A good excavator using a pick and shovel can recover a surprisingly high percentage of the artefacts and ecofacts in a deposit. The problem is that the sample recovered will be biased in favour of the big and against the small, and in favour of colours contrasting with the background soil matrix and

Figure 5.13   Coarse excavation: digging with a JCB 3c.

against those of similar colour. From a mid-grey soil, therefore, the sample recovered may include all cattle bones but few small fish bones, and all red pottery but only big grey sherds.

A finer level of recovery will involve small hand tools like the mason's pointing trowel. Usually the excavator is crouching or kneeling when trowelling, so is much closer to the area being dug than when standing up using a pick and shovel. By being closer and moving smaller quantities of soil, artefact and ecofact recovery will increase but it will still have a size and colour bias. Depending on the nature of the context and the type and period of site, this may not be important. If you are excavating a medieval pottery kiln site, for example, and already have a million potsherds, how useful are those few extra flecks of pottery missed? However, if excavating a native Amerindian site with perhaps few surviving inorganic artefacts, greater recovery may be considered advisable.

Increased recovery can be introduced by using sieves (screens or meshes) (Fig. 5.14). These are used on a regular basis in the USA but much more selectively in Britain. This partly relates to the relative volume of material on sites in the two countries, but also goes back to Richard Atkinson's statement in his text book, *Field Archaeology*: "A fairly coarse-meshed sieve may sometimes be needed to search for coins, beads, and other small objects, but its use should not be encouraged, as the exact original position of finds made in this way cannot be determined" (Atkinson 1953). If soil is simply shovelled through a sieve, this point is worth considering, but generally sieving takes place on soil already carefully trowelled, so the objects, although moved from their exact location, would be lost without sieving.

Figure 5.14   Fine recovery: sieving soil for artefacts and ecofacts.

Figure 5.15   Recovering metal objects: using a metal detector on an excavation.

Figure 5.16   Recovering carbonized material by water flotation.

By sieving soil from discrete contexts separately, objects can be tied clearly to their context of origin.

Sieving for tiny, abraded potsherds on sites that have hundred-weights of sherds is probably pointless, but small beads and coins can be missed in trowelling. Coins, however, are often crucial for dating on some sites, so their exact location may be important. These can often be located *in situ* by using a metal detector across a context about to be trowelled (Fig. 5.15). The location of metal readings, which may be coins or other datable metalwork, can be carefully marked so the troweller can look even more carefully in these areas. Sieving is, however, essential in reducing bias in bone assemblages, especially in the case of fish and small mammal bones. For these bones a 1 mm mesh size should be used. This may require wet sieving to get the fine soil particles to go through the sieve.

The next level of recovery will involve wet sieving or water flotation (Fig. 5.16). Wet sieving can be used to recover any small material, but water flotation is usually

Figure 5.17   Recovering carbonized material with a froth flotation unit.

used to recover carbonized seeds and charcoal. By sieving in water you will reduce
the abrasive effect of dry sieving. Lithics will not be re-touched and organics will
float to the surface of the water where unabraded charcoal, for example, can be
collected.

The process of recovering organic material can be greatly accelerated by using
a water flotation unit. Evolved by Gordon Hillman to recover plant remains in
the Near East (Williams 1973), it can be run either by using mains water or
by recycling the water using a pump. The flotation unit consists of a tank of water
with soil held in a 1 mm mesh in the top of the tank. Water is pumped through the
soil, breaking it up and releasing organic materials like seeds and charcoal. This
light fraction flows over the lip of the tank to be collected in a nest of sieves. The
water is then either passed through resettling tanks for recycling, or discarded if
mains water is used. A modification of water flotation using chemicals to break up
soil and create a froth was developed, but is now less used than simple water
flotation (Fig. 5.17).

The next level of recovery involves attempting to recover very small materials
or those not visible to the human eye. This can be done only by taking bits of the
site away (as soil samples) and undertaking extraction under laboratory conditions.
This is how land mollusca and pollen are recovered, both being identified and
counted under a microscope. Clearly, at this level sampling is crucial, as not all soil
can be removed from a site. Generally these samples should only be taken from
dated, uncontaminated, sealed deposits. Buried land surfaces are particularly suitable
for such sampling (Fig. 5.18).

Figure 5.18 Sampling for pollen.

The final level of recovery is locating the chemical traces of artefacts or ecofacts which simply do not exist any longer. A buried body, for example, may survive only as a concentration of chemicals, including phosphorus, in the soil. At every stage of an excavation the director or delegated site supervisors must make informed decisions about the level of recovery appropriate to a particular context. Remember, however, that whatever you do, you will be recovering only a sample.

CHAPTER SIX

Digging the site

When setting out an excavation, some care should be taken to consider the effective management of soil in relation to safety and the day-to-day running of the site. Much time and effort can be wasted in moving, and sometimes re-moving, soil. The first aspect to be considered will always be safety, then what is best for the archaeology of the site, and finally the most efficient way of moving and storing soil. From a safety point of view soil should never simply be dumped on the edge of the trench. Soil dumped in this way will not only increase the likelihood of trench-edge collapse but will also spill back into the trench, becoming particularly dangerous to site workers as the trench gets deeper. Archaeologically it is also bad, as objects from the spoil (soil) heap can fall into earlier layers, potentially confusing their date.

Soil should never be dumped closer than one metre from the trench edge, but if any great depth is involved it should be dumped well away from the trench. Having said that, you must, however, consider what is going to happen to the soil at the end of the excavation. If trenches are to be backfilled, which is usual – except in salvage archaeology – then you need to consider whether backfilling is going to be done by hand or by machine. With shovel tests and test units the soil is usually piled close to the hole, but still over a metre away, so it can be easily backfilled. For big sites, particularly if machine-stripped, there may be one or two main spoil heaps away from the excavation (Fig. 6.1).

When considering the location of these spoil heaps you should consider ease of access, sieving (screening) and photography. Ease of access includes the construction of short, safe barrow-runs or paths for carrying buckets. Steep barrow-runs can be extremely dangerous in wet conditions. Spiral barrow-runs up spoil heaps are safer than long, straight runs. Sieving should be done on or beside the spoil heap, so care should be taken to consider wind direction, or fine dust will be forever blowing over the excavation. It is also worth considering the location of spoil heaps in relation to photography. By constructing spoil heaps on only two sides of a rect-angular excavation, for example, not only do you have ready-built photographic platforms giving height, but also in photographing from the spoil heap you will avoid their appearance in the excavation photographs.

Restricted sites do, of course, have their own particular problems. On small urban sites, especially those to be followed by development, it may be worth paying, or negotiating with the developer to pay, for the soil to be removed from

Figure 6.1 The layout of an excavation. Note particularly the position of soil dumps (spoil heaps).

site by skip. Other sites may involve a multi-season excavation to resolve the soil dumping problem. When excavating the top of the motte at Lewes Castle, Sussex, for example, not only did the soil have to be kept on the top of the motte, but also half the top had to be kept accessible for tourists paying to visit the castle. The area excavation therefore had to take place over four seasons. Each season one quadrant was excavated, while another quadrant was used for soil dumping. The remaining two quadrants remained open to the public. Each year the excavation and spoil heap moved around one quadrant (Fig. 6.2). The location of site offices and facilities also has to be considered in relation to both the excavation and spoil heap, and also access into and out of the site for site huts, and so on. Usually these temporary buildings are best situated as near as possible to the road access.

The physical layout of the excavation will depend very much on how the site is to be dug. Do not expect machine drivers to be able to see thin string. If using machinery, it is often best either to lay out the trench roughly, and then cut back to its final shape by hand, or to dig a clear spade-width trench inside the edge of the trench as a marker. Rough shapes for machining can be marked with sand, spray paint or ranging poles. If hand-digging a trench, then the edge should be clearly marked with string held down with 6-inch (15 cm) nails – larger in sand. Remember that if you put a nail in the corner of a trench and then dig up to it, it will fall out. This problem can be avoided by placing the nails outside the trench and making sure the strings cross at the trench corner (Fig. 6.3). The edge of the trench can then be started with a spade to mark the vertical cut. Finally the excavation is under way.

Figure 6.2   Excavating a restricted site. Over four seasons one quadrant was excavated, a second being used to dump the soil.

Figure 6.3   Stringing up the corner of a trench.

Excavation

The aim of excavation is to identify, define, uncover, date, and – by understanding transformation processes – interpret each archaeological context on a site. Usually this process is carried out in the reverse order of the site's construction, cutting or deposition. I am using the term 'context' as it is used widely in British archaeology today. A context refers to any discrete archaeological entity on site, and so could refer to a layer, a pit or a posthole. It is often the result of a single action, whether it leaves a positive or a negative record on the site. The cut of a posthole, for example, leaves a negative record (that is, something has been removed) whereas the fill of a posthole leaves a positive record (that is, the content of the posthole has been added to the sequence). Contexts were traditionally known as layers and features in Britain, and these terms are still widely used elsewhere in the world. In the USA the term 'stratigraphic unit' is used. Some archaeologists argue strongly for one term or another, but as these are simply labels of convenience it really does not matter. No prehistoric person said "Let's go and make a context today"! For this discussion I will use the term 'context' as it is the shortest.

A context consists both of a discrete archaeological entity, and its interfaces with other contexts (Harris 1979). A specific deposit of soil will be above something, below something (unless the top layer), and beside any number of other deposits. At each of the junctions there is an interface. By isolating interfaces, sequences – the stratification of the site – can be established. Not all contexts and their interfaces cover the whole site, hence one of the many problems of digging small holes which may, or equally may not, be typical of the stratigraphy of the whole site.

Contexts are basically the result of natural erosion and deposition (Pyddoke 1961) and of human activity operating within the context of these natural processes. The natural process of erosion and deposition is well known on a geologically large scale. All hills are gradually eroding and the resulting erosion products are deposited in low-lying areas like valleys. This process also takes place on the very small scale. The soil dug out of a posthole, if left as a pile after the post is set in the hole, will erode down, mainly through the action of wind and rain. This soil will either wash into any hollows or spread out over a surface. Human activities like pit-digging will cut into lower deposits, creating new contexts: the pit and pile of soil will be used and transformed into the contexts the archaeologist isolates.

A crucial element of excavation is therefore the process of defining contexts. This may be easy or may be extremely difficult. It requires skill and experience. A wall, a hearth, a pit may be fairly easy to isolate, but the eroded pile of soil from a posthole may have simply blended away into adjacent contexts. To define a context one is essentially looking for differences, differences in colour, texture, consistency and coarse components, and the junction or interface of these differences. We will be returning to the description of these four elements when considering the record of contexts in Chapter Seven. Here the importance is simply to define elements of the site that are different. At its very simplest, an area with black soil is different from an area with red soil is different from an area of red soil with bits of stone in it. The context thus defined is recorded in plan (Chapter Seven) and then decisions have to be made about how to excavate it.

Recurrent types of context and their excavation

One of the most important things to remember when excavating is that people rarely lived on walls, down pits, in postholes or in ditches, and yet excavations are often dominated by these contexts. People lived on surfaces, and much of what they did on surfaces will leave only the slightest trace or none at all. Some surfaces, like the tiled floor of a medieval hall, are relatively easy to isolate and excavate. Other surfaces will include the natural land surface during the period of occupation. These are much more difficult to define and excavate. They may be traceable only through changes in soil chemistry or magnetic susceptibility (Chapter Three), by areas of trampling, or by artefact patterns.

Identification of living surfaces is made more difficult by post-depositional trans-formation processes (Chapter Two). Layers with low concentrations of artefacts (not middens or rubbish dumps) may represent the artefacts from a living surface that have been worm-sorted down the profile. The pattern of artefacts could still represent the activities on the occupation surface, but be 20 cm or so below the surface that was actually lived on (Darwin 1881). Trampling on that surface may have been worm-sorted out of existence. The surface as such will survive only if rapidly buried. Surfaces can really only be excavated in plan, hence the desirability of open-area excavation.

Black Patch (Drewett 1982), the bronze-age site in East Sussex, is an example of how careful plotting of worm-sorted artefacts made it possible to suggest where specific activities like weaving, leather-, wood-, and bone-working, and cooking took place (Fig. 6.4). The excavation technique employed was to grid the area under excavation into one-metre squares. These were all excavated at the same rate, with every artefact and ecofact left *in situ*. At the end of each day all objects were recorded directly onto field plans, lifted and bagged by grid square and, in the case of specific objects like bronze pieces, by two-dimensional co-ordinates (see Chapter Seven). Living surfaces will often merge into the surrounding landscape, making definition of extent almost impossible. Somewhat arbitrary decisions about extent may have to be made.

Some types of archaeological context are much easier to define than surfaces. These include recurrent contexts like pits, postholes, ditches and walls. These are the contexts traditionally – and often still – known as 'features'. Pits include a wide variety of holes dug from the living surface into underlying layers, and often into bedrock. Rarely are they actually dug as rubbish pits, although this may be their final use. Pits were dug for all sorts of reasons including to store grain or other foodstuffs, for water storage, as quarry pits, cesspits, cooking pits, earth ovens, manure stores, or for ritual functions. The purpose of excavating a pit is, like the excavation of the whole site, to establish sequence and event. When was the pit dug, used, abandoned and filled in? How was the pit dug, what was its size, shape,

Figure 6.4   Excavating a hut floor by one-metre squares.

and lining, and what events took place during its life? Then, how does it relate to other pits and contexts on the site?

To establish sequence, pits are often half-sectioned. The top edge of the pit is carefully defined and then divided into two halves with string and nails. Some excavators orientate all section lines north–south. Although this looks neat on the plan, it has no real advantage and orientation in relation to sunlight, both for photography and drawing, is worth consideration: drawing pit-sections is extremely difficult when half is in sun and half in shade. One half of the pit is then excavated following natural stratigraphic layers (Fig. 6.5). Arbitrary spits should be dug only if no natural layers can be determined. The surface of each new layer should be carefully excavated in plan. Even if you consider the deposit to be just domestic rubbish thrown in an old storage pit, there may be structure within the rubbish, or specifically placed offerings. What we see as 'rubbish' today may have had all sorts of meanings and taboos in the past. The edges and bottoms of pits should be treated with extra care as they may provide information concerning the primary function of the pit.

Having dug one half of the pit it should be recorded as part of the written, photographic and drawn record (Chapter Seven) and then the other half carefully removed in the same way. Pits, because of their depth, often have good preservation of carbonized organic material, so are often subjected to water flotation. Remember, however, that the contents of pits usually comprise secondary rubbish and tell you about activities elsewhere on the site, generally not about activities taking place in the pit itself (except, of course, the activity of rubbish disposal). An alternative way to excavate a pit is in plan. The top of each natural stratigraphic layer is carefully

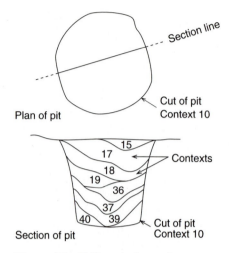

Figure 6.5   Half-sectioning a pit.

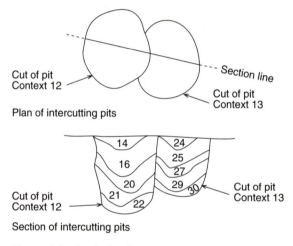

Figure 6.6   Sectioning intercutting pits.

cleared and levels taken. From these levels sections can be reconstructed through the deposits on any line. Excavating in plan has the advantage of allowing whole surfaces as well as any activities (like votive depositions) to be viewed. In a half-sectioned pit these deposits have to be dug and recorded in two halves.

If any pit cuts through another, it may be possible to establish a sequence of pit-digging. Again this can be done in plan, but the relationship is usually defined in section. To do this the edges of both pits should be defined in plan and then the section line laid out through both pits rather than treating each as a separate pit (Fig. 6.6). If you are lucky you may see how one pit cut through the fill of the other. Roots, worm-sorting or burrowing animals may, however, have removed this evidence, so if there is doubt record the sequence as doubtful. The relationship may be resolved when other factors, like datable artefacts, are taken into consideration.

Figure 6.7   Half-sectioning a posthole.

Timber posts set into the ground were, and in many areas still are, used for a wide variety of constructions, from the great Amerindian round houses to simple drying racks. The ability to recognize, define and excavate 'postholes' is essential on most excavations. There are three main elements to these contexts. Firstly a hole dug into the ground, often known as the 'post-pit' although sometimes as the 'posthole'. Secondly the post is put into the hole and then packed around with soil or rocks: the 'post-packing'. If left to rot or pulled out, the post may leave an imprint in the packing. This is variously known as the 'post mould', 'post pipe', or 'post socket', or sometimes this element on its own is known as the 'posthole'. For the erection of very large posts there may also be a 'post ramp' cut down into the post pit. Careful excavation of postholes is therefore essential as, firstly, they can be confused with many other holes both humanly-dug or natural, and secondly the size of the post pit may or may not relate directly to the size of the post, and the size of the post is what matters when reconstructing buildings.

The most usual way to excavate a posthole is to half-section it. This is best done when all postholes from an individual structure, like a round house, are visible in plan. Carefully clean the top of the posthole in plan. If you are lucky, the post pipe or mould may be visible, or more usually an erosion cone above the top of the post pipe may be seen (Fig. 6.7). If the position of the original post is visible in plan, then the half-section should be laid out through the post pipe and packing to the edge of the post pit. The half-section is then cut out carefully, keeping all finds from the post packing separate from any from the the post pipe. The section can then be recorded (a written, drawn and photographic record) and the other half removed. If no post pipe is visible in plan, then the posthole could be quadranted,

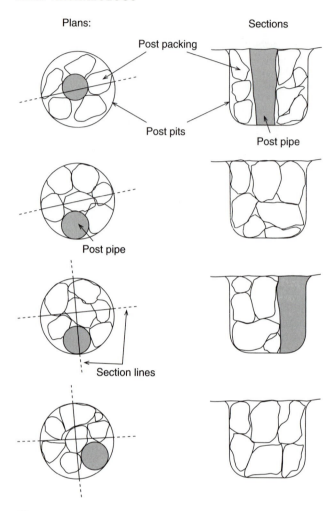

Figure 6.8 Problems with half-sectioning and quadranting postholes.

giving two cross-sections, or excavated in plan with a section reconstructed from the plans. Usually, however, an intelligent guess is made and a single section is cut through the middle of the hole. This can, however, either miss the post pipe altogether or produce totally erronous evidence (Fig. 6.8).

The dating of postholes is not at all straightforward. The date of objects within a posthole will provide only a *terminus post quem* date, that is, the posthole is from the same date as the latest object within the hole or later. Clearly, in terms of sequence of deposition, the objects within the packing material will be earlier in date than those in the post pipe. Usually, however, objects within postholes bear little relationship to the date of the hole, especially on multi-period sites. This is hardly surprising. When a posthole is dug, the hole-digger will cut through earlier occupation layers (with their artefact assemblages). The post is then set in the hole and either the soil dug out is packed in again, or only the big bits dug out, like potsherds, bones and stone packed in to hold the post steady. A medieval post put in on a site occupied in the neolithic period may therefore contain only neolithic artefacts in its packing.

The post may finally rot or be pulled out. If it rots *in situ*, fine particles of soil may fill in the void and no artefacts are likely to get into the post pipe. If, however, the post is pulled out, then surface rubbish may fall or be pushed into the hole. The material will provide a *terminus ante quem* for the removal of the post. The post has to have been removed at the time of the date of the latest object in the post pipe or later.

A safer way to date postholes is to attempt to date the surface from which they were dug. This is rarely easy on shallow sites where postholes are generally not recognized until seen cut into bedrock. This is particularly the case on ploughed sites. Again the surface from which the posthole was dug, if locatable, will provide only a *terminus post quem* although the layer above the surface will provide a *terminus ante quem*. Generally, individual postholes are undatable, but fortunately postholes are often part of a larger structure which may be dated either by the plan of the structure, or its relationship to other contexts like floors.

Ditches are, and were in the past, dug for a wide variety of reasons. Massive ditches could defend towns or hillforts. Little ditches or gullies could be dug around individual houses to prevent flooding. Whether big or small, they present the problem that, as linear features, the sequence at one spot may be totally different to the sequence at another. A single right-angled cross-section will only give the dimensions of the ditch, its sequence of filling, and possibly recutting, at that point. A section a metre away may give a totally different sequence. To understand fully a ditch sequence, it should ideally be excavated as a series of quadrants so that you end up with sections across the ditch, but also a continuous longitudinal section (Fig. 6.9). This process is, however, time consuming, so it may be better to spend time and resources on understanding what is happening within the ditched enclosure than working out minute sequences of ditch fills. The edges of ditches are usually quite clear if dug into bedrock, but if in doubt it is better to overcut, or even box-section into the adjacent bedrock (Fig. 6.10). This process, although often frowned upon in Britain, is widely used in some parts of the world.

When ditches are seen to cross in plan, it is essential to attempt to work out the sequence of digging as this will be important in working out the development of the site. Sometimes the sequence of cutting can be seen in plan, but if not, sections must be carefully located to provide sections through both ditches, so cuts can be determined (Fig. 6.11). As with pits and postholes, the date of objects within ditches can only provide a *terminus ante quem*.

Unlike the excavation of pits, postholes and ditches, which involve a cut-and-fill, walls present their own problems. Unless excavating standing structures, walls are generally represented archaeologically either by foundations, or even only by trenches left by stone robbers (robber trenches). It is rare for masonry structures to be built directly on the ground surface, except in the case of simple low-walled

Figure 6.9 Sectioning a length of ditch (M. Redknap and M. Millett for Sussex Archaeological Field Unit).

Figure 6.10 Box-sectioning a ditch.

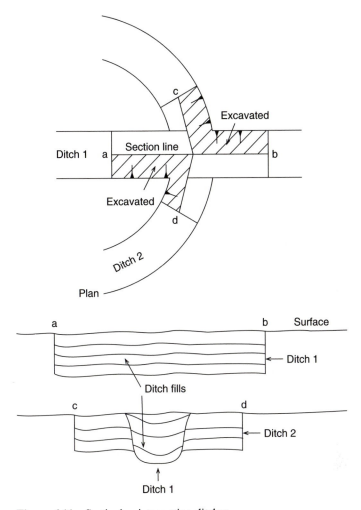

Figure 6.11   Sectioning intercutting ditches.

buildings. Usually walls are built on something solid like bedrock, or footings set in a foundation trench. Foundation trenches can be used in two ways. Either a trench the width of the wall footings is dug and filled with footings, or the trench is dug wider than the footings, the footings built, and the remainder of the trench backfilled. Objects found in the foundation trench are likely to pre-date the wall by years or even centuries, so again provide only a *terminus ante quem*. Every effort must be made to determine the layer from which the foundation trench was cut. The foundation trench has to be the date of that layer or later, but earlier than the date of the layer sealing the foundation trench cut (Fig. 6.12).

Sequences of construction of wall footings can sometimes be determined by looking at points where bits of wall meet. A straight join – where one wall butts against another – usually suggests different periods. This can often be confirmed by differences in building material, relative depth of the foundations, and perhaps

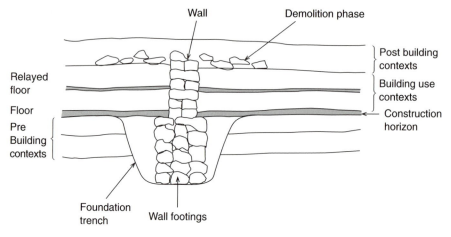

Figure 6.12   Excavation and dating of wall footings.

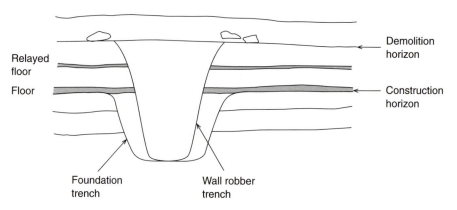

Figure 6.13   Excavation and dating of a robbed wall.

by differences in the mortar used. If the wall has been robbed completely, it may be possible to trace former walls only by the pattern of robber trenches. When excavating a robber trench, great care should be taken to determine its extent in relation to the original foundation trench (Fig. 6.13). The robber trench is likely to be more or less the actual width of the wall. Masonry buildings should always be excavated in plan with sections at right angles to walls.

The excavation of human burials presents legal, ethical and practical problems to field archaeologists. As mentioned in Chapter Five, the excavation of human remains in England (the position is somewhat different in other parts of the UK) requires a Licence for the Removal of Human Remains under the 1857 Burial Act. In the USA the Native American Graves Protection and Repatriation Act 1990 requires human skeletal material to be returned to tribal descendants for re-interment. Most countries have some legal control defining what can and what cannot be done to human remains. Regardless of what the law says, however, field archaeologists should always consider the ethical position of excavating what were, after all, human beings. Most people think that the dead, when laid to rest, should be allowed to do just that. Human remains are not put in the ground for the amusement of a minority group, however cleverly archaeologists wrap up their justification for what most people would see as desecration.

The removal of human remains during a rescue or salvage project can usually be justified, but on research excavations the ethics of the process must be considered in even greater detail. The main areas to consider are firstly, what is the real scientific justification for the excavation? This should be explained clearly to all interested parties. Secondly, how can the work be done with due propriety and respect, and finally, what is the most appropriate way to dispose of the remains after study? Many archaeologists now consider reburial is the most suitable way to conclude a burial excavation.

Having justified your proposal to excavate human remains, and having obtained all required agreements and consents, then the excavation of a burial should be treated in many ways as that of any other context. A burial is a specific discard process. The discard may, however, take place in a special area or special structure, for example, a graveyard or a round barrow. In some cultures, however, the dead are not clearly separated from the living, and burials take place in living areas, inside houses, yards or middens. A key element of burial excavation is, therefore, to consider the context of the burial. Where are the burials in relation to other areas of human activity? Are the related structures burial structures – like a round barrow – or are they domestic structures – like a midden – also used for burial?

Human remains found by archaeologists usually consist of articulated bones, disarticulated bones, or cremated bones. Very rarely do human bodies survive intact as a result of waterlogging, freezing or desiccation. The excavation of an articulated human body is, in many ways, the easiest as one can predict the relationship between a human head and its associated arms, legs and torso. An extended inhumation is, however, much easier to excavate than a crouched burial which, in turn, is easier to excavate if laid on its side rather than sitting up in a pit.

When excavating an extended burial in a grave pit, the top or front of the skull is usually found first. This immediately gives some idea of the orientation of the rest of the body. Ideally the excavator should work from planks resting on a scaffold frame positioned over, or carefully within, the pit. If the excavator is standing on the grave surface, bones and any associated grave goods could be crushed. Having located the skull, a centre line through the skeleton can be estimated and then soil carefully peeled back from this line to reveal all the bones. Standard small tools, the mason's pointing trowel, paint brush, bucket and hand-shovel are usually used for skeleton excavation, but as bone often softens in the ground, softer brushes and even wooden spatulae are sometimes used, togther with more delicate tools like a plasterer's leaf or dental picks. A range of small spoons, perhaps with their handles bent at right angles to the bowl, are useful for extracting soil from between bones. However careful the excavation, odd small bones, especially ear, hand and toe bones, are often not where you may expect them, so the soil content of graves should always be sieved (screened).

The excavation of disarticulated burials is more difficult as there may be no obvious relationship between bones. Here the excavation should proceed in the careful, systematic way that any rubbish deposit would be excavated, each bone being revealed and recorded. Great care must be taken to establish whether the disarticulation is pre-burial or perhaps the result of post-depositional changes like the scattering of bones by burrowing animals. Cremations, also disarticulated bone, are the result of bodies being burnt prior to burial. Bones may have been hand-picked from the cremation pyre and crushed before burial. The cremation may have been buried directly in a small pit, or contained in a pot, bag or box. Unless tightly contained in a surviving container, the bones are likely to be spread by post-depositional activity. Cremations usually, therefore, have a core deposit with odd bones moved away from the core. Careful sieving is really the only way to attempt to recover a complete cremation. If the soil is too acid for the survival of human bone (bone being calcareous), then bodies can sometimes be traced as body-shaped stains, or even as changes in soil chemistry resulting in a body-shaped area of high phosphate surviving, for example, under a round barrow.

Sites without features

Not all archaeological sites or parts of sites produce features like pits, postholes, walls or burials. Sites, particularly very early ones, may survive only as spreads of artefacts and ecofacts representing activity areas. Others, like field lynchets and dry valley sediments, indicate human activity and produce considerable data about the past, but may have no features as such, although the lynchet itself is a feature.

Activity areas without features can really only be thoroughly investigated through open-area excavation. The exact location of individual pieces of struck flint, for example, could indicate where on a site flint knapping took place, and also whether the person knapping was standing, sitting or crouching. Each knapping position could produce a distinct pattern of waste production. Negative areas within a site with no lithic waste may be equally important, indicating sitting areas or routes through the site. This sort of evidence will only, however, be retrievable when a site has been undisturbed since deposition. Usually this involves very rapid burial under sediment or a cliff collapse. Great care should be taken to establish whether the lithics are really *in situ* or not. Lithics deposited in flowing water, for example, have a single orientation in relation to the water flow, while all patterns may be lost through ploughing. Lithics with sharp edges are less likely to have moved far than those with rounded edges.

Two areas of mass soil movement which still have great archaeological signi-ficance, but require specific excavation techniques, are lynchets and dry valley sediments. I have linked these because their process of formation and methods of excavation can be similar. Both are the result of soil moving downslope and com-ing to rest at a specific spot in the landscape. Lynchets always, and dry valley sediments usually, involve some agricultural activity in the past. Lynchets are the

Figure 6.14   Excavating a lynchet section.

result of soil moving down slopes as a result of agriculture, and building up at the bottom of a field.

If they are part of a field system, as opposed to a single field, then the lynchets will have a positive and a negative element. At the bottom of the field the soil builds up as a positive lynchet, while at the top of the next field soil is eroding away to create a negative lynchet. It is the positive lynchet which provides most archaeological information. The lynchet may have built up against an unploughed strip of soil or against a barrier like a fenceline, wall or bank. If so, features like postholes may be involved. The usual way to exavate a lynchet is to cut a right-angle section through it (Fig. 6.14). Open-area excavation would be considered only if a whole field, or even a field system, were being excavated, a luxury usually limited to salvage or rescue excavations.

The purpose of lynchet excavations is to provide an agricultural history for the field or field system; this can only be effectively done where fields are regularly manured with domestic or farmyard manure which contains artefactual material like potsherds. These move down the slope of the field and are deposited in the lynchet in more or less the sequence of their introduction into the field with the manure. By two-dimensionally plotting artefacts (along the section and down the section) horizons with datable artefacts can be located, indicating broad periods of ploughing. These can be tied to environmental sequences derived perhaps from molluscan analysis (see below) which could suggest phases of pasture within arable sequences.

Lynchet excavations can be undertaken entirely by hand from the surface downwards, recording the exact location of each artefact. Alternatively, to accelerate the process when digging at Bullock Down, Sussex, in 1976, I cut one-metre wide machine trenches through the lynchets. The section was then drawn and a 50 cm section was cut back by hand on one side of the trench, with artefacts directly plotted onto the already-drawn section. This reduced the average time taken to section a lynchet by two-thirds, a considerable saving of time and therefore money.

Soil not stopped by lynchet formation will finally come to rest in the bottoms of valleys. These will, therefore, also preserve an agricultural and environmental history of the local area. Sections can be cut through dry valleys in the same way as through lynchets, with careful plotting of the artefacts to provide sequences of rapid soil accumulation suggestive of agriculture. The environmental history of the area can often be pushed back earlier than agricultural periods by studying the earlier, naturally accumulated, valley sediments.

Artefacts and ecofacts, their recovery and treatment

The recovery of artefacts, ecofacts and associated environmental data are essential for the understanding of a site. Although finds, particularly artefacts, may be important in their own right, for example as art objects, their importance generally lies in their association and their context on the site. They can provide information about what happened on a site, where it happened on the site, and when it happened on the site. How artefacts are excavated and recorded will depend very much on the type of site being excavated and the field archaeologist's assessment of the type of deposit involved, especially if it is primary or secondary rubbish (Chapter Two). Primary rubbish, discarded where it was generated, requires much more careful excavation and recording than secondary rubbish. Secondary rubbish is usually excavated, lifted and grouped by context, whereas the exact location of each bit of primary rubbish may be important for locating activity areas.

Unless the site being excavated is waterlogged, desiccated or frozen, most of the artefacts found are likely to be inorganic, particularly lithics and/or ceramics, depending on period. Both lithics and ceramics survive in most types of soil and can usually be safely excavated by carefully clearing the soil from around the object and, having established its full extent, carefully lifting it. Never pull an object out of the ground when first revealed; part of it may still be securely bedded in the ground and will break off. The object is then put into a finds tray or bag, clearly labelled with at least the site name or code and context number or, if exactly located, with three-dimensional co-ordinates (see Chapter Seven). Large, complete or fragile pots will require greater care in excavation and may need specialist conservation treatment *in situ*, followed by special lifting techniques. On larger projects there is usually a site conservator, or one may be on call for particular problems. If a conservator is not available, then the field archaeologist should have enough basic conservation knowledge to deal with the problem.

The main aim of field conservation is to provide an environment for the object to be safely lifted and transported, without sustaining any damage, but in such a way as not to impede future conservation (Payton 1992). Soft ceramics may require some consolidation before lifing. Polyvinyl acetate (PVA) in acetone is one of the most commonly used consolidants, but others such as Paraloid B-72 and Butvar B98 are also available. If the object needs support during lifting, it is advisable to place a barrier between it and the support. Plastic food wrapping (cling film), aluminium foil or acid-free tissue paper can be carefully moulded around the object. This is then encased in plaster of Paris, aerosol or two-component polyurethane foam, or wrapped in plaster bandages. If the object is large or heavy, a board can be slid under it to facilitate lifting. Great care must be taken when consolidating and lifting an object on an excavation not to damage either the site or adjacent objects, particularly when trying to undercut the object being consolidated.

Lithics also require care when being excavated, lifted and removed from the site. The main problem with lithics is that careless treatment can create secondary re-touch and apparent microwear. An *in situ* knapping floor must be treated with particular care. Fine-mesh sieving will be required to recover all the smallest chips of flint, but dry sieving may retouch many of the finest edges. Careful wet sieving of the soil will reduce the abrasive effect of the sieving. Lithics should then be packed separately to prevent retouch in transit. This is, of course, less of a problem when dealing with secondary or rolled contexts, like lithics in a lynchet section.

Most other artefactual materials require specific care when excavating, packing and storing. Metals are best lifted without touching them, and should be carefully sealed in aluminium foil with silica gel to keep them dry in order to slow down corrosion. Wet organic artefacts, like wood, should however be kept wet, with sufficient fungicide to stop them going mouldy, and should then either be taken to a conservation laboratory as soon as possible, or drawn, photographed and the wood identified prior to being thrown away. No museum will be prepared to take bits of mouldy, rotting wood!

Bone and shell will survive only in relatively calcareous soils or under special conditions. When first excavated they may be fairly soft, but often harden up when dry. If very soft, consolidation and careful lifting may be required but usually they can be treated in a similar way to ceramics. Again date and context will determine an appropriate method of excavation and treatment. An *in situ* human bone of 400,000 BC is likely to be treated more carefully than a nineteenth-century horn core in a residual context.

The methods of excavation of environmental data are quite different to the methods of excavation of artefacts and ecofacts of food-refuse type. Two key types of environmental data that can be recovered are pollen, generally from acid sites, and land mollusca from alkaline sites. Both involve taking samples of soil away and extracting the evidence under laboratory conditions. Ideally, sampling on site should be undertaken by an environmental archaeologist in co-operation with the field archaeologist. Sampling is usually taken from standing sections, but in open-area excavation, samples may need to be taken as the excavation progresses. Pollen samples are often obtained by taking columns of soil samples at 1 cm or 2 cm intervals through buried land surfaces (Fig. 5.18). Molluscan samples need to be larger, and are taken from discrete contexts like layers in a ditch. Soil samples, being damp, may well go mouldy if sealed in a plastic bag and kept in a warm site hut. Ideally, take the samples straight to the environmental laboratory. Otherwise keep the bags cool or even add a small amount of fungicide.

Matrices, phasing and dating sites

To work out the development of an archaeological site through time the stratigraphical sequence needs to be determined. Individual elements of stratification (contexts) are put into sequence, a process known as phasing. Phases may be grouped together into periods. On complex sites this process can be aided by the construction of matrices. The principles of *terminus post quem* and *terminus ante quem* are then applied to aid the dating of the phases and periods.

Phases are established from the bottom of the sequence upwards. Traditionally this would involve the careful study of standing sections to establish a sequence of deposits and any associated features or structures. In open-area excavation this is done through the context recording system. Each context is recorded as being below and above other contexts or having some other stratigraphical relationship with them (Fig. 6.15). Those contexts stratigraphically associated can be considered as forming a phase. This element of phasing is based only on the study of the stratigraphic evidence without any consideration of artefacts or dating. Phases can then be grouped into periods by considering elements like building levels and associated datable artefacts or ecofacts.

On complex sites sorting out the stratigraphic sequence and phasing can be greatly aided by producing a schematic diagram showing relationships between all contexts on the site (Harris 1979). Figure 6.16 is a simple example. Context 1 could be a plough soil resting on top of context 2, a layer, and contexts 3, 4 and 5, a pit cut and its fills. Context 2 overlays context 6 and all contexts overlay context 7.

The theory of stratification is an important tool in giving a sequence to phases and periods on a site. This layer is older than that layer. This gives a sequence to the site. What it does not do is date elements of the site. For this we need the additional theory of *terminus post quem* and *terminus ante quem*. We cannot simply say this layer has Clovis points in it so is, say, 9000 BC or has medieval pottery so is, say, AD 1400. We cannot simply get a radiocarbon date for a piece of charcoal in a layer and say the layer is 2000 BC. What we can do is apply the theories of *terminus post quem* and *terminus ante quem*.

Terminus post quem dating requires datable things to be found within a layer, say coins, pottery of a specific type, or organics suitable for radiocarbon dating. This theory then asserts that the layer is the same date as the latest datable object in the layer, *or later*. All layers above this 'dated' layer must therefore be younger than that date. This theory must, however, be applied in conjunction with theories of transformation processes outlined in Chapter Two. Is that datable object intrusive or residual? Have transformation processes like earthworms or tree roots moved the object? Consideration of one theory may need another one to qualify it.

Terminus ante quem dating is related in method to *terminus post quem* dating but relates to layers, deposits or features being earlier than a dated element rather

Field Archaeology Unit

CONTEXT RECORD FORM

DESCRIPTION

CO-ORDINATES	SITE CODE	SITE SUB-DIVISION	CONTEXT NO.
CATEGORY			

LENGTH	WIDTH	DIAMETER	HEIGHT/DEPTH

SOILS	COLOUR	
	TEXTURE	
	CONSISTENCE	
	COARSE COMPONENTS	

STRUC.	BONDING AGENT	
	CONSTITUENTS	

DESCRIPTIVE TEXT

EXCAVATION

METHOD OF EXCAVATION
FINDS
SAMPLES

PHYSICAL RELATIONSHIPS

EARLIER THAN	BELOW	
	FILLED BY	
	CUT BY	
	BUTTED BY (STRUCTURE)	
CONTEMP. WITH	WITHIN	
	CONTAINS	
	BONDED WITH (STRUCTURE)	
	SAME AS	
LATER THAN	ABOVE	
	FILL OF	
	CUTS	
	BUTTS (STRUCTURE)	
UNCERTAIN		

INTERPRETATION

INTERPRETATIVE COMMENTS

CHECKLIST

DRAWING NOS.	PLAN	SECTION	
PHOTO NOS.	MONOCHROME	COLOUR	
RECORDER	CHECKED		CONTINUED

Figure 6.15 Example of a context record form.

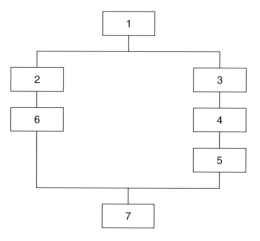

Figure 6.16   Stratigraphic matrix.

than later. If an element within the sequence can be given an 'absolute' date by, say, scientific (for example, carbon-14 dating) or architectural means (a datable construction technique) then all layers and features below it must pre-date it even if only by seconds. An area may, for example, be covered with rubble and then a floor laid immediately upon it. Archaeologically the rubble foundation and floor are contemporary, but in strict stratigraphic terms the rubble pre-dates the floor. The dated floor has provided a *terminus ante quem* for the foundations and everything below them.

The theory of *terminus post quem* and *terminus ante quem* dating is in principle, therefore, relatively straightforward. In practice, however, there are many problems, the main one being how reliable the dating of anything in an archaeological sequence really is. Very rarely can objects be precisely dated and even if they appear to be, like a post-medieval potsherd with an inscribed calendar date, can the date be believed, and how close to that date was deposition of the object? A commemorative pot inscribed *AD 1650* might still be being produced years later if the market for that particular pot continued. The pot might then be kept as an heirloom (curated) for generations. It could be broken in, say, 1750. The sherds could then be thrown into a rubbish pit which, fifty years later, could be used to level land for a new house. The sherd dated to 1650 might, therefore, be the only dated object in a layer in fact deposited in 1800. In this context the anomalous date might be recognized, but would this be the case in a prehistoric context?

On prehistoric sites 'absolute' dates are more likely to come from scientific dates like carbon-14 or thermoluminescence. Even here, what are referred to as 'absolute' dates are not quite what they appear to be. Most scientific dating techniques require some form of calibration to bring them nearer to calendar dates, and even then we are left with an approximate date bracket for the material. How and when the material ended up in a particular archaeological context always remains a debatable question.

Excavation and the public

Gone are the days when archaeological excavation was the private preserve of an aloof, academic elite. The past belongs to everyone, and everyone should be allowed access to it. This should involve access to sites in the field, artefacts in museums, and the excitement of archaeological discovery on excavations. Clearly, however, access to excavations must be carefully controlled, both for the safety of the public and for the protection of the site. Firstly the field archaeologist should assess likely demand. Where is the site, and what is likely to be found? Sites in areas of dense population or on tourist routes are more likely to generate large numbers of visitors than those in sparsely populated areas with no easy access. A Roman villa excavation is likely to attract more visitors than a lynchet section.

Basic visit provision could include a notice board, site tours, public lectures and finds exhibition, together with special provision for school parties. The notice board should say something more than *Archaeological Excavation: Keep Out*. If such a notice is required, at least let it read *For your own safety please keep out unless on an organized tour*. Ideally the notice should provide basic information about the site, and dates and times of site tours. In some areas one widely-advertised site tour may be all that is required. A key site in a major city could, however, require almost continuous site tours, especially if a major discovery has been announced. Site tours are best run by carefully selected site workers who can instil in visitors something of their own enthusiasm. Keep the tour to a reasonable length, speak clearly, and avoid too much jargon, though the use of some special terms, if adequately explained, adds to the special nature of the event: this is, after all, a 'scientific' operation.

Site tours can, of course, give only a 'snapshot' picture of the site at the moment of the visit, so a concluding public lecture is often a useful addition to site public relations. This is best organized in conjunction with the local archaeological or historical society, museum or college. Carefully selected objects should be put on show if this can be organized safely. Provision for schoolchildren should be considered separately. Schoolchildren rarely like standing on the edge of a trench being lectured at. If possible, get them involved. Is there a bit of the site they can safely trowel? Maybe there are some shells or potsherds they can wash, or if part of the site is finished with, perhaps they could 'reconstruct' the buildings by standing in the postholes. Remember they include the next generation of archaeologists and museum curators – even the politicians who could affect how archaeology develops in the future.

CHAPTER SEVEN

Recording archaeological excavations

The record of an archaeological excavation consists of four major elements: the written record, the drawn record, the photographic record and the materials taken away from the site, that is, the 'finds' consisting of artefacts, ecofacts and environmental samples. Finds will be considered further in Chapter Eight.

The written record

Traditionally the written record of an excavation was kept in field notebooks, perhaps separated into site, area and trench (or unit) books. These were kept by those in charge of particular parts of the excavation. Site notebooks should include details of every aspect of the excavation, from detailed notes about soil changes and structures to thoughts, ideas and interpretations. A well-kept field notebook can be a perfectly good written record of an excavation, but anyone who has attempted to write an excavation report from the field notebooks of a dead archaeologist will be aware of the many inconsistencies and outright omissions that can creep into an unstructured field notebook. They may be fine for recording the sociology of an excavation but are rarely adequate for systematic recording of data.

For this reason pre-printed context or feature/layer forms are now favoured by many archaeologists. In Britain they are used on virtually all excavations. The advantage of a pre-printed 'context record form' is that one can see at a glance whether all the data that should have been recorded are there. Context record forms vary a little from site to site, but all should include location information, soil or structure information, methods of excavation, stratigraphic relationships, interpretation and cross-references to the drawn and photographic record. Some forms include finds information while some archaeologists keep this separate. The redesign of context record forms has been something of a national sport in archaeological circles in Britain over the last twenty years or so, but usually it is only the detail and layout of the form which varies rather than the real content. Figure 6.15 shows a fairly typical context record form. It could be completed in the following way.

Co-ordinates These enable you to locate the position of the context. They give a measurement along the base of the site grid and another up the axis at right angles.

If the site grid is orientated north–south, then the co-ordinates are recorded as a measurement from west to east along the base line of the grid and then a second measurement from that point from south to north.

Site code Ideally the site code should be clear, simple and designed to reduce future remarking of finds, as this code is marked on all finds. If the finds are to end up in a public museum, as all finds should, then it is sensible to use the museum accession number as the site code. This saves remarking when accessioned into the museum collection. In Britain each museum accessions each object or group of objects by year and discrete number, so for 1999 objects are numbered 1999.1, 1999.2, 1999.3 and so on. The site code should then be the next number allocated by the museum, for example, 1999.51. Alternatively the site name can be abbreviated to create a site code, for example, Off76 being the site excavated at Offham in 1976. Clearly it is essential to establish that the code has not already been allocated in the region in which the finds will be stored.

Site sub-division This is recorded if the site is divided up in any way. For example, test pits or units may have their own numbers, or the site may be divided into areas by letter.

Category This describes the type of context represented. Is it, for example, a deposit or layer of soil, or is it the cut of a pit or ditch?

Length A measurement of the length of the context, this will follow national conventions using imperial or metric measurements. Metric measurements may be in metres and centimetres or, following architectural conventions, all in millimetres.

Diameter If a round pit or posthole, the diameter of the context is recorded. Some forms do not have length, width and diameter on them as this repeats information available on the context plan.

Height/depth The vertical measurement of the context is given usually as a range, for example, depth 50–25 mm, or simply a maximum measurement.

Soils The four main elements when describing soils are colour, texture, consistency and coarse components. Fine analysis can really only be undertaken in the laboratory, but for archaeological purposes simple field descriptions based on physical methods are generally more than adequate. It is interesting to note how much effort is put into describing soils on excavations and yet how little these data are actually used by archaeologists. It generally remains as raw archive data, never reaching synthetic works of archaeology.

Soil colour Depending how this information is going to be used, colours can be either divided at a very general level visually – for example, light brown, dark grey, black – or more precisely using a colour chart. The Munsell Soil Color Charts were developed in the United States especially to describe soil colours. Colour is divided into hue, value and chroma. Hue divides the whole spectrum into ten parts from red-purple (RP), red (R), yellow-red (YR), yellow (Y), green-yellow (GY), green (G), blue-green (BG), blue (B), purple-blue (PB) to purple (P). Each of these divisions is then divided into ten parts so 1B is blue bordering on blue-green, 5B is mid-blue and 10B is blue bordering on purple-blue. Value divides the shade of the colour from dark to pale in ten divisions, so 1 would represent the darkest and 10 the lightest value. Chroma refers to the purity of the colour as most soils contain some greyness, so 1 is close to grey while 10 is almost the pure colour. Any colour can therefore be given a simple code, for example, 9B 2/4. Blue soils are, however, not particularly common!

Soil texture For a basic textural description of soils, mineral particles can be divided into three size classes: Sand (0.06–2.00 mm), Silt (0.002–0.06 mm) and Clay (less than 0.002 mm). Although texture can be accurately ascertained only by laboratory analysis, general texture can be ascertained by rolling a soil sample in the hand. If the soil sample, when damp, can be rolled into long threads which can be bent into rings, then it is largely clay. If the threads will not bend to form a ring, then it is a silt, while sand cannot maintain any shape.

Soil consistency The consistency of a soil can again be determined by simple hand tests. A soil which is bound together with substances other than clay – calcium carbonate for example – may be described as cemented, while a soil which adheres to fingers when wet is sticky. A plastic soil can be rolled into 'worms' between the palms of the hands, while a loose soil cannot be moulded into a cube. A friable soil, however, can be moulded into a cube, but the cube will collapse with simple pressure. A firm soil requires considerable force to collapse a cube squeezed between two fingers, while a cube of hard soil cannot be crushed between two fingers. Most soils contain some larger bits which are referred to as 'the coarse component'. These can be described as small (up to 8 mm), medium (up to 16 mm), large (up to 32 mm) or very large (over 32 mm). The shape of pebbles in soil may be significant, so that should be described according to a roundness index ranging from very angular, through angular, sub-angular, sub-rounded and rounded, to well-rounded.

If the context consists of a structure like a well rather than a soil deposit, the boxes below the soil boxes are filled in. A structure usually consists of a material such as bricks (the constituents) held together with a bonding agent like mortar. Many stone walls were, however, constructed 'dry' in the past, so have no bonding agent. An important element of recording masonry structures is to record both the finish of individual stones (for example, ashlar, squared, rough) and how, particularly bricks, are laid (bonding). Bonds like English, Flemish or herringbone may provide dating information. The bonding agent should be described rather like soils, that is, colour, texture and coarse components. Samples of mortar can be taken for compositional analysis, which may be valuable in phasing masonry remains.

One of the early criticisms of context record forms was that they could be filled in mechanically and that there might be important observations which the excavator wanted to make that simply did not fit into any of the pre-printed categories. For this reason the 'descriptive text' box can be useful to describe anything else not recorded so far.

The second block on the form relates to the process of excavation, firstly 'method of excavation'. It is clearly important to record whether a context has been machined out, shovelled, carefully trowelled, or subjected to 1 mm – mesh sieving. To compare the bone assemblage from a fine-mesh sieved context with a shovelled context would clearly not be a good idea! Basic categories of find like pottery, bone, metal, can be listed in the Finds box and samples, for example soil, listed by sample number in the Sample box.

The third major section on the context form describes physical relationships of the context, that is its stratigraphic relationships. An alternative way of recording this is to show context numbers in little boxes above and below the context being described. This would be the first part of a stratigraphic matrix which could be constructed for the whole site. This particular form, however, groups relationships into 'earlier than', 'contemporary with' and 'later than'. There are four relationships which show the context being described is earlier than others. Firstly, if it is sealed below another context, it is earlier than the overlying context. Secondly, if it is filled with another context, it has to be earlier than the fill. For example, the cut of a dug pit is earlier than the rubbish put into the pit. Thirdly, if the context being described is (say) a ditch, and a pit had been dug into the edge of the ditch, then the ditch is cut by (that is, earlier than) the pit. Finally, if the context is a piece of masonry and another piece is built up against it, the first structure is butted by (that is, earlier than) the second structure.

It is clearly important to try to establish which contexts are contemporary with which others on a particular site. Broadly this can be done by establishing which groups of contexts are earlier and which are later than another group of contexts. However, to establish that one context represents an activity which took place at exactly the same time as another is more or less impossible. Some activities, like putting up a post for example, can produce more or less contemporary contexts. All the posts of a single-phase round house are likely to have been put up at more or less the same time. The post packing will be 'within' the context of the posthole cut, and more or less contemporary with it. The posthole cut 'contains' the post packing context. In the case of a masonry or brick wall where two walls at right angles are bonded together, they represent contemporary construction. Sometimes a context being described turns out to be the 'same as' one already recorded. A ditch, for example, may be excavated at either side of a site and not seen to be the same until other layers in the centre of the site are removed.

Relationships of time are shown by the 'Later than' box. The context being described is 'later than' any contexts it is above. Naturally this box cannot be filled in until the context beneath is reached. The soil silting into a ditch is clearly later than the date of the ditch cut. Therefore the silt context is the 'fill of', that is, later than the ditch-cut. If, however, the ditch-cut cuts through a pit, then the ditch 'cuts', that is, is later than, the pit. Finally, if the context is masonry or brick and it 'butts' against another structure, then that structure must be earlier. In theory all these relationships can be worked out by an experienced field archaeologist. In practice this is not always as easy as it sounds. Often natural transformation processes like worms, burrowing animals or roots destroy relationships which may never have been particularly clear in the first place. Further relationships may be established at the post-excavation stage when finds are dated, so if relationships are still uncertain in the field, say so in the 'Uncertain' box.

The fourth main section on this context record form concerns interpretation. The sections above are largely descriptive, though interpretation does enter into most sections. The 'interpretative comments' box, however, enables the excavator – or whoever fills in the form, with the context clearly visible in front of them – to consider its interpretation. Is it a rubbish deposit or could it be, or include, a ritual element? Is it deliberately laid to level the ground for building construction? Is it a naturally accumulating deposit resulting from erosion? Does the erosion have an anthropogenic cause? Leaving all interpretation to the post-excavation stage means interpretation can only be based on the record not on the actual context, and however good the record is, it is never as good as the *in situ* context when attempting interpretation.

The fifth and final section of this particular version of a context record form is a checklist enabling cross-reference to the drawn and photographic record. Each plan and section will be numbered, and the number filled in as 'drawing number', while each photographic image produced in either monochrome or colour is numbered and filled in as 'photo number'. The name of the recorder (and, if checked by a site supervisor, *their* name) is filled in along the bottom line. Sometimes more space may be needed for one or two categories on the form, so if continuation sheets are used make sure this is recorded. Some context record forms also have a reverse side to be filled in. This may include space for a sketch of the context and level information, although levels are often more appropriately put on the drawn record.

As each context is recorded on a separate loose-leaf sheet, these must clearly be kept together safely in a ring binder or folder and a single context register kept for each site. The context register simply records each context number as it is allocated, together with basic information about location of the context, by site subdivision for example, and what category of context it is. This way, information about all pits or all postholes can be easily recovered as well as making sure no two contexts are ever given the same number.

The written record also includes forms recording drawings (the drawing register), photographs (the photographic record) and finds (general and special finds registers). These will be considered as appropriate below. Special types of site may also require specially designed record forms appropriate for particular circumstances. Burial and waterlogged sites, for example, generally warrant special recording forms. A skeleton form could have a pre-printed drawing of a skeleton, so bones found can be simply coloured in on the form. A timber recording form would include information about tool marks, joints and type of wood. Remember, however, that forms can be designed for virtually anything and the multiplication of forms does not always lead to greater efficiency or better recording, just paper overload. Paper overload can, of course, be reduced by recording all this information directly onto hand-held computers, but information overload is still present if what is recorded is not carefully considered at all stages of the excavation.

The drawn record

The drawn record consists essentially of measured drawings of surfaces: vertical (sections) and horizontal (plans). Vertical sections are created by archaeologists at specific points on the site to give information about sequences of events (the stratigraphy). These sequences may be long-term, like the whole sequence of a site

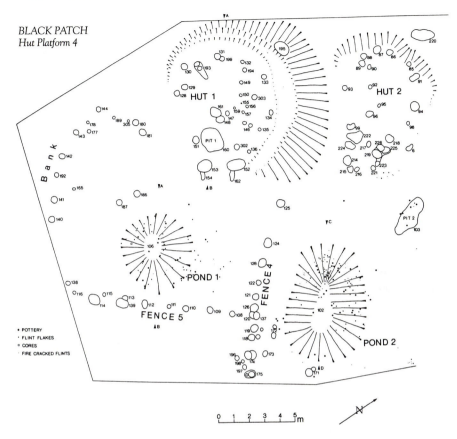

Figure 7.1   Multiple-feature plan.

over years or centuries, or very short-term like the sequence revealed by a single posthole section. The method of drawing a section is essentially the same, however big or small it is. Plans can, however, be produced in different ways. The appropriate type of plan should be determined by the type of site being excavated rather than any predetermined dogma. A shallow chalkland site ploughed into the chalk surface for centuries may survive largely, or only, as features dug into the bedrock (although see Chapter Three, Geophysical survey, on the archaeological potential of plough soil). These could best be illustrated as a multiple feature plan (Fig. 7.1) where each pit, posthole and ditch is clearly shown on the plan in relation to other features. With no surfaces other than the surface of the bedrock surviving, any sequence of features will have to be interpreted by the archaeologist, using intercutting features and attempts to date individual features.

Composite plans remain the most commonly produced archaeological plans (Fig. 7.2). These attempt to record surfaces with contexts like walls and floors related to contemporary ditches, working areas and rubbish deposits. They create a clear 'snapshot' view of what the archaeologist considers to be a major surface,

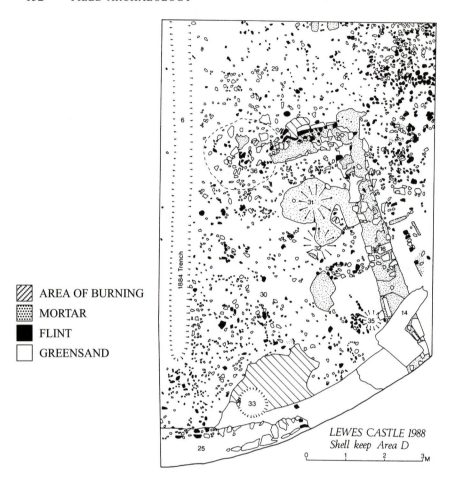

AREA OF BURNING

MORTAR

FLINT

GREENSAND

LEWES CASTLE 1988
Shell keep Area D

Figure 7.2   Composite plan.

usually representing a specific phase of activity. On single-phase sites this is clearly a good way to produce a visual representation of a site at a particular point in time. Problems however arise on multi-period sites, especially deep urban sites. Occasionally major surfaces can be determined, but usually contexts overlap, are interleaved, are cut into and built upon. Any archaeologically-produced surface will generally have revealed only bits of contexts of very different periods. In effect the surface is the creation of the archaeologists producing it: the trowellers somewhat arbitrarily decide where to 'end' a context which may be dipping under another on the produced surface.

One way around this problem is to record each context separately by producing single-layer (Harris 1979) or single-context (Spence 1990) plans (Fig. 7.3). In this method each context is defined to its full extent and then drawn in plan separately. These form the archive plans but can be combined to produce either composite plans or multiple-feature plans for publication as required. The only problem with

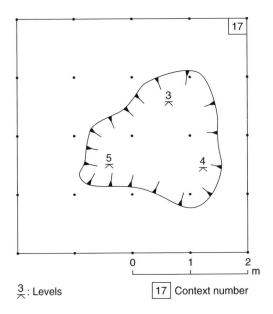

3/木 : Levels   17 Context number

Figure 7.3   Single-context plan (illustrating hachures
and spot-heights).

the single-context plan system is the sheer volume of the archive produced. Much
of the problem has, however, been reduced in recent years by developments in
computer-assisted cartography (CAC) and computer-aided design (CAD).

The actual process of producing plans in the field, whether multiple-feature,
composite, or single-context, is essentially similar. All plans must be related to
fixed points which must remain constant throughout the excavation. This is usually
achieved by establishing a site grid before the excavation starts and then maintain-
ing it throughout the excavation. Physically the site grid may be represented in
the field by just three fixed points, accurately surveyed and marked – either by pegs
or steel rods driven or cemented into the ground outside the area to be excavated.
One peg is set at each end of a baseline and one at right angles to the origin of
the baseline. A right angle can be laid out in a variety of ways, as described in
Chapter Four.

Site grids are usually laid out on true north, but on restricted sites other orientations
could be considered if more practical. From the basic three grid points any number
of intermediate points can be established. These could be pegs at one-, two-, five-
or ten-metre intervals along two or all four sides of the excavation, or permanently
established corners of grid squares across the site (Fig. 7.4). If permanently marking the corners of squares within an excavation, then thin steel rods hammered right
through the site are better than 6-inch (15 cm) nails which tend to be loosened, and
often moved about, as the excavation proceeds. Only very few types of sites, like *in
situ* palaeolithic flaking floors, require permanent squares marked with string in the
excavation area.

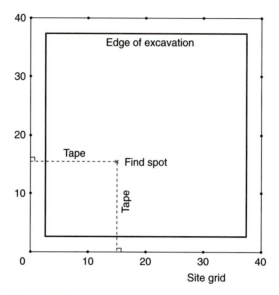

Figure 7.4   Site recording grid.

Plan drawing can be undertaken by offsets or triangulation from fixed points (Chapter Four), or by using a drawing frame which is an extension of offset survey-ing. Alternatively, plan making within an excavation can be undertaken using a total station (Chapter Four); but this, like triangulation, is best for recording large contexts like ditches and pits, and the extent of areas of cobbles or demolition debris, rather than its actual detail. The detail is best drawn with a drawing frame. The drawing frame consists of a square (usually 1 metre) of wood or metal strung up into 20 cm, or sometimes 10 cm, squares (Fig. 7.5). The area to be recorded is then gridded into 1-metre squares with string and nails. The relationship with the site grid is recorded. The drawing frame is then laid over the first square to be drawn and – with the planmaker's eye directly over a 20 cm square – detail, like cobble stones, can be drawn by eye to scale on a drawing board mounted with plastic tracing film. As most plans are drawn at a scale of 1:20, each 20 cm square on the ground is represented by 1 cm on the drawing board. Accuracy of 1 cm or less on the ground is therefore perfectly possible using a drawing frame. Inaccuracy will, however creep in, the further away the frame is from the surface being drawn, if for example large rocks are involved, or if drawing is done at an angle rather than from directly above each square.

Plans should ideally be drawn with north at the top of the plan, but whether or not the plan is drawn this way, a north point should be added onto the plan. If possible, everything should be drawn as seen from directly on top. Individual stones should be drawn, not just blocks of masonry. Different types of stones used in a wall or elsewhere can be recorded with different coloured pencils. Slopes, however, like a ditch edge, require conventions. Slopes are usually illustrated by using hachures (Fig. 7.3).

Figure 7.5 Drawing frame.

In order to relate plans vertically, contexts should be levelled in relation to the site datum. This is a fixed point outside the area to be excavated. It can either be tied into ordnance datum using a level or total station (Chapter Four) or simply given an arbitrary value of, say, 50 and referred to as a temporary benchmark (TBM). The level is usually set up outside the excavation and a reading taken on the TBM. If this back sight reads 1.2 metres, then the plane of collimation is 51.2 m (that is, the TBM value of 50 plus 1.2 m). A foresight is then taken to the context being levelled. The staff is held on the context and read. This example could read, say, 1.5 metres so the reduced level in relation to the TBM is 49.7 metres (that is, the plane of collimation value of 51.2 minus the reading of 1.5 metres). This process of reducing levels was described in Chapter Four. Spot heights (levels) can be recorded across the surface of the context and clearly marked on the plan above the level of a bar on an inverted V (Fig. 7.3).

An alternative method of producing a site plan is to use photographs, but unless complex piles of stones (like a cairn) are involved this process is rarely cheaper or much quicker than conventional planmaking. To produce reasonably accurate plans a mosaic of vertical photographs with 40–50 per cent overlap should be taken. This can only be done using a quadripod, bipod or monopod to raise the camera vertically above each section of the site (Dorrell 1989). The basic problem is one of distortion resulting from the rounded shape of the camera's lens. The image produced by a camera becomes more oblique towards the edge of the photograph, but by overlapping and only using the central part of the photograph, this problem is reduced (but never entirely removed). The image can then

Figure 7.6   Section drawing from a horizontal datum.

either be simply traced directly onto plastic tracing film, or digitized and plotted by computer.

Vertical sections are usually drawn in the field at a larger scale than plans. Where any detail is present, 1:10 is the usual scale, although large sections with little detail can be drawn at 1:20. Sections should be drawn from a horizontal datum fixed to the surface of the soil face, not above it where it can be slackened in the wind or tripped over. As measurements are taken at right angles from the datum it is best to fix it halfway up the section (Fig. 7.6). The datum is set up by firstly putting a six-inch (15 cm) nail or surveyor's arrow into one end of the section. Thin string is then tied to this and pulled tight along the section so it is approximately level. It can then be precisely levelled using a simple line level hung from a string. This is best done with two people, one to look at the level and tell the other to raise or lower the string. When level, the string is nailed into the other end of the section.

This process can also be done with a dumpy level, theodolite or transit. This is set up away from the face of the section, and then the staff is held on the face midway down the section. A nail is put in the face below the staff. The staff can then be moved along the section and nails put in wherever the staff has exactly the same reading. If all the readings are the same, then the line of nails must be horizontal. They can then be joined with string to create a horizontal datum. The height of the datum should be recorded in relation to the site datum. A measuring tape is then fixed parallel to the datum string either just above or more generally just below it. It should be fixed to separate nails, remembering never to tie the tape but only bend once over the nail and clip with a bulldog clip or peg.

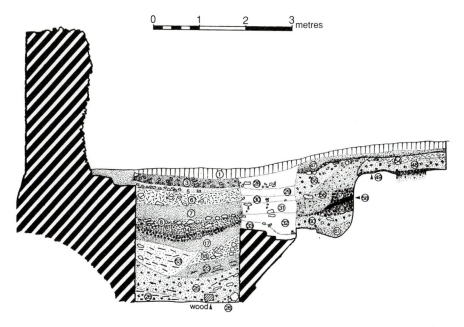

0   1   2   3 metres

Figure 7.7   Example of section drawing combining convention and pictorial representation.

The datum line is scaled down and drawn on plastic tracing film mounted on a drawing board. If wet or windy, the tracing film should be sealed all around with drafting tape. Otherwise a strip across each corner is usually adequate. If the tracing film is not pre-printed with graph squares, then a sheet of graph paper may be mounted under the tracing film to give a framework of guidelines. Usually sections are drawn using two people, one to draw and one to measure. Measurements are taken by creating a vertical from the datum, either by eye or using a plumb bob. Two measurements are read, one along the datum and one at right angles above or below the datum. It is generally best to plot the top and bottom of the section first. This gives a framework which is then filled in by following individual contexts, marking top and bottom of each context (the top of one usually being the bottom of the next) together with cuts like a pit edge.

The extent of all contexts visible in the section should be recorded, but then how much detail within a context should be drawn is a matter of opinion. Larger fragments of stone, bricks, pottery and the like should certainly be plotted on sections, but how small a piece should be recorded depends very much on the period and type of site being recorded. Generally, good sections involve a combination of convention and pictorial representation (Fig. 7.7). Each context drawn on a section must be given its context number, clearly marked on the section drawing. Do not try to describe contexts on the section: all the written description appears on the context record form. Cardinal points at each end of the section should be recorded, together with site name, section number, scale, name of recorder and date of drawing.

The photographic record

Unlike field surveys, where equipment has to be carefully selected for mobility, excavations are usually long-term and in one place. Generally, equipment is delivered by vehicle so its weight is less of a problem. The most important addition to the basic field photographic equipment outlined in Chapter Four is a strong, well-built, tripod. Avoid those which may be damaged by dust. Simple clamp legs and pan-and-tilt heads are best. Most excavators now use 35 mm cameras for basic site work, but large-format cameras or medium-format cameras with a shift lens may be needed to photograph masonry or deep, narrow trenches. The photography of high walls or deep trenches using a 35 mm camera usually produces unacceptable distortion (Dorrell 1989). For vertical photography or general site views tripod towers, quadripods or bipods may be added to the excavation photographer's equipment (Dorrell 1989). Specialized cameras, like polaroid and digital cameras, along with video, should also be considered.

Photography, together with the drawn record and the written record, is one of the key forms of excavation record. Ideally, a specialist archaeological photographer should be on site throughout the excavation. On smaller excavations this role may be combined with others on the excavation. It is essential, however, that one person has responsibility for the site photography, the equipment, film processing and record keeping: only in this way can consistency be maintained. If no specialist archaeological photographer is available, a photographer without archaeological training can be used, but they will require continuous advice as to what is required archaeologically. An archaeologist without photographic training may, of course, produce even worse results.

The photographic record of an archaeological excavation should start with general photographs of the site before work begins, together with details of any archaeological features visible. These should be taken in the same way as field survey photographs (described in Chapter Four). As with field survey photography, the basic record should be in black-and-white, with colour slides for lectures and publication. Colour prints should be restricted to temporary record and exhibitions. Each stage of the excavation should then be photographed, and each context and group of related contexts photographed for permanent record.

Some archaeologists separate photographs for record from photographs for publication; this sort of division is often ill-advised. In many cases the distinction is not always clear during the excavation, and a roughly-cleaned context photographed for record may be the context you finally wish to publish. It is generally better to take all photographs to publication standard. On a well-run excavation this should be no great problem as the site is always kept clean and tidy, but even on the best-run site, some preparation for photography will be required.

M. B. Cookson, in his classic – though now technically very dated book *Photography for archaeologists* considers the importance of "Cleanliness of the subject with a capital C". How this is done depends on the type of site and soil conditions, but it remains the basis of a good archaeological photograph. Firstly, remove everything that does not need to be in the photograph. This includes loose soil, buckets, trowels, shovels and, generally, people. However, occasionally, on a big site, carefully placed people may both aid visualization of scale and also add interest.

The context to be photographed should then be well cleaned, together with the whole area to be included in the shot. If the site is difficult to keep permanently clean, for example leaves or dust are constantly blowing onto it, it is well worth defining the actual area for detailed cleaning by viewing it through the viewfinder of the camera. Do not, however, leave the camera set up or dust may ruin it. The area to be photographed should then be cleaned from the centre outwards, or from one side to the other. Stiff brushing is often good for masonry or hard surfaces, but skimming with a trowel is better for soils, particularly damp soils, as brushing will smear different colours.

Ideally, edges of contexts should be defined simply by cleaning, and then colour differences enhanced by spraying with water and using appropriate colour-enhancing filters. Some archaeologists, however, define contexts by differential digging, lowering the top fill of a pit by a centimetre or two, for example. Cutting lines between layers in sections, however, should probably be avoided as it makes any re-interpretation from photographs very difficult. A possible exception could be the junction between fills in a pit or ditch and the natural bedrock. Slightly under-cutting this junction does make the shape of the fill clearer (Cookson 1954, Plate 2). Contrast is, however, better emphasized by dampening the soil and using appropriate filters. The soil should be dampened using a very fine spray of the type often used in gardens, but take great care. If too much water is applied, colours may merge and if applied too violently, the splash effect may mask all contrast. For publication the whole area to be photographed should be sprayed, although for lecturing with colour slides some differential spraying, for example just of the context under consideration, may be justifiable though you could be accused of 'faking' (Fig. 7.8)!

Filters are most important for black-and-white photography, as they can be used to accentuate contrast. Basically, a filter of a given colour will make colours on the opposite side of the spectrum appear darker, and will make its own colour appear lighter. Blue filters darken reds and yellows but lighten blue. Green filters darken reds and oranges but lighten green. Deep yellow filters darken blues but lighten yellow and orange, while red filters darken blues and greens but lighten red and orange (Dorrell 1989, 47). These filters are, of course, of no use for colour photography. For slight adjustment of colour balance Kodak produce colour correction filters, but generally only ultra-violet or polarizing filters are used to enhance the image of blue sky with white clouds. This may be important for exhibition work or to impress your lecture audience, but will rarely improve the image of the archaeological context itself.

Some form of scale is essential for virtually all photographs. If no scale is used, a small posthole can look like a huge pit when photographed to fill the frame. The scale does, however, only give an approximation due to distortion inherent in the photographic process. The round lens causes distortion and the scale appears smaller the further away the subject is from the camera. Photographed obliquely, a pit is smaller in scale at the top of the photo than where it is closer to the camera at the

Figure 7.8   Spraying a section to enhance colour variation.

bottom of the photo. Scales can therefore never be used to take measurements off a photograph. For that kind of detailed information use the plans and section. Scales should be clear and an appropriate size for the image. Remember it is the context or site you are photographing, so the scale should be clear but not dominant. A good variety of scales is needed for any excavation, varying from 2 m ranging poles, through 40 cm or 50 cm scales, down to 10 cm 5 cm or even smaller (Fig. 7.9). Red-and-white graduations stand out best in colour photographs, but black-and-white are better for monochrome. Ranging poles are normally only red-and-white, so unless you repaint them they will have to do for black-and-white photos.

Some archaeologists like to have an indication of orientation on their photographs, as opposed to simply recording details in the photographic record. If required, it is better to have a scale with a north point laid in the right orientation, than to clutter up the image with a separate scale and north point (Fig. 7.10). A photograph will look even more cluttered if an information board is introduced as well. These are essential for the disorganized field archaeologist, but it is generally better to put all valuable information about site, year, feature number, level, and so on, onto the photographic record sheet rather than try to cram it into the photograph. By the time you have laid out information board, scale and north point, there will not be much room left in the frame for the context itself! If information boards are considered essential, at least combine the scale into one edge and perhaps lay the board oriented north–south.

When photographing sections especially, although also most contexts, the scale looks much better if parallel to the frame of your photograph either vertically or

Figure 7.9   Ranging-pole scale.

Figure 7.10   North-point scale.

horizontally. To achieve this effect do not try to use a plumb-bob or spirit level, as distortion means that your frame edges are very rarely vertical or horizontal. The effect should be achieved by looking through your view finder and having someone else move the scale until it appears vertical or horizontal. Do not worry that in reality the scale may be 30° or more off vertical; it will produce a much better-looking photograph than one with scales at crazy-looking angles.

The basic photographic record should be produced on black-and-white film and colour slide, but polaroid, digital and video cameras all have their place. Instant polaroid photos can be produced immediately on site, so can be annotated as part of the working record. This may be useful where time is short, as on an emergency salvage project or to aid report preparation, but the life of polaroid photographs is uncertain and they should be used without delay, and never as a primary record.

Digital cameras and video are widely used on archaeological projects but the quality, unless you can afford top-of-the-range equipment, can rarely match traditional photography. Their importance, however, lies more in the realms of data storage, manipulation and electronic publication (see Chapter Ten) than the actual quality of the image. Video is still generally used to record how a site is dug rather than to record individual contexts which, as discrete static entities, are better recorded by conventional photography. Video can be used very much as a diary or aid to memory when producing excavation reports.

Recording the image you have created is almost as important as creating it in the first place. For video, a spoken commentary can be used, perhaps with information boards relating to specific contexts. For still photography, a detailed photographic record is required even if information boards are used. Each film must be numbered and then each roll has a separate photographic record sheet. This should include basic information common to the whole roll and then single-frame information. General information includes camera type, roll number, film type, film speed (DIN/ASA), sheet number, date started, date finished and date processed. Each frame should then have its own information recorded in columns including frame number, subject, context number, direction viewed from, date, time, exposure, lens and photographer's initials. To make sure films are not muddled during the processing stage, basic information like site name and film number could be put on an information board and photographed as frame one. The basic information is therefore always with the negatives, regardless of future labelling.

In the past it was normally the practice on large excavations for the site photographer to process films either on site or at least close by. This had the clear advantage that the whole process, from taking the photograph to final print, was under the control of the field project. Contexts could be left untouched on site until the photographs were confirmed to be satisfactory. The whole process could be done within hours. If working away from any population centre, a field processing laboratory is possibly still essential, but generally most towns worldwide have good local commercial laboratories and these are increasingly used by field archaeologists. It remains important, however, to get films developed quickly so that any faults of camera, photographer, film or processing can be rectified by re-photographing the context or area.

It is clearly better if resources and personnel are available at least to develop black-and-white films on site. The quality of the photos is established at once; the printing can come later. A temporary dark room can be established in any available room that can be light- and dust-proofed. This can be done using black plastic sheeting, although ventilation often creates a problem. A minimum of two benches, one for dry work, the other for wet, are needed. For developing, a ready supply of clean water close by is essential; for more than developing, electricity and running water are required (Dorrell 1989).

Basic equipment for developing black-and-white films includes developing tanks, developer, thermometer, plastic measures and funnels, a timing clock, a litre-graduated plastic bucket and drying clips. If your budget runs to it, a drying cabinet is a useful investment, otherwise a dust-free drying area must be created (Dorrell 1989).

Colour films are rarely processed in on-site dark rooms, but are generally sent as quickly as possible to commercial processing laboratories. Although this creates the risk of faults not being revealed until the excavation has progressed, colour photographs are generally considered less important than the black-and-white primary site archive photographs. In fact with modern films, cameras and a reasonably competent photographer there is little likelihood of finding yourself with no usable colour photographs.

The finds record

The finds record overlaps with the written, drawn and photographic record, but is perhaps best considered as a record in its own right. This is the site record covering all elements of the site that are removed, so it includes artefacts, ecofacts and environmental samples. Basically, this record includes no quantification or analysis, but in practice there may be an advantage in undertaking extra work on particular classes of material, like plain roof-tiles, so that they can be discarded on site. This could save huge amounts of time and money.

The location of artefacts and ecofacts can be recorded in two basic ways: either by context or by specific location. To record the exact position of every artefact and ecofact on a site when huge numbers are present is generally not practical, and is only really worth considering when there is good evidence that the objects are still in their area of primary use (Chapter Two). Redeposited rubbish generally needs only to be recorded by context. Specific rare objects may, however, also be worth locating precisely. Such objects are generally called 'special' or 'small' finds. General finds and special finds are treated differently from their moment of location, and each type has its own record.

General finds are grouped together by context on site. They are either put in a clearly-labelled finds tray or finds bag. The minimum of information recorded on the label should be the site name and/or number and the context number. If bags are used on site, each bag should be given a discrete bag number. If bagged from trays at the end of the excavation of a context or the working day, the bag should be numbered then. This is the only way to be certain that no bags of finds have been lost. When a numbered finds bag is issued it should be recorded on a Finds Register. This Finds Register should record bag number, context number, grid reference from site grid to locate the context, date, brief field comments (if required), and then some indication of the range of material in the bag, for example, pottery, stone or bone.

Special finds are kept separate from the moment of their location. If possible they should be left in place in the ground until a special finds bag has been labelled and the Special Finds Register completed. The bag requires to be labelled with, at a minimum, the site name and the small finds number (issued centrally from the Special Finds Register). The Special Finds Register records the special finds number, the context number, broad object type (for example, metal or coin), the site grid reference locating its horizontal location, and the level to locate its depth in relation to the site datum (and ultimately Ordnance datum). If recorded on a drawing or site photographs, cross-references can be made to drawing and photograph numbers. There may also be a section for general description of the object, whether it requires conservation, and the form-filler's initials and date. The last two enable mistakes to be followed up. Environmental samples have their own Environmental Sample Register, with each sample being given a sample number but then recorded in a similar way to special finds.

The aim of on-site finds processing and recording is essentially to enable finds to be got from the site to the post-excavation laboratory or workshop in a safe way so that each object or sample, or group of objects or samples, can be readily located. They should also be in a suitable state for the post-excavation work to begin. Generally, but not always, the excavation stage of a project has more available labour than the post-excavation stage. If this is the case it is essential to get as much of the basic processing as possible done on site. This will include finds washing and marking (to be considered further in Chapter Eight).

CHAPTER EIGHT

Post-fieldwork planning, processing and finds analysis

Post-fieldwork planning

Many field archaeologists attempt to go straight into the post-excavation stage of their fieldwork without considering fully what they are really letting themselves in for. Post-excavation work and publication preparation takes far longer, and is often more expensive in terms of time and money, than the actual excavation. At a general level, the field project design should have considered the post-excavation and publication stages of the project (Chapter One) but detailed post-excavation project-planning cannot be undertaken until the excavation is complete. Only then will you know fully the range, quality and quantity of data recovered.

The first stage of a post-excavation programme is therefore to assess what you have recovered, its potential importance, and what questions you want to ask of it. On the basis of this, appropriate forms of analysis can be considered. Most of the questions will, of course, have been formulated at the start of the project and then perhaps modified during the fieldwork phase. Obviously it would be too late at the post-fieldwork phase, for example, to decide to Carbon–14 date a particular context if samples had not been taken in the field. Likewise it would be impossible to ask many questions about the economy of the site if organic remains had not been recovered by flotation from suitable contexts. The post-excavation questioning therefore starts with a review of your primary research questions and whether the data obtained are suitable to answer these questions. Unexpected data may also have been recovered. For these data, new questions may be formulated.

If finds washing and marking have not been done on site, this should be done as soon as objects arrive at your home-base or museum. If soil is allowed to dry hard onto objects, it often becomes very difficult to remove. Most artefacts and many ecofacts, like animal bones and shells, should be cleaned before they move into the analysis stage, and certainly before they are finally stored in a museum or elsewhere. Pottery and stone artefacts, together with bones and shells, can be carefully washed in clean water using a soft toothbrush. Potsherds should be scanned for food residues or friable paint before washing. If either is present, it is better not to wash them but carefully pack them in plastic bubble wrap in suitably-sized plastic boxes.

Washed artefacts should be clearly marked with at least the site name (in abbreviated form) or site number, and the context number. Marking is done using a mapping or other suitable pen with black or white Indian ink. If the surface of the object is friable, use a dab of acetone (nail varnish remover) to create a surface on which you can write. The numbers can then be protected by applying another dab of acetone over them. Care should be taken only to do this on very dry pottery: water evaporating out of the sherd can lift off the acetone, and the numbers with it. Most stone artefacts, including flint or chert tools, can also be safely washed and marked.

Metals and most organic materials, other than strong bone and shell, should not be washed. Most metals, other than gold, are not stable and as soon as their environment is changed through excavation, will rapidly deteriorate. Exposure to the air and moisture will result in iron, for example, corroding rapidly; to introduce water through washing is, therefore, clearly a bad mistake. Strong metal can be carefully 'dry cleaned' with a soft brush, but fragile objects or those of greater archaeological significance like coins or brooches, are best left to the conservation laboratory. Metalwork should then be stored in hard polythene boxes with silica gel to keep the interior of the box dry. Make sure the boxes are fully labelled with site name or number, and context number. Metal objects themselves should not be written on.

Carbonized materials like charcoal are generally best kept dry, but in general organic materials should be kept in conditions similar to those in which they were found. Damp seeds are best keep damp, and waterlogged wood should always be kept wet. To stop it going mouldy, introduce a one per cent fungicide solution.

The site records also need to be checked and organized before the full post-excavation project can commence. All site drawings should be checked and put in order. This is a double check, as plans and sections must always have been checked on site. Drawing number, title, scale and north point are key elements to check. Security copies should be made. Drawings can be stored flat in portfolio cases during the post-excavation stage. The photographic record should also be put in order, making sure every photo is developed and labelled from the site photographic record. A set of prints can be made available for the post-excavation stage, while negatives should be stored in the dark in polyester pockets to protect them and keep off dust.

Once the finds, and the written, drawn and photographic records, are organized and readily accessible, a post-excavation programme can be prepared. Once again time, money and resources are involved so a project management diagram, like a Gantt chart, may be a useful tool to aid the process. For a complex post-excavation programme, the PERT may be more appropriate (Chapter One). The aim of the post-excavation programme is firstly to produce a basic site archive, and secondly from this to select elements of significance for widespread dissemination, either on the printed page or electronically. At the end of the day, the final result of any field project must be some form of published report. As General Pitt-Rivers said in 1898: "A discovery dates only from the time of the record of it, and not from the time of it being found in the soil" (Pitt-Rivers 1898).

It is essential to realize from the start of a post-excavation programme that not everything recovered from an excavation is of equal value in terms of advancement of knowledge about the past. Just because the site excavated has produced huge amounts of pottery does not necessarily mean that this is the area of finds research where most time and money should be concentrated. The pottery may be of such a common type that further detailed study may provide little new information. Such material could be studied at a minimal level and archived for future research when perhaps new methods, approaches, or techniques have been developed. Alternatively, samples could be selected for specific analyses that had perhaps not been formerly applied to an otherwise common type.

For practical reasons it is generally better to separate all classes of material into discrete groups for analysis, particularly if specialists in a specific material or artefact type are involved. When the final report is prepared for publication however, the *site* is what is perhaps more significant than specific types of material. Activity areas involving different materials, or pit groups containing a variety of materials grouped together in a deposit, should be regrouped to show associations which may have had great significance in the past. So although the next section considers discrete types of material, it is their association with other materials, and how and where they were deposited, that may be as important as a detailed analysis of their chemistry or typology.

Finds analysis

Pottery

Once the knowledge of how to make pottery arrives in an area, it is from then on often the dominant find on archaeological excavations. For this reason more detail is given here than for other classes of material. How one deals with the analysis of a pottery assemblage should be based very much on questions to be asked of it and the context of its discovery. An out-of-town rubbish dump will provide a different type of information to potsherds trampled into the mud floor of a house where the pots were used. Sherds from both contexts can, however, be used for dating. Date your potsherds and you at least have a *terminus post quem* for the date of the deposit in which they were found. Prior to the arrival of Carbon–14 dating, pottery was often used to provide the most reliable chronologies in a region, although as in the case of British prehistory, these chronologies were often too short.

The second major form of information that pottery can provide is about movement of the pots themselves. If you can demonstrate that the clay or materials added to the clay (fillers) used in the pot have a particular geographic source, and the pot is found away from that source, then it is obvious that it must have been taken there, perhaps through trade, gift exchange or movement of the pot's owners. Dating and distribution studies have always dominated archaeological studies of ceramics, but equally important is the function of the pottery in its living context, and what it may indicate about the organization of settlements, and the social, economic, ritual and symbolic life of past societies. Before these considerations are made, the pots, or more likely the sherds from the pots, have to be classified in some way.

The three key elements of pottery analysis are fabric, form and decoration. The form of a pot consists of four main elements: its base, body, neck and rim. If a

Figure 8.1 Thin-sectioning laboratory.

whole pot is found, all four elements can be used to describe its form; but most pottery from archaeological sites is found as sherds, so division by fabric is often considered the most valuable first stage in sorting pottery. It is rare for a single pot to be made of different fabrics, although this could of course happen, particularly with hand-made pottery. The fabric of the pot, sometimes known as its paste, although this term has a more restricted use among potters (Rhodes 1989), consists of the clay matrix and inclusions, tempering or filler. 'Inclusions', 'tempering' or 'filler' are all terms used for material of little or no plasticity, added to the clay body to control its shrinkage during drying and firing.

The first stage of fabric analysis involves the visual inspection of a fresh break. This may require snipping the sherd with pliers. Some inclusions are readily identifiable by eye or under a binocular microscope, while others may require simple tests, or cutting of thin sections and examination using a polarizing microscope. If inclusions are of a reasonable size, fabrics containing grog (ground down old pots), flint, shell or quartz can be readily identified. Shell, and other calcareous inclusions like limestone, can be confirmed using a ten per cent solution of hydrochloric acid, while a magnet can confirm the presence of iron compounds. Many rock fragments added to clay by potters cannot be simply identified by eye, so a sample may be needed for analysis.

Petrological analysis requires thin-section samples: to make these, firstly a slice is cut off the sherd using the diamond-edged blade of a stone-cutting saw (Fig. 8.1). The resulting edge is then polished with successively finer particles of corundum: 220 grits, 600 grits and 1,000 grits per cubic millimetre, on flat wet glass surfaces.

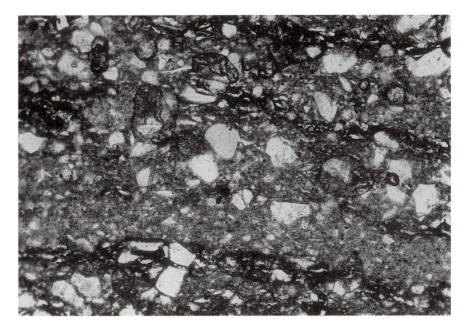

Figure 8.2   Ceramic thin section (section and photo: Lys Drewett).

The corundum particles are then washed off and any that have worked their way into the fabric are removed by immersion in an ultrasonic bath. After careful drying, a glass slide is attached to the clean sherd section using hot-cure resin. When the resin is hard, the sherd is mechanically ground to a thickness of approximately 0.01 mm. This section is then hand-polished with corundum particles to a thickness of 0.003 mm, the optimum thickness at which most minerals are rendered translucent or transparent, allowing their optical properties to be studied. There are now also semi-automated systems for grinding and polishing. Finally the new surface is cleaned and sealed with a glass slide cover using resin, which also fills any voids in the specimen to maximise clarity of vision. The slide is then studied under a petrological microscope which has a polarizing light source with a rotating stage. A good knowledge of optical mineralogy (Kerr 1977) is needed to identify the characteristics of different minerals under polarized light (Fig. 8.2).

Colour and hardness may also be considered when dividing sherds by fabric. Both characteristics are determined more by firing conditions than by the clay or inclusions used by the potter. Colour is best described in relation to a standard colour system rather than using terms to modify basic colours like reddish-brown which, being non-precise, will mean something different to everyone using it. The most commonly used colour system is the American Munsell system which uses colour charts. Each colour is considered to have three variables: hue, intensity and saturation. The hues are the basic colours of the spectrum. Each colour varies in chroma or saturation from black or grey to a clear, pure colour. It also varies in intensity or value from dark to light. A colour can therefore be described by

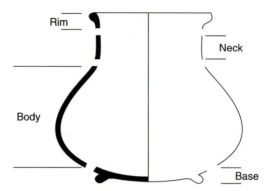

Figure 8.3   Pot elements: base, body, neck and rim.

Munsell chart page number and colour (for example, 10YR, that is, page ten, colour yellow-red) followed by a value number (for example, 5) separated from a chroma number (for example, 8) by a slash. A unique colour description to which anyone with a Munsell colour chart can refer would be expressed as, for example 10YR 5/8. A colour may be recorded for both the core of the sherd and its surfaces if they differ.

Hardness also needs a standard if it is to mean anything comparatively. Moh's scale, devised by the German mineralogist Friedrich Moh, is a universal standard. Moh divided hardness of minerals into a scale of ten:

1 Talc
2 Gypsum
3 Calcite
4 Fluorite
5 Apatite
6 Orthoclase
7 Quartz
8 Topaz
9 Sapphire
10 Diamond

For pottery hardness, 1–2 on Moh's scale can be scratched by the fingernail so are considered soft. 3–5 cannot be scratched with the fingernail, so are considered hard, while 6–10 are very hard as they cannot be scratched with a steel knife. From the fabric analysis, a type series of fabrics can be established against which new sherds can be compared.

Once sherds have been divided by fabric they can then be divided by form. In sherds this includes four main elements: base, body, neck and rim (Fig. 8.3). Of these generally, but not always, the rim is the most diagnostic, and undecorated body sherds are the least diagnostic. The diagnostic value of necks and bases depends very much on period and geographical origin of the assemblage under study. The bases of early neolithic pottery in Britain for example (they are all round-based) are not particularly diagnostic, while chronologically significant changes are made to bases in dynastic China.

Rims are one of the most visible elements of a pot in everyday use, so it is hardly surprising that potters varied their forms in every conceivable way. Rims can be made – and therefore classified into – a wide variety of forms, from plain to thickened, vertical, flaring, incurving, T-shaped, pendant or horizontal. Likewise bases can be divided into round, flat, concave, disk, pointed, and a variety of other regional forms (Joukowsky 1980). Individual body and neck sherds are often difficult to give a form to, but if a whole pot is present it can be given a form description based on geometric solids like spherical, ovoid or cylindrical (Shepard 1956). From these shapes a type-series for the assemblage should be established.

The third key element in pottery analysis is a consideration and classification of decoration. The damp surfaces of newly-made pottery before firing are an ideal medium for decoration by grooving, combing, incising and impressing. Fired surfaces can be painted, while glazes can be used to fire a coating of coloured glass onto the pot's surface. Alternatively, moulded pieces of clay can be added to the surface prior to firing. All these techniques of decoration can be applied in a variety of shapes, some as pure decoration, others providing particular meaning to the people using the pottery. In analysing a decorated pottery assemblage, a type-series of decorative techniques and designs should be established.

The first stage of the analysis of any pottery assemblage therefore involves creating a type-series of fabrics, forms and decoration. Clearly a single sherd will have a fabric and a form and may have decoration, so the three elements can be combined on a single record form to create a type-series for the whole assemblage (Orton, Tyers and Vince 1993).

The second stage involves attempting to establish how much of which types of pottery are present in a particular assemblage. This involves some form of counting or quantification. The basic problem with this is that archaeologists generally work with sherds, while people in the past used pots. Ideally archaeologists should want to know how many pots of a particular type are present, not how many sherds. However, more often than not, archaeologists have to compare quantities of sherds of different types between areas on a site, between sites, or between periods.

One of the easiest ways of quantifying a pottery assemblage is to count the number of sherds of each type defined in the type series. This will give a rough idea of, say, coarse ware sherds compared with finely decorated sherds, an observation that could probably be made without counting! The problem of counting is that pots of different types break up differently, so sherd counts are biased when attempting to establish proportions of different types. There is also the problem that the degree of fragmentation varies between assemblages (Orton 1975).

An alternative way of quantifying pottery is to weigh sherds of different type. The problem here is that heavy types of pottery, for example flint-gritted storage vessels, will be over-represented in comparison with lighter types, like grass-tempered wares. Weighing sherds, therefore, also introduces bias, but at least the bias is the same between assemblages. In fact, although problems in quantification by weight are well known, it remains a popular method (Orton, Tyers and Vince 1993).

Given that people in the past used pots rather than sherds, it would clearly be more satisfactory to quantify numbers of pots of different types rather than numbers of sherds. Without whole or fully-reconstructed pots, this can only ever be an estimate. A very rough estimate can be made by grouping together all sherds apparently from the same pot, that is, sherds that appear to be from the same pot but do not actually fit together. This can be used to suggest the minimum number of pots present of a particular type. This type of estimate is so rough that it is of uncertain value. An alternative is to weigh whole pots of each type (if they are available) and divide the weight of sherds of a particular type by the weight of a whole pot of the same type. This again gives a minimum number of pots present.

If the assemblage consists of wheel-turned pottery with round rims, an estimated vessel-equivalent (*eve*) can be calculated (Orton, Tyers and Vince 1993). This involves measuring rim diameters of pots of the same fabric and form using a rim diameter chart. Each rim sherd will be a fraction of a full rim (360°). Therefore by measuring the proportion of the circumference formed by each rim sherd of the same circumference, adding all these together and dividing the total by 360°, you have estimated the minimum number of pots that could be represented (that is, the *eve*). It remains, however, a minimum number – probably many less pots than were actually present in the living context.

Stone

Prior to the introduction of metal, stone was a key tool-making raw material. Its domination in some archaeological assemblages is, however, partly a result of its largely indestructible nature. Tools made of organic material only survive in special circumstances. Stone was also used in the past for a variety of purposes other than making tools. We will start, however, by looking at the analysis of stone tools.

Stone tools can be broadly divided into those that are chipped or flaked and those that are pecked and/or ground. Flaked tools may, however, also be ground or polished, like some neolithic flint axes in Britain. Where available, rocks that fracture concoidally like flint, chert, obsidian and quartz are favoured for flaking, while igneous, some volcanic and some sedimentary rocks are best pecked or ground. The first stage in the analysis of stone tools is to identify the stone used. Broad identification can often be done with a very basic geological knowledge. Flint, obsidian or quartz are readily identifiable, while igneous and sedimentary rocks will require more specialized knowledge. Cutting thin sections, as done for pottery sherds, may be needed to identify rocks petrologically under a polarizing microscope.

Having identified the raw materials being used, the primary division of lithic material is into pieces that have been used, and waste material resulting from making those worked tools. This division requires some basic knowledge of how the tools are made. We will consider chipped and flake tools first. These are generally made of silica like flint, chert, obsidian and quartz, and have a concoidal fracture. Hit these rocks at the right angle and the pressure passes through them as a series of waves, rather like dropping a pebble into water. The flake which breaks off will show these rings or waves radiating out from the point of percussion.

Below this point is the bulb of percussion and often a bulbar scar and fissures (Crabtree 1972). Flakes made with a hard hammer (stone) can be separated from those made with a soft hammer (bone or wood). The angle and depth of flake scar is much less when a soft hammer is used. Other waste material or debitage includes the cores from which flakes were struck, except in industries where the core was then made into a tool.

Analysis of waste material or debitage is important, as not only can it provide information about reduction sequences, but it will also provide information about what tools may have been made on the site, perhaps to be used and lost elsewhere. As with pottery, quantification is important, with counts of different types by context or period. Measurements may also be taken to chart technological change through time. Length, width, thickness and flake angle are commonly-taken measurements, but do this only if you have a particular aim in view. Measurement for measurement's sake is a waste of time, even if it does make your final report look 'scientific'.

The actual tools produced by chipping or flaking were clearly more important to the people making them than the waste material they generated. Tools should be classified by form and, where possible, by function. Flaked axes, arrowheads, scrapers and sickles can be classified as such, divided into types and counted. The real function of some tools is not always clear, so terms like 'biface' (a tool flaked on two sides) or 'uniface' (flaked on one side) are used. Many areas or periods in the world now have agreed flaked tool typologies and labels. To aid comparison, where possible, it is better to use these than introduce new terms, unless the agreed name is demonstrably inappropriate.

Pecked and ground stone tools generally do not produce classifiable debitage. Pecking may produce tiny chips, but grinding generates dust lost to the archaeologist unless production is on a big enough scale. Analysis therefore rests with the tools themselves. As with flint tools, function and form should be the basis of classification, together with the identification of the stone. Axes and adzes dominate most polished stone tool assemblages, with many other types having a regional or chronological distribution.

Stone is not used only to make tools, so all other utilized or foreign stone recovered from an excavation requires analysis. As with stone tools, geological identification is the first stage of analysis. Building stone is generally identified on site and then discarded, unless in the form of carved architectural fragments which may, on stylistic grounds, be as closely datable as pottery. Chips of stone should be carefully examined to locate areas of polishing or grinding, which could indicate they are from a quern or whetstone. There may also be just bits of stone clearly foreign to the site. If not in a glacial or riverine situation, they perhaps represent stones brought onto the site for a variety of reasons. Their significance will vary from site to site, but they may have served as hearthstones, as filler for pottery, or they could have had some symbolic value or been playthings for children.

Metals

Metal objects are much less common on archaeological sites than either pottery or stone. This is partly due to the fact that in the first place metal was probably much less common, but also it can be recycled and, even when buried, most soil conditions will reduce nearly all metals to a corroded mass, making identification difficult or impossible. Only gold, one of the rarest of all metals, survives well in most soils.

The significance of metal finds, and therefore how much effort is worth expending on their analysis, depends very much on the date and context of the find. A bronze age axe perhaps warrants more time than a corroded mass of eighteenth-century nails. The importance of the nails may simply be that they are nails, present in the context in which they were found.

The first stage of analysis is, therefore, to establish what the metal is and what the object was. Visual inspection can usually identify the metal as iron (badly rusted), copper or copper alloy (green corrosion), gold, lead or silver. Alloys are more of a problem, and require laboratory analysis to identify trace elements. Optical emission spectrometry, atomic absorption spectrometry, or x-ray fluorescence can all be used to establish the composition of an alloy.

If not badly corroded, identification of the object may be straightforward: an axe, a knife or a coin. If corroded, the object may be unidentifiable by surface observation. Often the object survives in a casing of corrosion, so can be revealed by x-ray, which is far quicker and cheaper than full conservation. Fragments of objects are, however, more difficult to identify except by a specialist in the field. If metal appears in any quantity, types should be defined and numbers counted by context.

Organic artefacts

In most periods in the past, many artefacts were made of organic materials like wood, skin, bark, feathers and bone. The preservation of organic materials requires specific burial conditions, so most archaeological sites reveal no organic materials unless the objects are carbonized. Except on waterlogged or desiccated sites, one must presume a strong bias against organic finds and in favour of inorganic materials like stone and pottery.

Wooden objects will survive only if waterlogged, desiccated or carbonized, although an indication of wood may also survive when buried against metal objects, as the corrosion products can replace the wood. Most organic materials require conservation before analysis can begin. Until recently the most common form of wood conservation was to replace the water content of the object with a solution of polyethylene glycol (PEG), but now freeze-drying is often used for smaller artefacts (Dowman 1970).

Having stabilized the wooden object, the first stage of analysis is to identify the wood. This may involve cutting a cube out of the object to examine transverse, radial longitudinal and tangential longitudinal sections (Dimbleby 1978). This enables the cellular structure of the wood to be examined under a lens or microscope (Fig. 8.4). Each species of wood has its own structure (Jane 1956). The next stage of analysis is a consideration of how the object was made, by identifying traces of cutting, scraping, carving, polishing and – in later periods – planing. Finally the nature and possible use of the wooden object should be determined if possible. Some objects like bows, arrow shafts, pins and axe handles are reasonably easy

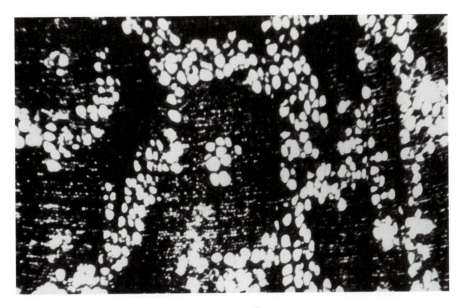

Figure 8.4   Cellular structure of wood under a microscope.

to identify while others, especially in fragmentary form, require specialized know-ledge (Taylor 1981).

Bone artefacts survive in a wider range of soil conditions than wooden ones. Bone consists of a combination of calcium and collagen. The collagen element survives well in waterlogged acidic conditions, while the calcium element survives in many dry calcareous soils. As with wood, the post-excavation analysis should proceed from conservation (if required) to species identification, manufacturing process, and functional identification. Other organic materials like basketry, textiles, skin, bark and feather artefacts are rare finds and generally require specialist con-servation and identification.

Artefacts of other materials like glass, amber and ivory all require specialist conservation treatment prior to analysis by finds specialists in these fields.

Finds analysis: ecofacts

The analysis of ecofacts and environmental samples at the post-excavation stage is usually undertaken by specialists in these fields rather than by the field archae-ologist who directed the excavation, although not infrequently the latter may have expertise in these areas. The field archaeologist's role may therefore be restricted to safely packaging and delivering samples to the specialist, providing detailed con-textual information, and incorporating the results of the analyses into the final archive and published report.

The term 'ecofact' is generally taken to cover all non-artefactual materials which have been modified by humans, and so have cultural relevance. This would cover food refuse like animal bones and shells from shellfish, but also pollen, land snails and humanly-modified soils. I propose in this section, however, to separate evidence that provides economic data from that which essentially provides environmental data, although clearly the two overlap and are interrelated.

Bones   Bones usually survive well in soils that are not too acidic, but they must have been buried fairly quickly to avoid attrition by scavengers and natural erosion through weathering. The collagen element of bone will, however, survive well in acidic waterlogged conditions, as in the case of the bog people of Europe. Food refuse bones from excavations will probably have been recovered in slightly different ways. Bird and fish bones require fine mesh sieving (1 mm) while large mammal bones are generally recovered through trowelling, perhaps with coarse mesh sieving (1 cm). Bones should be carefully cleaned with water and a soft brush prior to analysis. Fragile bones may require dry brushing or consolidation with a dilute solution of polyvinyl acetate (PVA).

The first stage of bone analysis is to identify what species, and what part of the body, each bone comes from. This is best done by use of a comparative reference collection, although a start can often be made by consulting illustrations (Ryder 1968). Fragmented bones, particularly shaft splinters, are naturally more difficult to identify than whole bones. A proportion of any bone assemblage may not be identifiable to species level.

Having identified the bones to species and to part of the skeleton, the bone assemblage should be quantified. As with pots and potsherds, the archaeologist should be more interested in how many whole animals are represented than how many bones are represented. A simple count of the number of identified species can give a very biased picture, although this may be appropriate if very small numbers are present. Generally a count of minimum number of individuals (MNI) is undertaken to compare abundance of species between contexts, periods and sites. The minimum number of individuals is calculated by counting only those bones which appear once in an animal, like a left scapula. If 100 left ox scapulae are present, the minimum number of oxen present is 100. This can then be translated into protein available to the people herding or hunting the various species by calculating meat weight represented by each animal. Zooarchaeology is now a significant subdiscipline of archaeology, so more complex analyses are generally beyond the expertise of the field archaeologist (Chaplin 1971). Sites crucial for the understanding of animal domestication, for example, would almost certainly have involved a zooarchaeologist in the initial planning, as well as the field element and post-excavation stages of a project.

Shells   The preliminary analysis of shells from archaeological excavations can be approached in a similar way to the analysis of bones, although the excavation of shell middens requires rigorous sampling in the field to keep the job to manageable proportions. Shells survive remarkably well and, if middened, can even survive on quite acid soils which would otherwise dissolve calcareous material.

Sites of many periods, particularly near coastlines or rivers, produce shells mixed with other domestic rubbish. Care should be taken to attempt to sort out shells which could be food debris, shells which have been utilized (some after the shell-fish has been eaten), and shells that arrived on site in other ways. A site on a sand bar, for example, will have natural residual shells. Shells may have been collected dead from beaches and brought back as toys or trinkets; others may have been carried onto the site by hermit crabs. Worn or abraded shells should generally be excluded from dietary calculations. In fact shellfish, except perhaps the conch (*Strombus gigas*) or giant clam (*Tridacna gigas*) provide surprisingly little in the way of calories, so are unlikely ever to have been a significant contribution to diet except in periods or areas of hardship. Often shellfish are simply an additional luxury, as in the case of oysters in Roman Britain.

The analysis of small shell assemblages involves firstly identification of species, preferably from a comparative reference collection, but otherwise from a range of well illustrated books available for some regions of the world (for example, Humfrey 1975). Minimum numbers of individuals (MNI) can then be calculated in a way similar to bones. Each gastropod has only one apex, while all left valves of bivalves can be counted. It is also possible in some parts of the world to establish the time of year that shells were harvested by counting growth lines. The thicker lines grow in the summer while thin lines indicate winter growth.

Seeds and other plant remains Plants were, and still are, a major form of human food and yet there is a strong bias against their remains surviving in the archaeological record. Plant remains survive only if waterlogged, desiccated or carbonized. Carbonized plant remains are the most common on archaeological sites. The fact that most plants remains survive only if burnt inevitably introduces bias into the archaeological record. Certain plant remains are more likely to get burnt than others. Perhaps the carbonized barley found in a later bronze age pit at Black Patch, East Sussex (Drewett 1982) was being prepared for brewing. Of the 21 kg found in Pit 3, 96 per cent was barley while only 4 per cent was wheat. In fact more wheat could have been grown on the farm, but most was perhaps successfully ground for flour. There is also the problem that some plants produce thousands of small seeds, while others produce few, bigger ones, so simply count-ing or weighing plant remains may in no way represent the relative importance of different species.

Seeds must, however, first be identified to species level. This is done under a microscope and, as with bones and shells, compared with a reference collection. With small numbers of seeds, results should perhaps only be expressed in terms of presence or absence, but with larger assemblages quantification is generally under-taken by weight or minimum number of individuals. Explanatory text, however, must emphasize that these figures may be strongly biased by a variety of factors and do not necessarily represent real proportions of plants grown and/or consumed.

The other most common plant on archaeological sites are charcoal. This pro-vides both evidence of human use, for example for firewoods, but also gives hints at the local environment. Humans will, however, select woods, so the use of char-coal in environmental reconstruction is limited. Unless large quantities of charcoal are present, it is probably best to identify it to species level (or sometimes only genus) in the same way as for a wood sample (see above) and then simply express in presence or absence terms. Counting or weighing charcoal is of dubious value, as one burnt apple branch can produce thousands of charcoal fragments while it may in fact not have been the most common species used on site.

Finds analysis: environmental samples

The analysis of environmental samples collected from archaeological sites and their environs requires specialist knowledge, and generally a considerable outlay in terms of time and money. It is always best to involve the environmental archaeologist from the initial planning of the project right through to analysis and final publication. What environmental indicators survive on a particular site depends entirely on its location, whether the soil is acid or alkaline, wet or dry, and its post-depositional history. Rarely do all types of environmental data survive on one site, although they may survive within a varied local environ (Evans 1978).

Pollen analysis   Pollen derives from all flowering plants and will generally survive well in any conditions lacking aerobic bacteria. It survives best in peat bogs, but also survives well in many other archaeological contexts, like land surfaces buried under round barrows or other earthworks, damp ditches or pits, and well fills. Samples are usually taken in columns at regular intervals, and immediately sealed to prevent contamination from modern pollen (Fig. 5.12). Each sample, or part of it, is examined under a microscope to extract and identify the pollen present. This is a long, laborious task, particularly as pollen can often be identified only to family or at least genus level rather than to species (Dimbleby 1978).

The pollen grains of each plant are counted and then expressed as a percentage of the total number of grains in the particular sample. These data are then usually illustrated graphically to show variations through the stratigraphic sequence sampled. Although the identification of pollen is essentially a mechanical process, comparing pollen shapes with pollen from known plants, the interpretation of the data requires considerable knowledge of plants and particularly how pollen is dispersed. Wind-dispersed pollen like pine can travel great distances, while insect-dispersed pollen, like lime, is likely to be more local. Some plants are even pollinated by slugs and snails, so their pollen moves only very small distances (Dimbleby 1978).

Land snails   Pollen rarely survives well in alkaline conditions, but fortunately in these areas land molluscs do survive well. These are the snails that live in abundance in many environments. When they die, their shells become incorporated into sediments in the landscape and deposits on archaeological sites. There are many species of land snails and many, but not all, have ecological preferences. Some prefer woodland, others short grass, while some can tolerate arable conditions (Evans 1972). Soil samples are taken from sealed deposits and all the land snails are carefully sieved out using fine mesh laboratory sieves (Fig. 8.5). Samples hand-picked on site are of little use, as it is the percentage of different species that

Figure 8.5   Extracting land snails in an environmental laboratory.

is important, not simply the presence or absence of particularly big shells. Counting is undertaken under a microscope, for many land snails are extremely small. The counting process is basically the same as for marine mollusca. What is important is how many individuals are present, not how many shell fragments. The minimum number of individuals (MNI) is calculated by counting apexes only, as each shell has only one.

The interpretation of land molluscan counts requires detailed knowledge of the habitats of the species involved and their speed and ability to adapt to changing conditions. The results of the analysis are often presented in absolute frequencies and percentage frequencies of different ecological groups, together with explanatory text.

Soils and sediments   The analysis of soils and sediments (soils contain an organic element which can support plant life while sediments are entirely inorganic) can provide considerable information about the environment of a site. The first stage of soil or sediment analysis takes place in the field and involves basic description of colour, texture, consistency and coarse components (Chapter Seven). Far more information can, however, be obtained through laboratory analysis (Cornwall 1958, Limbrey 1975). As with the analysis of all archaeological materials, broad questions will have been formulated at the start of the project, but during the excavation new questions may arise, for example, "is this context a buried soil?".

Techniques of soil and sediment analysis can be broadly divided into physical and chemical methods. Physical methods involve either separating deposits into their constituents and quantifying their size, shape and type, or preparing thin sections of the deposit for study under a microscope. Either way, the aim is to identify elements that may be characteristic of a particular formation process. Rounded particles, for example, may indicate rolling in water, whereas angular particles with limited attrition may indicate colluvial deposits. Mechanical separation of sediments can be undertaken using nests of sieves from, say, 2 mm down to 0.063 mm.

A high percentage of many sediments consists of quartz and other common 'light' (that is, having a specific gravity of less than 2.89) minerals. It is the other 'heavy' minerals that often indicate differences which can help determine the origin of the deposit and how it arrived at the site, so heavy-mineral analysis is often the key physical method applied to sediments. Greater detail of the composition of a soil, and particularly how the various elements present relate to each other, can be obtained by preparing thin sections rather like those prepared for pottery. With soils, however, the sample always has to be consolidated prior to grinding and mounting on a glass slide (Cornwall 1958).

A wide range of optical and other equipment is available for the chemical analysis of soils. However, simply listing chemicals in the soil or a sediment is rarely going to contribute much to the archaeology of a site. Again, specific questions should be asked of specific contexts. For example, is there no burial under this barrow because the pH is too high for the survival of bones, or, does the carbon or phosphate content of this context suggest human activity?

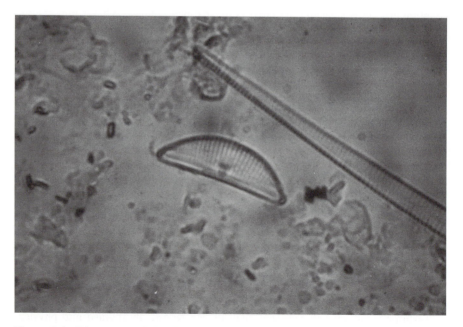

Figure 8.6   Diatom: unicellular algae with environmental preferences.

Other environmental analyses   Although the study of pollen, land snails, soils and sediments are the most commonly used analyses for determining the natural environment of specific archaeological sites, many other plant and animal remains may be analysed to help reconstruct the past environment of an archaeological site. Some, like diatoms, require particular local conditions, others, like phytoliths, are more widespread. Diatoms are unicellular algae which live, and die, in bodies of water (Fig. 8.6). Different species have different ecological preferences, so – as with land snails – they can provide a broad picture of the immediate environment. Phytoliths, the silica element of plant cells, can also be recovered from archaeological deposits and add to our environmental knowledge of a site. Finally, identification of small mammal and rodent bones, worm egg cases, mites and insects can fill out the environmental picture or provide detailed insights into specific contexts on an excavation.

CHAPTER NINE

Interpreting the evidence

Interpretation of the evidence revealed through excavation is not something that happens after the site has been dug and the finds have been analysed. It is an on-going process that takes place throughout the project. Having said that, inevitably interpretations change as new information is recovered, both during the excavation and in the post-excavation and analysis phase. At some stage in the project, however, an interpretation or a range of interpretations for the recovered data has to be decided upon. Raw data is just that. Archaeology is the study of the past *through* the study of material remains, not simply the study *of* material remains.

How one interprets material remains of the past does, of course, depend very much on one's theoretical perspective. The past has gone; we cannot reconstruct it, we can only present our interpretations of it based on the material evidence recovered. The aim of this chapter is to consider the interpretation of elements of *an* archaeological site excavated by a field archaeologist. It does not extend into broader archaeological interpretation of culture history or cultural processes. For this level of interpretation a wide and ever-expanding literature is available (for example, Willey and Phillips 1958, Binford 1983, Hodder 1982, and Shanks and Tilley 1987).

Interpreting the site's environment

To understand how a site may have worked in the past requires some knowledge of the environment in which it existed (Vita-Finzi 1978). The environment in the past may have been very different to the environment today. Clearly, large-scale environmental changes, like the movement of ice sheets and rises or falls in sea level, can dramatically change whole landscapes. Equally, very small-scale changes through human or natural agencies can change local landscapes, both during the life of a site and after its desertion.

Much work has been done on large-scale environmental and climatic change, particularly through the study of foraminifera from deep-sea cores (Butzer 1983). These single-celled organisms have environmental preferences, so as sea levels and the associated salinity fluctuate, so do the ranges of species of foraminifera. Changes in the oxygen isotopes in water as a result of environmental change are also reflected in differences in foraminifera calcium shells. When working on sites of post-glacial date, however, archaeologists are often more involved with the site's local environment.

The area around a site that is perhaps most important for the understanding of the site is the area used by the inhabitants. Defining such an area is naturally fraught with difficulties. Early attempts used ethnographic data to suggest that hunters and foragers generally utilized an area some 10 km in radius from their home-base, while farmers worked closer to home, rarely travelling more than 5 km to work the landscape. Circles were drawn around the site, and resources within the circles calculated, for example the percentage of good arable land (Higgs 1975). It was soon realized, however, that distance was less important than the actual time taken to get to a resource or work area: it takes longer to walk across rough, undulating or densely overgrown land than across level grassland. Circles were modified to produce zones around sites that took two hours to reach (in the case of hunters and foragers) or one hour (in the case of farmers). Although this technique of site catchment analysis gives a good idea of the potential around a site, it is perhaps more important to know what was actually used on-site and the zone of exploitation indicated by 'real' evidence (Flannery 1982).

Having decided upon the area to be considered in determining the local environment, a range of approaches can be brought to bear on the problem of what that environment was like in the past and how it changed through the life of the site. Direct observation of the present local environment is a good starting point. Hills, valleys and the solid geology are unlikely to have changed much in the more recent past. Water sources can however change, with rivers meandering across flood plains and springs drying up through climatic change or even current local water-pumping. The greatest changes will, however, be in the soils, vegetation and local fauna. These are the key areas of investigation when attempting to reconstruct the local environment of a site. Much data may be available from the excavation of the site itself, but more will be available from the wider landscape if suitable deposits can be located.

River alluvium and dry-valley colluvial deposits will provide information about soils formerly on the slopes above the deposits (Fig. 9.1). If calcareous, these deposits may contain land snails which, as we have seen in Chapter Eight, provide a broad ecological picture. For a more detailed picture of the local vegetation, attempts should be made to locate suitable deposits where pollen may survive. Peat is one of the best deposits, but pollen may survive in any anaerobic sediments or buried soils. Ideally a range of studies should be applied to the area to determine both the environment in which the site was constructed, and then changes in the local environment resulting from the use of the site. It should always be remembered that most environments are constantly changing under natural and human pressures, and such changes could affect how the site is used and even, on occasion, be a contributing factor in its change or even final desertion.

Figure 9.1   Sampling river valley alluvium: a major source of local environmental history.

Interpretation of the household and its activity areas

The household, in its many and varied forms, is a fundamental unit in human societies worldwide, so it is an essential element in the interpretation of archaeological data from most domestic sites. Evidence for the household consists of the house itself and evidence for activity in and around the house. The activities may be represented by sets of artefacts and/or features.

The house may be extrapolated from clusters of postholes, beam slots, masonry walls or robber trenches where walls have been robbed away (Fig. 9.2). Sometimes the structure itself leaves no trace and the site of a house can be determined only through careful plotting of artefact and ecofact distributions (Bradley 1970). Archaeologists generally recover only the plan of the house at ground level, so the nature of the structure above ground level is always open to interpretation. Such interpretations are based on a combination of known architectural parameters (for example, weight and stress of structural elements), available raw materials, ethnographic or surviving architectural analogy, and guesswork. Reconstructions can be built to show that a suggested interpretation *could* work, but not that it is necessarily the right interpretation (Fig. 9.3). The failure to achieve an agreed interpretation for the superstructure of sunken-feature buildings from early medieval Britain underlines the problem.

The plan of a house is generally laid out with some consideration of functional and social necessities, but it may also be subject to symbolic and cosmic interpretation (Guidoni 1975). Ethnographic data can provide detailed insights into why

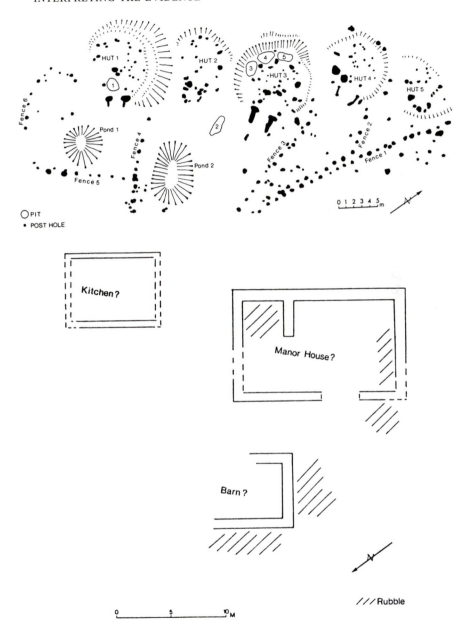

Figure 9.2 House plans from posthole patterns and wall footings.

particular house-plans and orientations are used in a specific context by a particular people at a particular time. The lowland South American Malocas are a good example. These oval houses are orientated on an east–west axis with the men's door at the east and the women's door at the west end. The posts supporting the

Figure 9.3   Experimental archaeology: house reconstruction.

roof are mountains, the roof itself represents the sky, the edge of the world is marked by hills represented by the walls. The ridge pole is the path of the sun, and an imaginary river flows through the middle of the house which becomes the river of the dead under the house (Hugh-Jones 1985). To apply such mythology outside the geographical and temporal area of the myth would clearly be unacceptable; what it does show, however, is that the interpretation, even of house plans, should perhaps take into consideration more than simply the functional aspects of the house. The same may apply to the location of activity areas. In a Dogan house (Mali), for example, the kitchen represents the head, the main room the trunk, and larders represent limbs. The head is therefore always on the trunk with limbs on either side (Griaule 1938). The location of activity areas may, therefore, also have a symbolic and cosmic element.

The interpretation of a particular area as the site of a particular activity is not always straightforward: some activities leave clear archaeological traces while others do not. A sleeping area may leave little or no trace, while a cooking hearth could leave clear traces. The residues of activities will probably be regularly cleared during the life of a household, and perhaps dumped as middens or into old storage pits. This secondary rubbish indicates the range of activities but not where they took place.

Household activity areas are best interpreted by combining the evidence of features with artefact spreads, and relating these to information gleaned from possible reconstructions of the house itself. Bronze age round houses in Britain, for example, often show discrete spreads of artefacts on their floors. One interpretation of these data is that they show actual areas where final activities took place prior to

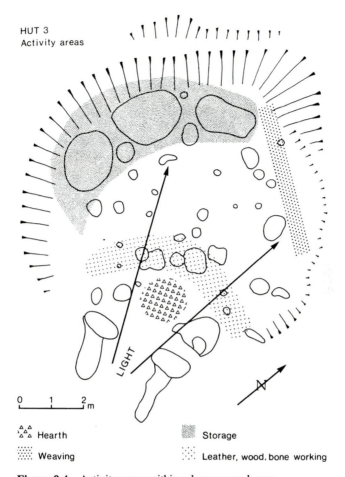

HUT 3
Activity areas

LIGHT

0   1   2 m

△△ Hearth   Storage

Weaving   Leather, wood, bone working

Figure 9.4 Activity areas within a bronze-age house.

desertion of the site (Fig. 9.4). The way the round houses were lit shows that these areas may have always had similar activities taking place at the same location in them, although the artefactual evidence was probably being regularly cleared away and discarded elsewhere. The orientation of these bronze age round houses may have had symbolic or cosmic meaning, but they were also functional workplaces.

Some activities generate specific patterns of artefact spreads without any surviving association features. Flint-, chert-, obsidian- and quartz-knapping are good examples. Many prehistoric sites produce secondary evidence of such activity, but where a knapping area is left *in situ*, and survives through rapid protection of the area following desertion, patterns of activity can be determined. A person knapping silica-based stone tools will generally either sit or crouch on the floor. Flakes will be knocked off the nodule to prepare a core. The flakes fall directly onto the ground between and beside the legs of the knapper. Areas clear of flakes may represent where the knapper was sitting and where his or her legs were (Fig. 9.5).

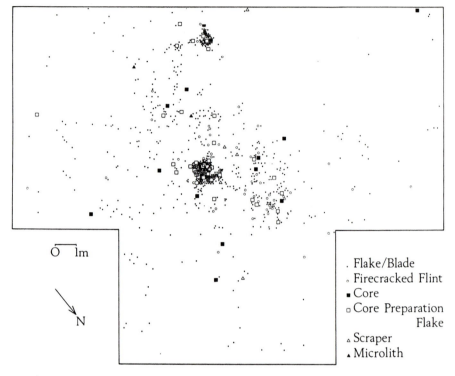

. Flake/Blade
∘ Firecracked Flint
▪ Core
▫ Core Preparation
          Flake
▵ Scraper
▴ Microlith

Figure 9.5   Activity areas: *in situ* flint knapping area (D. Garton for Sussex Archaeological Field Unit).

Tools, once finished, were taken away for use and cores were discarded around the knapping area.

The suggestion that a particular pattern of bits of flint found by the archaeologist represents a knapping episode involves a process of interpretation. The event happened in the past and nobody can say that this is what *was* done at a particular spot on the site. The living past is gone forever. Attempts to cross the gap between data from a current archaeological excavation and what really happened in the past requires extrapolation from the present into the past. The sociological term *middle-range theory* was first adopted by the American archaeologist Lewis Binford to cover the range of theory used to link material remains and their interpretation (Binford 1977).

Ethnoarchaeology and experimental archaeology are two key areas of middle range theory. Ethnoarchaeology essentially involves archaeologists living with peoples still generating the sort of residues found in the archaeological record, and then using their modern data to suggest how things *may* have happened in the past. Classic studies include those of the !Kung bushmen in Africa (Yellen 1977) and the Nunamiut Eskimo (Binford 1978). Experimental archaeology, like building a timber round house or knapping a flint axe, also shows how things *could* have

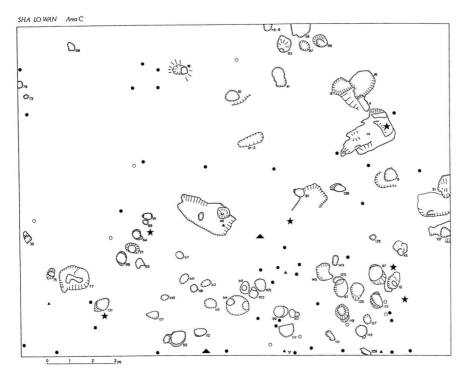

Figure 9.6   Neolithic domestic rubbish (broken pottery and axe fragments).

happened in the past and how a particular way of doing something may produce a residue *like* that found in an archaeological excavation (Coles 1979). Ethno-archaeology and experimental archaeology certainly show that particular patterns of waste flint flakes could best be interpreted as actual knapping sites.

Although the knapping floor will produce few or no actual tools, such tools may be found elsewhere on the site. To suggest what these tools were probably used for in the past involves the process of analogy. Analogy assumes that if something found on an archaeological excavation is perhaps the same size, shape and weight as something currently used in a particular way, then it *may* have been used in a similar way in the past. Roughly triangular or leaf-shaped flaked flint points may be similar to modern-day arrowheads, so could be interpreted as such if found on an excavation.

Although analogy and experimental archaeology can help suggest specific prac-tical uses of, say, stone axes, ethnoarchaeology and wider anthropological studies show that many artefacts hold symbolic value and may well have done so in the past (for example, Hodder 1982a). The context of the discovery of a pot or an axe may suggest its deposition as a symbolic act, in addition to the object itself having symbolic meaning. On the small middle neolithic domestic site at Sha Lo Wan, Hong Kong, for example, broken pottery and axe fragments were found in what appeared to be an occupation layer (Fig. 9.6), while similar whole pots and axes

SHA LO WAN   Area C

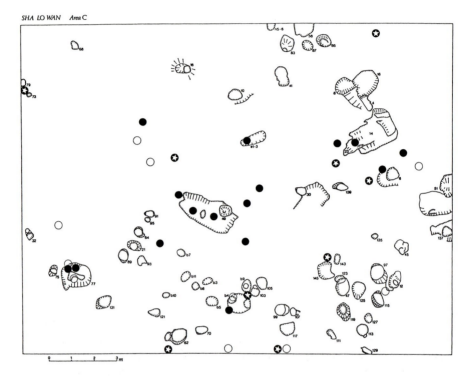

Figure 9.7   Neolithic ritual depositions of whole pots and axes on same site as Fig. 9.6.

were found carefully deposited in the ground (Fig. 9.7). The symbolic meaning of buried objects was clearly different to those used and discarded in everyday household use (Drewett 1995).

Interpretation of the community and its activity areas

Although the basic domestic unit excavated by archaeologists is generally the household, these are often grouped together into a community, either consisting of just a few households in the case of many hunter-gathering groups, or of thousands of households in a city. In addition to interpreting the individual household, the archaeologist may also be faced with interpreting the layout of several households, the space between households, variations in size of households, communal areas, structures and activities. As the communities became bigger there is a tendency for more evidence of specialization and increasing social complexity, with evidence of variation in social status sometimes detectable in the archaeological record.

The layout of a settlement may have been determined by many factors, some economic, some environmental, some social and some religious or symbolic. The local landscape, hills, valleys, rivers may predetermine the shape of a settlement, while its location may be partly determined by access to resources. The structure of the society, however, usually determines the elements within the community. A late Saxon village in England, for example, would have a church and manor house in addition to several households.

Among some communities the whole layout of the community has symbolism, perhaps representing creation myths. Among the Dogan, for example, the settlement represents a person, with the households representing the chest with blacksmith's forge at the head and shrines at the feet (Griaule and Dieterlen 1954). Although creation myths will be defined by time and space, recurring patterns within communities excavated by the field archaeologist will suggest a recurring need to lay out settlements in the same way. The reason may be symbolic, cosmological, functional, or a combination of reasons.

Most communities have some area or areas within or near the settlement for communal activities. The medieval village in England, for example, generally had a church and often a village green. In the Americas many communities had a central plaza for public ceremonies. These areas may be defined by special structures of some type or artefactual evidence of special activities. Sometimes communal activities took place away from settlement sites, as in the case of causewayed enclosures, often on the hillslopes above valley-bottom settlements in the neolithic of southern Britain (Drewett, Rudling and Gardiner 1988).

Another important area of interpretation at the community level is social ranking. Special or larger households, perhaps with rarer or more exotic artefacts associated, may perhaps indicate an individual or group of greater wealth and therefore higher status. Social ranking may also be reflected in burial structures and grave goods (Renfrew 1984).

Interpretation of how people lived

The interpretation of how people lived within a community of households is one of the key areas of study by field archaeologists. Artefacts and ecofacts can be used to interpret diet and subsistence patterns, resource use and manufacture, trade and exchange, ritual and religion, and social organization.

The interpretation of diet and subsistence patterns is derived mainly from the study of animal and plant remains found during excavation, together with associated artefacts. In Chapter Eight the basic process of identifying and quantifying plant and animal remains and calculating minimum numbers of animals present was considered. This analysis of data requires interpretation to understand how it may reflect the diet of the people living on the site and how they prepared their food.

Bone assemblages should be considered from a taphonomic point of view. Taphonomy considers the changes from the living animal community, through changes at death to the bone assemblage that survives in the ground, and on to the sample assemblage actually studied by the zooarchaeologist in the laboratory (Klein and Cruz-Uribe 1984). Although clearly of great importance when considering bone assemblages from caves, for example where wild animals like wolves and hyaenas may bring in and mix bones with those of humanly-killed animals, taphonomy is equally important in the study of any bone assemblage. Thin, small, soft bones are less likely to survive than big, robust leg bones. Dogs or wild animals can extract bones from midden deposits.

There may also be bias in the bone assemblage through human butchery practices or taboos. Wild animals, for example, could be butchered away from settlements, or the remains of certain animals may have been disposed of in a different way to those of other species. All archaeologists can really do is consider the archaeological assemblage, that is, the one they can recover from their excavations. The finds can be interpreted in terms of age, sex, butchery practices and perhaps seasonal use of animals. From this evidence, inferences can be drawn as to the dietary and other use of animals during particular periods, and in particular areas of the site excavated. Although based on good scientific data, the final conclusions can only be an intepretation based on the available information. The quality of the interpretation depends partly on the quality of the interpreter, but also on factors of survival and the quality of the work done by the field archaeologist recovering the remains.

The interpretation of plant remains from archaeological excavations in terms of diet is, in many ways, even more problematic than that of animal remains. Survival of the evidence is biased towards the results of certain elements of processing the plants and to particular conditions for their survival. Sometimes the evidence for the use of particular plants can only be deduced from the presence of specialized processing or cooking artefacts. Manioc, for example, was a staple crop in the Lesser Antilles and yet the palaeobotanical evidence for it is virtually non-existent in the area. What survives in the archaeological record are the tiny stone chips from manioc graters and the large flat griddles on which the cassava bread was cooked (Drewett 1991).

On most archaeological sites, plant remains survive only if carbonized. This is likely to happen by accident, only at specific stages in the processing of the plants. Many of the processing activities required, for example to turn wheat into bread, will leave no archaeological trace. They can be inferred from known traditional processing methods (Hillman 1981) and the surviving remains of seeds, specialized artefacts and structures. Traditional processes involve threshing, raking, winnowing, sieving, sometimes roasting or drying, storing, milling and finally cooking. The processes of roasting, drying and cooking all involve fire, and so are the most likely stages during which seeds may be carbonized. Accidental or deliberate burning of stored grain may also happen. Bulk burning could give a very biased view of plant-use, as in the case of a burnt barley store, for example. Ideally, interpretation of plants used in diet should be based on many smaller samples from contexts all over the site. Even so, such samples will be biased in terms of their preservation, so interpretation of plant remains in diet should also consider actual food residues, perhaps burnt inside cooking pots. Chemical analyses of food residues have been used to identify animal and plant fats, honey and wheat flour used in cooking (Hill and Evans 1987).

Although we now have access to detailed analyses of plant remains, the meaning of these remains in a particular context, of a particular date on a particular site, is always open to interpretation. Take, for example, the 21 kg of bronze-age carbonized grain from Pit 3 at Black Patch in Southern England (Drewett 1982). Although it tells us a great deal about crops grown and weeds thriving at the time, was the actual deposit accidentally burnt while malting for beer and dumped in the pit, was it ritually buried following its burning in a symbolic act, or was a small child playing with fire? The field archaeologist has to make an interpretation based on the data, and using his or her theoretical perspective. It is a 'fact' that the pit was filled mainly with carbonized barley. How it got there and what it meant to the people putting it there will forever remain speculation.

Another area requiring interpretation is the making of objects, their trade and exchange. Techniques of analysis are now so advanced that it is often possible to locate exact sources for raw materials and details of manufacturing processes (Parkes 1986, Hodges 1964). The source of a stone axe, for example, can sometimes be determined through detailed petrological and/or chemical analysis. Its exact method of manufacture and use may be understood through replication studies and microwear analysis, but why it was placed in a particular spot in the site or landscape, at a particular time, in a particular way, is open to interpretation. How far you believe you can go with that interpretation depends on your theoretical perspective (Chapter One).

Much has been written in recent years about how the distribution of artefacts can be interpreted in terms of trade and ways of redistribution (for example, Earle and Ericson 1977). If working in an historic period, it may be clear from documentary evidence that your site has a market for example. In prehistory you have to rely on the distribution and density of objects. From ethnography and history we know objects can be distributed in many ways: you can simply go and collect something from its primary source (direct access), you can exchange products you have for those you want but someone else has (reciprocity), trade down the line (repeated reciprocal exchange), or there may be markets as central places where people bring things from a wide area to exchange (Renfrew 1975).

The many forms of redistribution known in ethnography and history do not all leave clear archaeological traces. Trade down the line often does produce a fairly clear pattern with greatest densities nearest the source of the material, while trading ports, like medieval Southampton, with a wide range of European imports, can be recognized. Much of the trade and other forms of redistribution did not, of course, deal in exotic items like fine stonewares, obsidian or jade, but in everyday goods such as meat, skins, fat and honey which, even if recognized in the archaeological record, are generally impossible to identify as trade goods.

Prior to Lewis Binford's bold statement that "data relevant to most, if not all, components of past socio-cultural systems *are* preserved in the archaeological record" (Binford 1968), few archaeologists believed that their data could provide much information for the interpretation of social organization. Since then, however, it has become clear that societies organized in particular ways may leave a recurrent range of material remains in the form of settlement patterns, objects and structures. Correlation between particular material remains and particular social organization is, however, rarely straightforward, and a simple 'checklist' approach is clearly unacceptable.

One of the most widely-used frameworks for considering social organization is that suggested by the anthropologist Elman Service (Service 1971). Service's division of social organization into bands, tribes, chiefdoms and states remains a useful basis, but has been "criticized for its arbitrary rigidity" (Fagan 1991a). Used flexibly, however, it remains a useful starting point for considering social organization.

Bands are generally small groups of hunters and gatherers who move regularly to obtain wild resources. In theory they are all related equals with no established leadership. Tribes or 'segmentary societies' generally involve much larger numbers than bands, perhaps up to a thousand people who, although they may live in separate farmsteads or villages, are related through kinship ties. Like bands they are egalitarian. Generally, segmentary societies are composed of settled agriculturalists or mobile pastoralists. It is often difficult to distinguish archaeologically a chiefdom from a segmentary society. The main difference is some form of social ranking, with a hereditary chief. The chief, and other high-ranking individuals like warriors, often amass greater wealth than others in the society, which may be reflected both in artefact assemblages in and around the chief's house, but also in burial goods. Chiefdoms often have centres of power with prestige structures, fortified centres and ritual centres. Partly as a result of the numbers of people involved in chiefdoms, sometimes more than 20,000, specialization, particularly in craft production, is possible.

Bands, segmentary societies and chiefdoms are all pre-state societies. The development of early states involves fundamental changes with the development of ranked classes, usually under a king or emperor. Cities and towns develop with palaces, temples and other public buildings run by a priestly class and centralized bureaucracy. Specialization, including craft specialization, is the norm and may be reflected in discrete activity areas within the settlement, representing different crafts and other activities.

The interpretation of evidence suggesting the two extremes of Service's divisions – that is, hunter–gatherer bands or big city states like dynastic Egypt or the Roman Empire – is fairly clear, but the distinction between segmentary societies (tribes) and chiefdoms is rarely as clear, with the identification of 'chiefdoms' in the archaeological record often open to dispute. The evidence from a single settlement is never enough, as the whole settlement pattern has to be considered when looking at site specialization and ranking.

Field archaeologists recover data, some would say *facts*; for example, a pot of such a type was found buried under a wall of a building of such a type. Why the pot was buried, and what sort of society was responsible for that act of burial, is interpretation; and how you interpret depends on your theoretical perspective. There is no 'right' interpretation that one can prove to be correct, in the same way that there is no 'right' way to dig a site; but one suspects there are many wrong interpretations.

CHAPTER TEN

Publishing the report

The end product of most field projects should be an archive of material remains, field records and material analyses, together with a report. The archive must be deposited in a professionally-curated institution like a museum, and the report should be published. Both must be publicly available. The archive essentially comprises all primary data relating to the field project. In the case of an excavation or field survey involving surface collection, the artefacts, ecofacts and residues of any environmental samples will form the bulk of the archive, although this material will be of little use without its associated archive record.

Most museums will define the size and type of containers required for the storage of material remains and what packing materials should or should not be used. The size and shape of boxes required is usually determined by the type of storage system used in the museum. Ideally, the curator of the museum where the material will be finally deposited should be consulted both before the project starts and as it progresses. With increasing pressure on museum storage space, do not assume that a particular museum will accept all, or even some, of what you wish to deposit. They may take the view that the cost of long-term storage is so high that certain classes of material, like environmental sample residues or burnt flint, should be disposed of in some alternative way (for example, dumped back on the site).

Ideally, the material remains from a site will be stored by context and material. Researchers in the future may be interested in the whole site, a particular pit group, or perhaps a particular artefact type. Different materials do, however, require different storage conditions. All require some form of strong containers which may be of wood but in many museums are made of thick cardboard. These should have lids to keep off dust. Small objects are often stored in polythene containers within the standard storage box, which should be clearly labelled with museum accession number, site name, context numbers and type of material. Most pottery and stone artefacts do not require special conditions, but ideally should be loosely packed to prevent sherds rubbing against each other or even breaking because of the weight of sherds on top. Acid-free tissue paper can be used to wrap glass and bone, while metals should be kept immobile in padded polyethylene boxes containing silica gel to remove excess moisture. Metals and organic material are ideally stored in closely environmentally-monitored storage areas within museums.

The records element of the project archive will include the drawn, written and photographic site record together with records of post-excavation analyses. Ideally all documentation related to the field project should be included in the archive, but as with the material remains, long-term storage of records is an increasing problem so some weeding out of low-grade information is advisable.

In addition to the raw data, the archive should include summaries of the site's stratigraphy, the context record, the artefact record and the environmental record. Some archaeologists divide the archive into the primary site archive which is simply all data obtained in the field, ordered, but not amended, and the research archive (Andrews 1991). The research archive includes all the data obtained during the analysis phase, together with an interpretation of the history of the site and full artefact and environmental reports. When finally deposited, however, these archives effectively become one.

The long-term storage of the archive is expensive and needs expert curation in the same way that objects do. The costs and success of long-term storage can be considerably helped by the field archaeologist adhering to a number of basic rules. Plans, for example, survive best if stored flat in polyester packets or acid-free card folders. This cannot easily be done if drawings are larger than A1 (594 mm × 841 mm), a fact that must be considered by the field archaeologist when drawing in the field. Original drawings should be on polyester film, using a hard (4H) pencil. They are best stored in the dark within a temperature range of 13–20°C and relative humidity of 45–50 per cent. The outside of all folders must be clearly labelled, so that researchers can go straight to the plan they want without touching unwanted drawings. The written paper record should be stored in similar conditions, in acid-free dust-proof boxes. Care must be taken not to use metal paper clips, staples, sticky tape or adhesives, all of which create problems in long-term storage. Use plastic paper clips to group papers if required (Ferguson and Murray 1997).

The photographic element of the archive also requires special care in storage, with negatives and colour slides being stored separately from prints in polyester sleeves in cool, total darkness. Storage of prints is less crucial, as they can always be reprinted. They are, however, the section of the photographic archive most likely to be consulted, so ideally they should be stored in archive boxes at 16–21°C. And a relative humidity of 40–50 per cent (Ferguson and Murray 1997).

Some people assume that if field data are stored on computer disks their life will be greatly enhanced. Unfortunately this is not the case; magnetic media and computing programmes have a comparatively short life, probably shorter than paper, and frequent copying and up-dating of format are essential if records are to survive.

Archaeological illustration

Archaeological illustrations form a significant part of the archive and a crucial part of the published report. Indeed, the final published report should, in many ways, be hung on the illustrations. These will consist of maps, plans and sections, object illustrations, photographs and perhaps reconstructions. Increasingly maps, plans, sections and reconstructions are computer-drawn using CAD software, but object drawing usually requires the skill of a draftsperson, although flat-bed scanning of an object is possible (Houk and Moses 1998).

Many archaeologists still draw site plans and sections by hand for publication. If drawn this way, field drawings may be traced using tubular-nibbed drawing pens on plastic drafting film. Tracing paper is not suitable due to its differential expansion and contraction under changes of humidity. Original pencil field drawings should never be directly inked-up as they are an essential element of the primary site archive. Correcting errors on drawings for publication has always been a major concern using traditional materials, so highly-skilled archaeological draftspeople were in great demand. Since about 1963 however, the skills of draftspeople have, initially slowly and in recent years very rapidly, been overtaken by computers. The SKETCHPAD system developed at the Massachusetts Institute of Technology by Ivor Sutherland started this process (Sutherland 1965). Now field drawings can be simply scanned into computers and images enlarged or reduced, lines made thinner or thicker as required. Both the available hardware and software are developing so fast that any particular system recommended here would almost certainly be out of date before this book is published. It is perhaps more important for the field archaeologist to know what illustrations are needed in what form to convey information about a site.

The one area of archaeological illustration that has remained firmly the province of the draftsperson is the illustration of objects. This is partly because it is not a purely mechanical process like producing a map, but involves interpretation, and to some extent selection. Archaeological object illustration has developed independently in different parts of the world, and indeed within different parts of individual countries. There are, therefore, no universally-accepted conventions, although there are general guiding principles. The basic aim is that the drawing should be produced in such a way that anyone understanding the principles used can understand the drawing and use it for purposes of comparison.

The first stage of drawing an object is to examine it and, perhaps in conjunction with a specialist, understand what the object is, how it was used and how it was made, and what it is made of. Without this level of knowledge it is perfectly possible to produce an artistic image of the object, but perhaps not a drawing of use to an archaeologist. For this reason sometimes people trained in art require an element of retraining to produce archaeological illustrations. The aim is to produce objective drawings, although how far this is possible is open to debate (Orton, Tyers and Vince 1993, Fig. 7.3).

Archaeological objects always have three dimensions, but publication, other than electronically, is in two dimensions. To give an impression of the third dimension, objects are always drawn as if the light were coming from the top left-hand corner of the illustration. Orientation is also an important principle. The vertical axis of the object should be parallel to the side of the page with side views achieved by rotating the object by 90°. Most object drawings should also include a representation of a reconstructed section cut through the object (Griffiths and Jenner 1990).

Basic drawing equipment used for archaeological illustration includes a drawing board, pencils (2H to HB), eraser, dividers, bleed-proof drawing paper or plastic

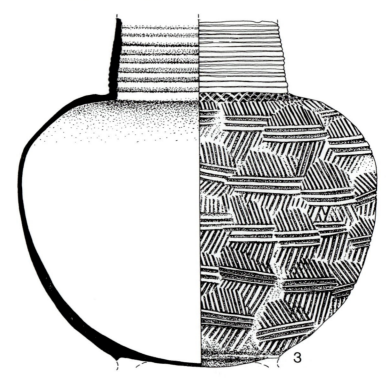

Figure 10.1   Conventional archaeological drawing of a pot (Lys Drewett).

drafting film, an engineer's square, calipers and tubular-nibbed drawing pens. If a properly equipped drawing office is not available, the illustrator will also require a well-lit space with adjustable desk and chair. Natural daylight is best enhanced with a desk lamp to light the object from the top left-hand corner.

Archaeological drawing of pottery is in many ways the most conventionalized form of archaeological illustration. The conventions are best understood by looking at a whole-pot and a whole-pot drawing before attempting to draw a sherd. The convention is to draw the pot as though it were standing upright and was then cut into two with the outside and its profile on the right and the section and interior on the left (Fig. 10.1). The two halves of the pot are bisected with a vertical line. In the United States the convention is reversed, with the section and interior on the right.

Most illustrators evolve their own ways of drawing whole pots, but the basic framework required is the base diameter, the rim diameter and the height of the vessel. If the pot is wheel-turned the rim and base are likely to be roughly circular and parallel to each other. Hand-made pots are rarely so regular. To draw the pot, place the whole pot on its side on the drawing paper (it can be held by small wooden blocks or re-usable adhesive). Then, with an engineer's square, project points around the pot down onto the paper. By joining these spots you have the shape of the pot. A line is then drawn from halfway along the rim down to halfway across the base.

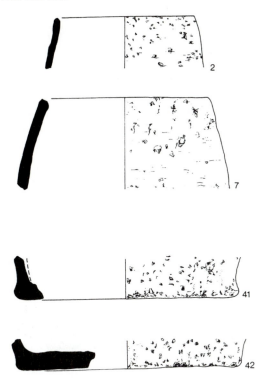

Figure 10.2 Conventional archaeological drawings of rim and base sherds (Lys Drewett).

Using a rigid frame of drawn right angles, as some illustrators recommend, generally has the effect of evening up irregularly-shaped pots and should be avoided. Alternatively you could use a profile gauge to register the shape of the pot, then draw carefully around it. The thickness of the pot for the section drawing can be measured using calipers. Remember to take several measurements as the thickness of a pot is not always constant. If the pot is of a fine wheel-turned fabric, parallel lines of variable thickness are used both to represent the marks of wheel-turning and to illustrate shape. For coarser wares the actual components of the fabric are usually drawn, particularly larger pieces of filler like grog or burnt flint. Simple repetitive decoration can be drawn directly onto the pot drawing, but complex non-repetitive decoration may need to be drawn separately, 'rolled out' (Griffiths and Jenner 1990).

Potsherds should, where possible, be incorporated in their correct position in a reconstruction drawing of the whole pot. A rim sherd should become the top of a whole-pot drawing, the base sherd the bottom (Fig. 10.2). Diameters of rim and base sherds can be calculated by using a radius chart. This is simply a series of concentric circles drawn at 1 cm intervals. By placing the rim or base curve on the radius chart its diameter can be easily estimated. Care should be taken, particularly with the angle of rim sherds. If the sherd is from a wheel-turned pot it should be

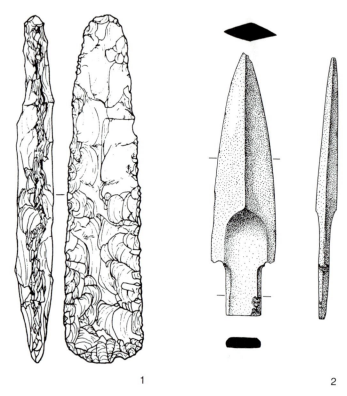

Figure 10.3 Line drawing of flaked flint tool (1) and stippled polished stone tool (2) (Lys Drewett).

placed with the top of the rim flat on the radius chart. The angle is correct when no light can be seen passing under the sherd. Body sherds are often more difficult to locate correctly as if they were part of a whole pot. They are, however, usually drawn only if their decoration is of particular interest.

For illustration purposes, stone artefacts are generally divided into those with evidence of conchoidal fracture, like flint and obsidian, and those without, like sandstone. Flake scars showing conchoidal fracture are illustrated by roughly parallel curved lines, the lines thinning out across the flake scar surface, while other worked stone is stippled (Fig. 10.3). Most flaked tools are drawn in three views with the dorsal view on the left, ventral on the right, and lateral profile between, although there is no great standardization in lithic drawings. Basically, draw enough views to show the size and shape of the object, and how it has been chipped. The outline can be created by fixing the object to your drawing paper with re-usable adhesive and carefully projecting the edge down on to the paper using a set square. The points where the flake facets hit the edge of the object can be recorded in the same way. The flake facets are then drawn using a combination of dividers and eye. Flake facets are indicated using hatching, which not only shows the direction of flaking but also gives an impression of depth.

The principles of drawing all other classes of object are basically the same. Understand the object, decide how many views are required, create a measured outline and then, using dividers, measure in detail, remembering to show depth by lighting from the top left-hand corner. Each class of object does, however, have its own problems. Generally corrosion is not drawn on metal objects, as it only creates confusion and often alters the original shape of the object. If totally corroded, the real shape may only be obtained by tracing off an x-ray of the object. The drawn surfaces of metal objects are generally shown as smooth, indicated by parallel lines, or cross-hatching in shaped areas. Likewise polished bone should be shown as smooth; natural variations in the bone structure are generally not shown. The natural surface of rough materials like antler may, however, be stippled. Wooden objects are generally line-shaded while leather may be line-shaded or stippled.

Most objects are drawn at a scale of 1:1, for reduction to 1:4. However, small objects are often published at 1:1 so should be drawn at double scale. Given that final published drawings are reductions, care should be taken to use ink lines thick enough to reduce, and never too close or they will black in on reduction. The traditional way of preparing object drawings for publication was to mount them on white mounting card, numbering each object and adding a linear scale. Now drawings can be scanned into a computer, moved into place, numbered, and scales added.

Many people question why so much effort is put into archaeological illustration of objects rather than simply using photographs. The proportion of object drawings to photographs does in fact vary considerably around the world. British archaeologists, for example, tend to publish more drawings and fewer photographs than Chinese archaeologists. Drawings and photographs both have advantages and disadvantages. A good photograph can give a 'real' view of an object with fine detail of texture, while drawings can incorporate sections and provide more accurate dimensional information.

Although photographs adequate for lecturing can be produced using 35 mm cameras, large-format cameras are better for producing publication-quality object photographs. These can record finer detail, and using camera-movements foreshortening can be eliminated. If a 5 × 4 inch (12.8 × 10.2 cm) camera is used, a standard 150 mm lens is suitable for most work. In addition a strong tripod, contrast filters, light meter and object stand will be required (Dorrell 1989, 155–77). Care should be taken to select a suitable background against which to photograph an object, and all photographs should include a small, unobtrusive, but clear and well-made scale.

For black-and-white photographs, a background of either black or white is usually best as other colours appear as variations of grey. Colour photographs look better with a coloured background, although not one that will dominate the object. To bring out the texture of an object, careful lighting is required. Continuous tungsten lighting has the advantage that it can be moved around the object and the photographer can see the best angles, but such lighting becomes hot which may not be good for some objects. Electronic flash is safer but it is less easy to predict what

Figure 10.4   Photograph of whole pot for publication (photo: C. S. Fung).

the finished image will be like. Cameras with built-in flash units are usually unsuitable, except for record shots, as they tend to flatten the image. Flash units need to be carefully positioned at an angle to the object to bring out fine texture.

Most archaeological publications only use black-and-white photographs, essentially for reasons of cost (Fig. 10.4). The prints should be on glossy paper and generally either at publication size or double size. It is essential to discuss with the editor or printer exactly how photographs should be presented. All should, however, be clearly labelled on the back of the print with the article and author's name, and figure or plate number. This should be done in soft pencil or fibre-tip pen, not ball-point which can impress the surface of the photograph or adhesive labels which can fall off. Also mark any required cropping of the photograph in soft pencil on the back.

Writing a report

There are essentially three types of field reports being written by archaeologists today: archive reports, technical reports in developer-funded archaeology, and reports for publication. The three types have different aims, readership, and therefore content.

The archive report has already been touched on earlier in this chapter. This is basically a record of data ordered in such a way as to be accessible, and with an interpretation of the history of the site. It will include detailed, quantified artefact and environmental reports. The actual structure of an archive report will depend on the type and period of a site, but in many ways it is similar to the structure of a traditional published excavation report considered below. The aim of archive reports is the long-term preservation of data.

Technical reports produced in developer-funded (contract) archaeology are, by contrast, for immediate use, and used often not by archaeologists. Unfortunately, however, they are increasingly becoming the sole record of much salvage archaeology. Cultural resource management in North America has created an enormous number of these technical reports, often referred to as 'grey literature' as it is desk-top published in small numbers, essentially for commercial clients. Some reports, particularly based on work done on military property, are never available to the wider archaeological community. This problem of 'grey literature' is increasingly becoming an issue in Britain as most excavation, following PPG 16, is now developer-led.

Technical reports are the product a developer will expect if funding an evaluation excavation, or indeed a full site excavation. Evaluation reports must be produced quickly as they are often an essential element in the planning process. They should be clear, well written and illustrated, jargon-free and easy to use by developers, planners and lawyers who may need to cite them at a public inquiry into a planning application.

Although there is no agreed standard for such technical reports, most roughly follow a set pattern. A clear, dated title page is followed by a contents list of chapter headings, appendices, plans and figures, and photographs. The text should start with a brief, clear non-technical summary. This should outline exactly what was done and what was found. Here, and throughout the text, each paragraph should be numbered (Section 1, 1.1, 1.2, 1.3 and so on, Section 2, 2.1, 2.2, 2.3 and so on) as specific points may need to be referred to in public inquiries or other parts of the planning process.

The main text then starts with an introduction stating where the site was, who commissioned the work and why, an outline of previous knowledge, what form the current work took and when it was undertaken, and finally who did the fieldwork and prepared the report. Section 2 considers the aims and objectives of the project, while Section 3 describes the methodology used. Section 4 describes in clear terms the evaluation results, particularly where what features were found and the stratigraphy of the site. Section 5 outlines the finds, artefacts and ecofacts found, while the final section discusses the evidence and draws conclusions. Fine detail in all these sections is best left to appendices. These can include tables summarizing contexts found and listing artefacts and ecofacts, together with any specialist finds reports. A clear stratigraphic matrix is a good way of summarizing the sequence of contexts on a site. Finally location maps, trench and context plans and sections, and site photographs are included.

Ideally these technical reports should be considered simply as temporary documents and any field project must have a site archive and published report. The sheer volume of field archaeology now being undertaken, and the detail of information that can be obtained from the smallest excavation is, however, creating a severe problem in the area of archaeological publication. Added to this are concerns expressed by some archaeologists about the actual process of writing up field projects (Hodder 1989).

Traditional excavation reports are essentially designed so that future archaeologists can reinterpret a site from the data published without recourse to an archive, except perhaps a re-examination of selected finds. Such a report should start with a clear abstract of about 200 words outlining the project and the importance of key discoveries. With so much archaeology being published, this is probably the most read section of the report. Ideally it will be published not only in the language of the country in which the site is located, but also in major international languages. The introduction should locate the site, place it in its environmental and historical context, and explain the reasons for the excavation and the methodology employed. The main body of the text involves a description of the contexts found on the site, including dimensions, stratification, and soil descriptions. This is followed by finds reports covering artefacts and ecofacts. Details may, however, be relegated to appendices. The final section in the main report is a discussion of the interpretation of the site, and conclusions.

Each of these sections will include illustrations, location plans and photographs in the introduction; site plans, sections and photographs in the site description; and object drawings and photographs in the finds reports. Much of the specialist data has always been relegated to appendices which, from the 1960s onwards, often became larger than the main report. If appendices are used they should be relevant and clearly cross-referenced to the main body of the report. Finally, every report should have clear acknowledgements to all who contributed, and a bibliography of sources referred to.

This traditional form of excavation report (Joukowsky 1980, 457–66) goes back over a hundred years to pioneers of field archaeology like General Pitt-Rivers and Sir Mortimer Wheeler (Grinsell, Rahtz and Warhurst 1966). The aim is to publish all data recovered so that anyone in the future can understand, check and, if required, reinterpret the site. As already mentioned, however, there are problems with this type of report. The sheer amount of archaeological data available is becoming overwhelming and the cost of conventional publication is becoming prohibitive. Published reports must therefore be far more selective in what appears on the printed page, with reference back to the unpublished archive. Only findings of significance should be published, with sufficient data to support these findings. Most excavations produce a great deal of low-grade data which will be reported in detail in the archive, and simply referenced in the published report. Finds reports should relate to the interpretation of the site, and not simply be lists of finds common on any similar site excavated in the area. Ideally, regional synthetic finds reports will be published, which can then be cross-referenced in the published excavation report. Endless publication of similar material, simply because it is there, is not a good use of limited resources.

One of the problems with brief, synthetic published reports with a full but unpublished archive is that the archive has to be stored in a single place which may not be convenient to the researcher wishing to access it. Archive stores have to have opening and closing times and restrictions on the use of data. Hard-pressed researchers may need to access hundreds of archives in different locations. There will always be a tendency to use and accept the published version of the excavation report without detailed checking of the archive data. Archives therefore really must be accessible. Fortunately this can now be done with electronic publishing, which will almost certainly be the way forward in archaeological publishing. The entire archive can then become available through the Internet, but only accessed when researchers wish to follow up specific information referred to in the published report.

Getting a report published

No field archaeology project is complete until a report is published. Getting reports published is a combination of skill, careful judgement and luck. Skill is required in the actual production of the report, careful judgement is required in selecting a suitable journal, and luck is required in relation to editors, referees and available space. Some archaeologists appear to have terrible trouble getting anything published; others manage to get everything, however awful, published.

If you are attempting to get a field report published, it is essential that firstly you select the right journal, and secondly you adhere to the 'notes for contributors' provided by the editors of virtually all journals. Publication in monograph form will require detailed discussion with the publishing organization. Most archaeological reports, however, appear in journals.

Archaeological journals are in three basic tiers: international, national and local. Few international journals publish excavation reports. Journals like *World Archaeology* publish thematic volumes of potential international interest. *Antiquity* will publish short articles on major new field discoveries, but not excavation reports as such. Most continents or countries have journals which will publish major discoveries derived from field projects within the area, but most have a preference for synthetic articles rather than straight excavation reports, unless of major significance. The Society for American Archaeology, for example, publishes *American Antiquity* for North America and *Latin American Antiquity* for South America and the Caribbean.

Britain's major national journals are period-based, being the journals of societies with period interests: *Proceedings of the Prehistoric Society*, *Britannia* (for Roman Britain), *Medieval Archaeology* and *Post-Medieval Archaeology*, although there are also wider-based journals like *The Antiquaries Journal* and *The Archaeological Journal*. All will accept British excavation reports, although only if clearly of national importance. Most excavation reports are published at the local level, in Britain generally by the county archaeological societies. Journals such as *Wiltshire Archaeological Magazine* or *Sussex Archaeological Collections* have been published annually for over a hundred years. In the United States, State historical societies like the Idaho State Historical Society or the Minnesota Historical Society fulfil a similar role to the British county archaeological societies.

Having selected a suitable journal, consult the editor to see whether he or she also agrees that your report would be suitable. Most journals produce detailed 'notes for contributors' which, if you want an article published quickly, you must follow closely. Also, use recently published reports in the same journal as models. If a word limit is prescribed, stick to it. Many journals have word limits of about 8,000 words. Most journals have a 'house style' which will include how references should be presented, and possibly even illustration style. Do not use footnotes if the journal clearly does not allow them. Most editors require two or more hard copies of the report plus a version on disc. Remember, however, that editors, printers and postmen are human and do sometimes lose things, so always keep your own back-up copies of everything sent out.

References

Andrews, G. 1991. *Management of archaeological projects*. London: English Heritage.

Atkinson, R. J. C. 1953. *Field archaeology* (2nd edn). London: Methuen.

Barker, P. 1977. *Techniques of archaeological excavation*. London: Batsford.

Bersu, G. 1940. Excavations at Little Woodbury. *Proceedings Prehistoric Society* **4**, 30–111.

Binford, L. R. 1968. Archaeological perspectives. In S. R. Binford & L. R. Binford, *New perspectives in archaeology*. Chicago: Aldine.

Binford, L. (ed.) 1977. *For theory building in archaeology*. Orlando, Florida: Academic Press.

Binford, L. 1978. *Nunamiut ethnoarchaeology*. Orlando, Florida: Academic Press.

Binford, L. R. 1983. *Pursuit of the past*. New York: Thames and Hudson.

Binford, S. R., & L. R. Binford. 1968. *New perspectives in archaeology*. Chicago: Aldine.

Bradley, R. 1970. The excavation of a Beaker settlement at Belle Tout, East Sussex, England. *Proceedings Prehistoric Society* **36**, 312–79.

Butzer, K. W. 1983. Global sea-level stratigraphy on appraisal. *Quaternary Science Reviews* **2**, 1–15.

Chaplin, R. E. 1971. *The study of animal bones from archaeological sites*. London and New York: Seminar Press.

Clark, A. 1990. *Seeing beneath the soil: prospecting methods in archaeology*. London: Batsford.

Coles, J. 1979. *Experimental archaeology*. London: Academic Press.

Columbus, C. 1960. *The journal of Christopher Columbus*. London: Anthony Blond & The Orion Press.

Conyers, L. B., & D. Goodman. 1997. *Ground-penetrating radar*. Walnut Creek, California: Altamira Press.

Cookson, M. B. 1954. *Photography for archaeologists*. London: Max Parrish, p. 13.

Cornwall, I. W. 1958. *Soils for the archaeologist*. London: Phoenix House.

Coventry, W. F., & J. L. Barker. 1981. *Management*. London: Heinemann.

Crabtree, D. 1972. *An introduction to flintworking*. Pocatello, Idaho: Idaho State Museum.

Crawford, O. G. S., & A. Keiller. 1928. *Wessex from the air*. Oxford: Oxford University Press.

Cunnington, R. H. 1975. *From antiquary to archaeologist: a biography of William Cunnington, 1754–1810*. Princes Risborough, Bucks: Shire Publications.

Dallas, R. 1980. Surveying with a camera: rectified photography. *Architectural Journal*, 20 February 1980, 395–9.

Darwin, C. 1881. *The formation of vegetable mould through the action of worms*. London: John Murray.

Dillon, Brian D. 1989. The archaeological field vehicle. In *Practical archaeology: field and laboratory techniques and archaeological logistics*, Brian D. Dillon (ed.) Los Angeles: University of California.

Dimbleby, G. W. 1978. *Plants and archaeology*. London: Paladin Books.

Donachie, J. D., & D. J. Field. 1994. Cissbury Ring: a survey by the Royal Commission on the Historical Monuments of England. *Sussex Archaeological Collections* **132**, 25–32.

Dorrell, P. 1989. *Photography in archaeology and conservation*. Cambridge: Cambridge University Press.

Dowman, E. 1970. *Conservation in the field*. London: Methuen.

Drewett, P. L. 1975. Excavations at Hadleigh Castle, Essex, 1971–72. *Journal British Archaeological Association* **38**, 90–154.

Drewett, P. L. 1982. Later bronze-age downland economy and excavations at Black Patch, East Sussex. *Proceedings Prehistoric Society* **48**, 321–409.

Drewett, P. L. 1982a. *The archaeology of Bullock Down, Eastbourne, East Sussex: the development of a landscape*. Lewes: Sussex Archaeological Society Monograph no. 1.

Drewett, P. L. 1991. *Prehistoric Barbados*. Denbigh: Archetype Publications.

Drewett, P. L. 1995. *Neolithic Sha Lo Wan*. Hong Kong: Antiquities and Monuments Office Occasional Paper no. 2.

Drewett, P. L., D. Rudling, M. Gardiner. 1988. *The south-east to 1000 A.D. A regional history of England*. London and New York: Longman.

Earle, T. K., & J. E. Ericson (eds). 1977. *Exchange systems in prehistory*. New York: Academic Press.

Eidt, R. C. 1977. Detection and examination of anthrosols by phosphate analysis. *Science* **197**, 1327–33.

Evans, J. G. 1972. *Land snails in archaeology*. London: Seminar Press.

Evans, J. G. 1978. *An introduction to environmental archaeology*. London: Paul Elek.

Fagan, B. M. 1991. *Ancient North America*. New York: Thames and Hudson.

Fagan, B. M. 1991a. *In the beginning: an introduction to archaeology*. New York: Harper Collins.

Ferguson, L. M., & D. M. Murray. 1997. *Archaeological documentary archives*. Manchester: Institute of Field Archaeologists Paper no. 1.

Flannery, K. V. (ed.) 1976. *The early Mesoamerican village*. New York: Academic Press.

Flannery, K. V. (ed.) 1982. *Maya subsistence*. New York and London: Academic Press.

Griaule, M. 1938. *Masques Dogons*. Paris: Institut d'Ethnologie.

Griaule, M., & G. Dieterlen. 1954. The Dogon of the French Sudan. In D. Forde (ed.), *African worlds*, 83–110. London: Oxford University Press.

Griffiths, N., & A. Jenner. 1990. *Drawing archaeological finds*. London: Archetype Publications.

Grinsell, L., P. Rahtz, A. Warhurst. 1966. *The preparation of archaeological reports*. London: John Baker.

Guidoni, E. 1975. *Primitive architecture*. Milan: Electa Enditrice.

Haggett, P. 1965. *Locational analysis in human geography*. London: Edward Arnold.

Hampton, J. N. 1978. The mapping and analysis of archaeological evidence provided by aerial photographs. *Aerial photography* **2**, 18–24.

Harris, E. C. 1979. *Principles of archaeological stratigraphy*. New York: Academic Press.

Higgs, E. S. (ed.) 1975. *Palaeoeconomy*. Cambridge: Cambridge University Press.

Hill, H. E., & J. Evans. 1987. The identification of plants used in prehistory from organic residues. In W. R. Ambrose & J. M. J. Mummery (eds), *Archaeometry: further Australasian studies*, 90–96. Canberra: Australian National University.

Hillman, G. 1981. Reconstructing crop husbandry practices from charred remains of crops. In R. Mercer (ed.), *Farming practice in British prehistory*. Edinburgh: Edinburgh University Press.

Hodder, I. (ed.) 1982. *Symbolic and structural archaeology*. Cambridge: Cambridge University Press.

Hodder, I. 1982a. *Symbols in action*. Cambridge: Cambridge University Press.

Hodder, I. 1989. Writing archaeology: site reports in context. *Antiquity* **63**, 268–74.

Hodges, H. 1964. *Artifacts: an introduction to early materials and technology*. London: John Baker.

Houk, B. A, & B. K. Moses. 1998. Scanning artefacts: using a flat-bed scanner to image three-dimensional objects. *Bulletin of the Society for American Archaeology* **16**, no. 3, 36–9.

Hugh-Jones, S. 1985. The Maloca: a world in house. In E. Carmichael, S. Hugh-Jones, B. Moser, D. Tayler, *The hidden peoples of the Amazon*, 77–93. London: British Museum Publications.

Humfrey, M. 1975. *Sea shells of the West Indies*. London: Collins.

Hutt, S., E. W. Jones, M. E. McAllister. 1992. *Archaeological resource protection*. Washington: The Preservation Press.

Jane, F. W. 1956. *The structure of wood*. London: Adam and Charles Black.

Joukowsky, M. 1980. *A complete manual of field archaeology*. New Jersey: Prentice-Hall.

Kerr, P. F. 1977. *Optical mineralogy*. New York: McGraw-Hill.

Klein, R. G., & K. Cruz-Uribe. 1984. *The analysis of animal bones from archaeological sites*. Chicago: University of Chicago Press.

Langford, M. J. 1986. *Basic photography*. London and Boston: Focal Press.

Ligon, R. 1657. *A true and exact history of the island of Barbadoes*. Reprinted by Frank Cass, London, 1976.

Limbrey, S. 1975. *Soil science and archaeology*. London and New York: Academic Press.

Meighan, C. W., & Brian D. Dillon. 1989. Small Boats in Archaeological Exploration. In Brian D. Dillon (ed.), *Practical archaeology: field and laboratory techniques and archaeological logistics*. Los Angeles: University of California.

Orton, C. R. 1975. Quantitative pottery studies: some progress, problems and prospects. *Science and Archaeology* **16**, 30–35.

Orton, C., P. Tyers, A. Vince. 1993. *Pottery in archaeology*. Cambridge: Cambridge University Press.

Parkes, P. A. 1986. *Current scientific techniques in archaeology*. London: Croom Helm.

Palmer, R. 1977. A computer method of transcribing information graphically from oblique aerial photographs to maps. *Journal Archaeological Science* **4**, 283–90.

Patent Rolls, 1225–32, in H. M. Colvin (ed.). 1963. *The history of the king's works*, London: HMSO, pp. 417–22.

Payton, R. 1992. *Retrieval of objects from archaeological sites*. Denbigh: Archetype Publications.

Pitt-Rivers, A. L. F. 1898. *Excavations in Cranborne Chase*. Dorset: privately printed.

Proudfoot, B. 1976. The analysis and interpretation of soil phosphorus in archaeological contexts. In D. A. Davidson & M. L. Shackley (eds), *Geoarchaeology*, 93–113. London: Duckworth.

Pyddoke, E. 1961. *Stratification for the archaeologist*. London: Phoenix.

Renfrew, C. 1975. *The emergence of civilization*. London: Methuen.

Renfrew, C. 1984. *Approaches to social archaeology*. Edinburgh: Edinburgh University Press.

Renfrew, C., & P. Bahn. 1991. *Archaeology: theories, methods and practice*. London: Thames and Hudson.

Rhodes, D. 1989. *Clay and glazes for the potter*. London: Adam and Charles Black.

Roth, W. E. 1970. *An introductory study of the arts, crafts and customs of the Guiana Indians*. New York: Johnson Reprint.

Rouse, I. 1992. *The Tainos*. New Haven, Connecticut: Yale University Press.

Ryder, M. L. 1968. *Animal bones in archaeology*. Oxford: Oxford University Press.

Schiffer, M. B. 1976. *Behavioural archaeology*. New York: Academic Press.

Schiffer, M. B. 1987. *Formation processes of the archaeological record*. Albuquerque, New Mexico: University of New Mexico Press.

Service, E. 1971. *Primitive social organization*. New York: Random House.

Shanks, M., & C. Tilley. 1987. *Social theory and archaeology*. Albuquerque, New Mexico: University of New Mexico Press.

Shepard, A. O. 1956. *Ceramics for the archaeologist*. Washington D.C.: Carnegie Institution.

Spence, C. (ed.) 1990. *Archaeological site manual*. London: Museum of London.

Startin, B. 1993. Preservation and the academically viable sample. *Antiquity* **67**, 421–6.

Stove, G. C., & P. V. Addyman. 1989. Ground-probing impulse radar: an experiment in archaeological remote sensing in York. *Antiquity* **63**, 337–42.

Sutherland, I. E. 1965. SKETCHPAD: a man–machine graphic communications system. *MIT Lincoln Laboratory Technical Report* 296, May 1965.

Swadling, M. (ed.) 1992. *Masterworks of man and nature: preserving our world heritage*. Australia: Harper–MacRae.

Synnott, P. 1996. Geographical information systems – an archaeological application. In *Discovery Programme Reports* no. 4. Dublin: The Discovery Programme.

Taylor, F. W. 1911. *Principles of scientific management*. New York: Harper.

Taylor, M. 1981. *Wood in archaeology*. Princes Risborough, Bucks: Shire Publications.

Trigger, B. G. 1994. *A history of archaeological thought*. Cambridge: Cambridge University Press.

Vita-Finzi, C. 1978. *Archaeological sites in their setting*. London and New York: Thames and Hudson.

Willey, G. R., & P. Phillips. 1958. *Method and theory in American archaeology*. Chicago: University of Chicago Press.

Williams, D. 1973. Flotation at Siraf. *Antiquity* **47**, 288–92.

Yellen, J. E. 1977. *Archaeological approaches to the present: models for predicting the past*. Orlando, Florida: Academic Press.

Index